NewsLady

CAROLE SIMPSON

authorHOUSE®

AuthorHouse™
1663 Liberty Drive
Bloomington, IN 47403
www.authorhouse.com
Phone: 1-800-839-8640

First published by AuthorHouse 2/23/2011

ISBN: 978-1-4520-6236-5 (hc)
ISBN: 978-1-4520-6237-2 (e)

Library of Congress Control Number: 2010916010

Printed in the United States of America

This book is printed on acid-free paper.

Certain stock imagery © Thinkstock.

Dedicated to Jim, Mallika and Adam Marshall,
without whose love and support I could never have made it.

TO MY READERS

As a literary device, I have taken the liberty of recreating conversations I had with persons over the four decades of my broadcast journalism career. They include dialogues which occurred with family members, newsmakers, former co-workers, former employers and ordinary citizens. Quotations, of course, are not necessarily verbatim. There were no recorders or cameras present, but I did maintain diaries from 1974 to 2006. I have made every effort to express the words that were used both by me and by others to the best of my honest recollections.

Carole Simpson

CONTENTS

PROLOGUE

"Didn't I used to know you?" the TSA screener at Washington Reagan Airport asked me as I waited barefoot for the trays of my stuff to come off the conveyor belt. I looked at the older black gentleman and in nanoseconds I sorted faces through my brain: school, college, Chicago, neighbor, New York, somebody I used to work with? Nothing registered.

"I don't think so," I answered with a smile.

"Yeah, it's you. You know who you are." I thought I did. Another disgusted passenger going through the agony of airport security.

"The news lady on television," he said excitedly. "You the news lady on ABC. What's your name again?"

"I'm Carole Simpson." It had been two years since I had been anchoring "World News Tonight Sunday" on ABC. The man seemed ecstatic to hear my name.

"You absolutely right. That's your name. You good. I like the way you talk. How come I don't see you no more on Sunday night?"

"It's a long story, sir. But thanks for remembering me."

He wouldn't stop. "They should let you do the Peter Jennings show. I liked him but he gone now. I wanna see you."

An extremely complimentary proposal, but one that I knew, no matter what, ABC would never, ever, even consider.

As we chatted the passenger line through security was getting longer and people were getting impatient. They squeezed past me, turning their heads for a look at who was holding up the line and making this man so giddy.

"I'd better go," I said, grabbing my trays of belongings. "G'bye."

"Goodbye to you, lovely news lady," he shouted much too loudly.

It was a bittersweet moment. It reminded me of all the viewers I had reached over 30 years on national television. How could this nice man have known that from the beginning of my career, that's what people in the streets, the ordinary folks, would always shout to me, "Hey, news lady." No doubt it was because I was one of the first female reporters they had seen on television.

News Lady. I always loved the name. It not only described what I did but also the manner in which I tried to do it.

TIME TO GO

How did it come to this? It's 2:20 in the morning on March 19, 2003, a beautiful balmy night. I stand alone on a seventh floor balcony of Washington's historic Hay Adams Hotel. Gazing across Lafayette Park I can see the darkened White House, the Washington Monument looming majestically behind it. My eyes well with tears.

At this very moment tens of thousands of U.S. troops are engaged in the ballyhooed "shock and awe" bombing attacks and troop invasion of Iraq, sent there by President George W. Bush to annihilate Saddam Hussein and "liberate" the Iraqi people. I weep about the start of another war, and I weep for myself.

Although a Senior Correspondent and longtime Weekend News Anchor, ABC News assigned me to watch the White House from nine at night until nine the next morning. My assignment is to call the news desk and tell everybody if terrorists blow up the White House. It is a job, no doubt, one of our youngest and most inexperienced desk assistants could have managed, and I had to beg for this assignment.

At the time I had been a broadcast journalist for thirty-seven years, the last fifteen spent anchoring ABC's World News Tonight Saturday and Sunday, while still covering stories for other news programs. I was the first African American woman to anchor an

1

evening newscast for one of the major television networks. And I had a big following. I had received virtually every award presented to journalists and African Americans for professional excellence. I had spent the past twenty years being an outspoken advocate for diversity in the nation's newsrooms, with particular emphasis on women and people of color.

But why was I here, now? On this night, on that balcony I suspected that I was given such a lowly assignment because I had become a nobody. Everybody says I don't look or act my age, but I am among Americans in the least desirable demographic for television advertisers: over fifty-four. Add my color and sex, and apparently, no matter how good I may look, how good I feel, how enthusiastic I am about the news, my star had fallen.

It seemed to me that I was now dispensable. ABC's planning of the Iraqi war coverage took six months. As our military forces were building up in the Middle East, our producers, anchors, and correspondents were receiving their assignments. Not only was there none for me, the executives decided I couldn't even handle anchoring my Sunday night show during our important war coverage. When I demanded an official explanation, I was told that the executives wanted to try out some of the newer correspondents to see if--in five to ten years--they could become credible anchors.

But the scuttlebutt was I was no longer good enough to "go live." Since when? A person who has spent her life in front of cameras, microphones, and live audiences, is all of a sudden no longer capable?

So, for the first ten days of one of the biggest news stories in recent history, I had nothing to do. It seemed all the other correspondents and anchors were assigned to some special show, some special story, some special event, or some prime time documentary. But not the only African American anchor.

During those early days of Operation Iraqi Freedom, I reported for work everyday seething. I watched all the coverage and read everything in the newspapers and magazines, thinking that, at least if I were ever needed, I would be prepared. All my "boning up" was for naught. There was never an urgent call or email saying, "Carole, we need you to do…"

It was during that dark hour, on the balcony of the Hay Adams, that I decided I could not, would not, allow anyone to insult my work. Despite the years of struggle to prove myself as good as a white man, white woman, or black man, I surrendered. I was tired of fighting. It was time to leave a career that I loved. The triple pressures of being female, black and older--had finally taken their toll.

BECOMING ME

I don't know for sure when I was born. My birth certificate says December 7, 1940. But my mother told me she was in labor with me when news of the Japanese aerial attacks on U.S. Navy ships moored in Pearl Harbor blared from the radio, striking much more fear in her than my impending Caesarean birth. One of my aunts was with her and swears she heard the same alarming reports from the hallways of St. Luke's hospital in Chicago. In all the excitement, were the nurses so nervous they put down the wrong year on birth record? I would like to think so.

I always preferred the Pearl Harbor date. It made me a year younger and I would have been born on the day President Franklin Delano Roosevelt called, "a day that will live in infamy." I always had a flair for the dramatic. But that official 1940 birth certificate date follows me. I always want to correct it with, "Hey, I was really born in 1941."

Although I took my first breath in Chicago, I always felt that my roots sprang from the South. My mother, Doretha Viola Wilbon, was born in the small rural town of Washington, Georgia. Her father was a white man, one of the sons of the richest man in town, Pembroke Pope. When my grandfather, Frank Wilbon, was sixteen years old, he fell in love with a young black girl named Hilda Stalnaker. She was only twelve. Frank had seen her playing jump rope and ball in her front yard. One day he got up the courage to stop at her house to ask her father if he could court his daughter. My great grandfather must have been astonished. The son of the richest white man in town wanted to court Hilda? He told Frank that Hilda was a little too young to be courting, and suggested he wait until she was older, maybe in three years. Frank agreed. Over the years he would steal peeks of her around her house and waited.

No Negro girl was courted by a white man in the 1880's. If a man wanted to have anything to do with a black girl, he just had his way with her, and a black father better not complain.

When Hilda was fifteen Frank came "a'callin'." My white grandfather followed the etiquette expected of a proper young gentleman of his time. After a year of visiting in the front parlor and sitting outdoors on the big porch swing, he asked Hilda's father for her hand in marriage. My great grandfather gave his blessing. Once Frank had taken a black woman for his wife, unheard of in that place and at that time, he was treated as a black man for the rest of his life. To see his own father, he had to go to the back door with his hat in his hand.

My mother, Doretha, was the eldest of Frank's eight children. Hilda died in childbirth at age twenty-nine and little Doretha was only nine years old. She had to become the "woman of the house," caring for her little brothers and sisters, cleaning and cooking for Poppa and the family. She always regretted that she didn't have her mother in her growing up years. She had no one she could ask questions or who could teach her things. Her childhood was cut short with no time for fun and play. When my mother was twelve, Poppa realized Doretha couldn't handle the increasingly difficult job that had fallen to her, so he took a new wife, another black woman, Eva Hayes. Together they had thirteen more children. That's a total of twenty-one children that Poppa sired. Between the two sets of siblings, there was never any distinction made between half-brothers or whole sisters. They were all Poppa's children and my mother, as the eldest, became the matriarch to them all.

My grandfather owned 160 acres of land deeded to him by his father when he was a boy. Like other farmers of his day, he wanted lots of children to help him in the fields. He had cows, pigs, a horse and a mule, chickens, cotton and vegetable crops. He was also a Baptist preacher who had a circuit of four small black churches around Wilkes County.

Every Sunday he would drive his horse miles from home to minister to one of his various flocks. He was one of those "hell and brimstone" preachers, too. He would jump and shout in the pulpits of the tiny, white frame churches until he got red in the face and had to pull out his big white handkerchief to wipe the sweat that glistened around his whole face. As a little girl I watched him baptize people in small creeks, pushing each nervous man, woman and child face up under the muddy water for a few seconds, and then pulling them up dripping wet and shouting for joy. He told the family: "I leave some of 'em underwater a little longer than necessary 'cause it scares the love of Jesus into 'em. And some of these sinful folks really need to love them some Jesus." Poppa sounded just like a black preacher.

Once Mama Eva took over the household, my mother was able to go to school, but she didn't get past the ninth grade. Photographs of her at thirteen show that she was already beautiful, with dark brown hair so long she could sit on the ends of it. One day one of the white men in town told my grandfather he wanted her, and he said if he didn't turn her over to him, he would take her. Poppa said, "Over my dead body."

Poppa was an incredible shot. My uncles say he could shoot a rabbit running toward him right between the eyes. He got out his best rifle and sat at the door of his house all day and all night waiting for that white man to show up. He had arranged to put my mother on the next morning's train to Chicago, to live with his white half brother, John, and his black wife, Rosa, in Kankakee, Illinois. Poppa would later say it was one of the hardest days of his life, sending his oldest daughter away so quickly and for such a hateful reason. My mother had to work on Uncle John's farm to pay for her keep, so there was no more school for her. A couple of years later she and her uncle and aunt kept the farm but moved from the country to the big city, Chicago.

After they got settled, Aunt Rosa took my mother to Mr. Stephen Simpson's Barber Shop to get her cut. My great aunt thought Doretha's hair attracted way too much attention from men, who were always leering at the young teenage girl. It certainly got the attention of a handsome shoeshine boy in the shop who would become my father. He and my mother stole glances at each other. Daddy would later say that the moment he saw my mother he vowed to make her his wife.

That shoeshine boy was the barber's son, Lytle. He was born in 1905 in Terre Haute, Indiana, to Stephen, who was born a slave, and Amanda, a Cherokee Indian. He was the youngest of five children. Life was not easy. In the early 1900's, Indiana may as well have been in the Deep South. Negroes lived on the other side of the tracks.

Before he became a barber, Stephen Simpson was a county circuit schoolteacher who taught colored children for a week at a time in one-room schoolhouses in rural Indiana. The work paid little and he felt he spent too much time away from his wife and children. During the first great migration of blacks from the South, 1910 to 1930, Stephen Simpson moved his family to Chicago. With the little money he saved from teaching, my grandfather opened a barbershop. And his youngest child, Lytle, went to the shop after school and on weekends to shine shoes.

My father was a gifted artist. He wanted to become an architect, but his father said there was no money for him to go to college and besides, "No Negro's going to be allowed to design buildings and houses. You need to get a real job, a government job." For many lucky black men, that meant the U.S. Post Office.

While waiting for a postal job to open up, my teenage father painted signs for food specials at a nearby High 'n' Low supermarket. "Roast Beef, 15 cents a pound." "Pound of butter, 5 cents." He enjoyed it. Even though his hand-painted signs weren't the landscapes and portraits he longed to paint, he could point to his work in a store window. His dreams of becoming an architect were never realized. But he continued to sketch and paint throughout his life and even took art lessons when he was in his 70's. We treasure his paintings which are still hanging on the walls of several family members' homes.

A letter carrier job opened up and soon Daddy was getting up at 3:30 in the morning working at the U.S. Postal Service. In 1926, Doretha was seventeen when she married 21-year-old Lytle. Poppa was proud because his daughter married a man with a "government job." The young couple settled into a small apartment on Chicago's Southside and began a life together that would last forty-seven years, producing two daughters, my sister Jacquelyn, nine years older, and me. My parents' first child, who would have been called Peter, was stillborn.

My folks were God-fearin', church-goin', hard-workin', no drinkin', no smokin', and no swearin' working class people who instilled in Jackie and me the desire to be successful, college-educated black women. They succeeded. My sister finished Northwestern University with a degree in Voice and I earned my degree from the University of Michigan in Journalism.

I believe one influential person shapes every human being for ill or good. In my case, it was "Mama." She died of lung cancer when she was sixty-four years old. Too young, too soon, too painfully. But she gave me self-confidence, strength, gumption, faith, and a desire to be the best. What would I have been without her?

She was a simple housewife raising two daughters in a small Chicago apartment. My father also had a business with his brother-in-law installing and servicing radios in hotels (twenty-five cents for an hour's worth of music), and he managed a three-flat apartment building he and my mother saved every extra nickel to buy. Mama had three jobs, too: running the house, working at the apartment building, but mainly sewing for white and well-to-do black women. She often

9

worked into the wee hours of the morning sewing for someone who just had to "have this dress by tomorrow, please?"

Mama was a talented dressmaker and fashion designer. She made her own patterns and could tailor men's suits. If something wasn't exactly right on a garment, she would rip it up and start all over. "Anything worth doing is worth doing well," I overheard her say to herself again and again.

As a pre-school child I still have memories of lying on the floor beside her old Singer sewing machine, with paper, pencils and crayons. To the incessant sounds of the clackety-clack of her foot pedal and the punches of the needle through fabric, she taught me the alphabet, numbers, colors and the names of animals. I remember she had one eye on her sewing and the other on what I was doing. "Carole, show me your work," she'd say.

By the time I entered kindergarten I was the only kid who could count to a hundred, say my ABC's, and print my full name. That was almost unheard of in my neighborhood.

This must seem so quaint in this day of Leap Frog and Baby Einstein products. She was an excellent teacher given her pitiable education. Once I started going to school, she could no longer help me with arithmetic and English. She made it clear that school was *my* work and I would have to conquer it by myself. That's what I had to do. I skipped a grade in my public elementary school and my teachers recommended me to the University of Chicago Laboratory School, one of the most prestigious private schools in the city. I was accepted, but my parents couldn't afford the tuition even with the school's financial aid. Mama always regretted her inability to send me to that school. But when I had a similar opportunity, I could afford it and I sent my own daughter to the Lab School. That was one for you, Mama.

I grew up doing the usual chores of washing dishes, emptying trash, and cleaning my room. But because she had to work so hard, my mother laid more housework on me. At age twelve I was cooking dinner, setting the table, *and* washing the dishes, so Mama could continue sewing. She also made me get on my hands and knees to scrub the kitchen and bathroom floors two times a week. On Saturdays, I had to do work in the apartment building my parents purchased. I had to polish all the wood in the three-story building, the floors, stairs, and front doors. If I was real fast, I could meet my friends at noon at the Tivoli Theater to watch the afternoon cartoon festival.

One day I made the mistake of asking my mother why I had to do so much more work at home than my friends.

"I don't want to hear anything about them other kids. What happens in their house is not your business. Your business is in this house." I cringed in anticipation of a slap across my face. Mama could be hard sometimes. "You are my child and you will do what I say," she said sharply. "You're going to learn everything I teach you. Just because you're smart in school, you're still gonna know how to cook, iron, clean, and how to squeeze a quarter out of a dime."

She would get right up in my face. "I want you to be somebody special and high. But if you end up being a washerwoman, you're going to be the best washerwoman there is."

That time I was spared the stinging slap that sometimes accompanied my questioning her authority. She was all about tough love, before the term was coined. I feared her, but I respected her. But make no mistake, I had great times with her. Like all of Poppa Wilbon's children, she inherited a quick wit; she was a good mimic; and she was funny. I was her best audience, laughing hysterically at her jokes.

I came to realize that Mama gave me the most important gifts she could bestow. Life. Love. Moral values. Determination. Ambition. And she taught me about racism. She wanted me to be prepared to face it and fight it, if I could.

A CHILD'S EYE VIEW OF RACISM

I must have been about nine years old when Mama told me about the time she was my age and Poppa took her and two of her brothers to see what he said a "nigger-hating, white lynch mob can get away with in Georgia." The year was probably 1916. Folks at that time, black and white, came from all over to see the horrors of white on black hatred. The race crime occurred a few miles from Washington, Georgia, where my grandfather, my mother and her seven brothers and sisters lived.

Her description of what she saw was horrifying. She said she remembered begging Poppa to let her hide her eyes. She didn't want to look. But he said it was important that she and her elder siblings bear witness to it. To survive in the South, he said, his children needed to learn an essential lesson. They could be killed for being Negroes.

What they saw was the burnt out hulk of a car with its four occupants charred beyond recognition. The car bore a New York license plate. The story circulating among the crowd was that two black couples had been driving down from Brooklyn to visit relatives, who lived not far from the scene of the crime. People said a mob of white men set upon the car, first taunting and cursing the occupants, then pouring gasoline on the vehicle, burning them alive. Mama said there was a sign near the charred bodies that Poppa read to her: "No Yankee Niggers allowed. Stay out."

13

Mama said she had nightmares for weeks, unable to erase the terrible images of white hate against her people.

When she told me the story I asked her, "Why did those white people do such a bad thing?"

"Because the Negroes came from the North and had a car," she said. "They didn't want them to think they were better than they were."

"But we're not Negroes," I replied, examining my own beige arms and looking into my mother's white face. She was a mulatto who had a white father and a black mother. Today, of course, she would be called bi-racial.

Mama said, "Negroes are colored people who have skin that comes in all shades, from light brown to dark brown. Even white. We don't have dark skin, but we are still Negroes. She said if any of our people had mixed with any black person, that would make us a Negro, no matter what color they were."

I didn't know what "mixed" meant, but like Scarlett O'Hara I decided I would think about that tomorrow. It was just too much for a nine-year-old to understand.

Two years after that upsetting lesson, my mother, father and I piled into the old family Buick to drive to Georgia for a long overdue visit with Poppa and our other relatives. I had been there as a five-year-old to be the flower girl in my aunt's wedding. My mother and I took the train from Chicago to Atlanta. I remember having great fun because there were white children my age on the train. We laughed and played together in the aisle. Then I remember my sharp disappointment when my mother told me to say goodbye to my "new friends." We had to gather our belongings and move to a car filled only with Negroes and there were no children. Only later did I learn we had crossed from Illinois into Kentucky and were forced to sit in the Jim Crow car for the rest of the journey. It was lonely for a little girl.

On this trip my father planned to take two days, spending the night in a motel halfway through the 700-mile drive. He wanted to have enough time for a stop at Great Smoky Mountains National Park in Tennessee, so I could see mountains for the first time. When it started getting dark that first night, Daddy stopped the car and went into the office of a motel which was flashing a bright red VACANCY sign. I was eleven years old and had never stayed in a motel, and I was excited by the prospect.

Daddy emerged from the office a couple of minutes later, looking disgusted. In the car he and my mother exchanged knowing glances.

"What's wrong Daddy? Aren't we going to stay?" I asked.

"No, honey. They didn't have a room for us."

"But the sign says…" I pointed to it. Daddy told me not to worry because we would find another motel.

There were several of them lining both sides of the highway, and they were all advertising vacancies. Daddy went into one after another and at the last motel, he walked out of the door saying angrily to someone behind him, "You ought to change your sign."

It was about 10 o'clock at night and we were so tired. The three of us slept cramped in the car. I missed out on my treat of sleeping in a motel. I knew something was wrong but I wasn't sure what or why. My parents were mum.

The next morning we awoke to a beautiful morning and I could see the foothills of the Great Smokies. The woods were our toilet. We changed out of our wrinkled clothes but couldn't wash up. We began driving and followed signs to the entrance of the National Park. My father saw a coffee shop and wanted to fill his Thermos with coffee for himself and my mother and buy some milk for me. Mama, thankfully, had packed food for the trip.

Daddy went into the cafe. When the door closed behind him I saw a sign I would never forget. I read it aloud. "No Jews, no Catholics, no dogs, no niggers allowed." Niggers were lower than dogs.

"Mama, look! Why is that sign on the door?" She finally explained that we were in the South now and that's how white people feel down here. She said "nigger" was a really bad name they use for Negroes.

She added they didn't like Jews and Catholics either, but "niggers" they hated the most.

"Are we niggers?" I asked.

"No, we're not niggers. There are just stupid white people that use that word to make us feel bad, like we're not as good as them."

"But we are as good, Mama. Aren't we?"

"Yes, of course we are. And don't you ever let anyone make you think you aren't." Those words stuck with me for life.

Daddy came out of the shop. Despite the sign, the proprietor sold him coffee to pour into his Thermos at the back of the small dining room where white people sat. But Daddy said they wouldn't sell him any milk, because it was in a case up front. He couldn't walk up there. We sat in the car and we all drank coffee and ate some fruit and cake Mama had packed in a basket.

As we waited in the line of cars entering the Park, I started getting worried they wouldn't let us in. Daddy said the park was a "national park," and we wouldn't have any trouble. I didn't know what "national" meant, but I liked the word that might prevent any trouble.

Once in the park, we followed the winding roads that would take us to the highest peak in the park with an elevation of more than six thousand feet. Round and round the winding roads to the observation deck, my excitement was building with each ascent. When we reached the summit, I jumped out of the car and ran from one end of the platform to the other. It was the most beautiful sight I had ever seen at age eleven. On a clear day you can see seven states from there. It was a clear day.

My mother says I looked like a butterfly flitting about in my yellow dress, my pigtails, tied with yellow bows, bouncing in the air. I was having the time of my life.

I only had coffee to drink and I saw a water fountain. I went to get a drink and as my hand pushed the lever and my lips pursed in anticipation, I felt myself literally snatched away from the fountain. I was startled to see the strange white woman who brusquely pulled my arm and me away from the fountain.

"Don't you see that sign?" she demanded while pointing to a wooden placard that said "Whites Only." I was frightened. I didn't see my parents. The woman pulled me to the other side of a stone divider and said, "This is where you drink. Stay away from the white fountain." She stormed off.

She left me, not in front of a fountain, but a spigot that had dirt and trash underneath it and chewed gum sticking all over it. Above it was another wooden plaque, more crudely printed, with the words "Coloreds Only." I burst into tears and ran to find my parents. I told them what happened. My father was angry and wanted me to point out the woman who had done this to me. He said he wanted to have a talk with her. But my innocence was lost. I knew he wouldn't say anything, that he couldn't say anything. I hated the South and the Great Smokies. I wanted to go and never come back.

Years later I recounted this incident to a white friend who said she had journeyed with her family from Michigan to the Smokies when she was a young girl, too. She had been on the observation deck as well and went to the colored sign because she didn't want clear water, which she thought would be boring. She wanted colored water. She thought red, blue and green water would flow from it. Her mother guided her to the "white fountain." She at least got to drink. I didn't. I refused to drink from the nasty "colored" spigot.

I was so upset my parents decided to leave the Park and drive straight to Poppa's house with no more stops. Being there was a safe haven after just one day of my experiences in the segregated South. Poppa lived with his wife and my mother's younger siblings in a big old farmhouse with a big wraparound porch and lots of bedrooms. Awaiting us was one of the enormous meals typical at Poppa's house. The table was groaning, with platters of fried chicken and baked ham, big bowls of butter beans, mashed potatoes, fried corn, collard greens, cornbread and biscuits, and later homemade ice cream and fruit cobbler. We never ate like that in Chicago. What I didn't like about Poppa's house was the fact that there were no bathrooms. Outhouses in the day, chamber pots under the bed at night.

My grandfather was the wittiest, most humorous man I ever knew. After dinner he would "hold court." We'd sit around and listen to his funny stories that made our sides split with laughter. He talked about his church people, about white people, black people, and "hants," his name for all the ghosts supposedly wandering his land. His ghost stories were so vivid and scary we young'uns slept with the covers over our heads many nights.

Poppa always treated me special because I was the daughter of his beloved first child, whom he called "Feet." As a toddler he told her she was sweet, and she tried to repeat it and what came out was, "I feet."

"Feet," he told my mother during out visit, "I'm going to take Carole to town with me to buy some groceries. I want to teach her a few things." He had already taught me how to gather eggs from the hen house, how to pick a ripe watermelon in the field, the epicurean delight of eating a juicy, ripe tomato right off the vine. And the worst lesson: how to kill and pluck a chicken. What would I learn in town?

Poppa helped me into his old truck and we headed to the business district of sleepy Washington, Georgia, with a population of four thousand.

We parked near the market and Poppa said he needed to warn me about how a little colored girl had to act in the South. He told me if we were on the wooden sidewalk and white people were coming toward us, we would have to step off and walk in the street until they went past us. If a white person spoke to me, he said, whether they were old or another child, I was to say "Yes, sir," or "No, Ma'am."

"To kids, Poppa? That's silly." I scoffed.

"It's not silly down here, sweetheart. That's why I wanted to tell you before we got out of the car that you aren't in Chicago anymore, and if you want to stay safe you have to do what's expected between the races down here."

"But, Poppa, what if I forget?" I was getting scared.

"You won't forget. Your Poppa is right here with you. I'll take care of you, but you've got to learn how to act around these crackers'."

We went into the store and white people were all saying, "Hi, Frank" or "Hi, Rev." I kept my eyes on my shoes as we walked throughout the store picking up items. I never uttered a mumbling word.

My vacation to the South had been one of highs and lows. The highs were of the love of my big family. The lows were becoming afraid of white people and losing the self-esteem I had as a spirited 11-year-old girl.

Just two years later, lynching became more than a story told to me by my mother and my grandfather. In 1954, a boy my age, who lived just a few blocks from my house, had gone to visit his family in Mississippi just like I visited my family in Georgia. He whistled at a white woman in a store. That night, a white lynch mob dragged him out of the family house, beat, shot, castrated him, and threw his body into a river. That boy was Emmett Till. What Poppa had told me about Georgia suddenly became too real.

My family joined tens of thousands of people who flocked to the funeral home to view the boy's body in an open casket. His mother wanted everybody to see what "they" had done to her only child. I begged my parents not to make me view the body. I cried. My mother understood what viewing lynching victims had done to her, so my parents left me outside the funeral parlor for the almost two hours it took for them to go through the line of mourners and gawkers. People came out wailing and crying because Emmett Till's face looked so grotesque. I concluded I had made the right decision.

Then I learned about "white flight" on the South Side of Chicago. Twice our family moved into so-called changing neighborhoods where my parents hoped to get my sister and me away from growing crime rates and into better schools. We moved in and white people started moving out. It was almost laughable. A couple of black families in the neighborhood, and the "For Sale" signs went up almost overnight.

Of course, the neighborhoods went from white, to integrated, to all black. I am sorry I lost some good white friends whose families headed to the Northside or the growing suburbs around Chicago. I asked my parents why they were leaving. My father told me in a sad voice that white people didn't want to live in neighborhoods with colored people.

"It's racial prejudice," Mama said. "I've told you this before. They don't think we are as good as they are. They think we are inferior. Blonde hair is better than brown hair. Blue eyes, better than black. White skin better than dark."

She went on to explain that white people considered Negroes "ugly" because of our darker skin, kinky hair, broad noses, and full lips.

Then she recited a poem common in the black community at the time.

> *"If you're white you're alright;*
> *If you're yellow, you're mellow;*
> *If you're brown, stick around;*
> *But if you're black, stay back."*

She laughed about it. Most black people did. I didn't think it was funny.

I stared at my face in the mirror. Will white people think I'm ugly? I had a broad nose and full lips, long sandy brown braids and beige skin. My family didn't think I was ugly, but I grew up convinced I was. The white girls in school had straight hair that hung down their backs which they could fling into their faces and across their shoulders. They could wash and wear it. Some had blue, green, and gray eyes. The boys talked about their good looks. The black boys, too.

I decided that while I might not be as pretty as the white girls, someday I would be smarter and more important than they would ever be. Thirteen-year-old bravado.

THE "COLORED" LOIS LANE

Throughout my public school years I excelled. My grades, except for math, won me honor roll status every year. I joined school clubs and tried things other girls didn't, like becoming the first girl to run for president of the eighth grade class at Wadsworth Elementary School on the Southside of Chicago. It was always a foregone conclusion that the most popular boy in school won. He only had to be good looking and popular. But I really wanted to win, so I mounted a campaign. I got permission from the principal to put up posters and I passed out to the "voters" penny candy—"Mary Janes" and those little wax Coke bottles which contained that disgusting sugary colored liquid. I did grow up in Chicago where politics was, shall I say, always a bit unorthodox.

I lost the election by one vote. Mine. I cast it for my male opponent thinking that was the sportsmanlike-thing to do. I never made that mistake again.

Until I reached high school and saw my birth certificate for the first time, my name had been "Carol Estelle Simpson." But on the official document my first name was spelled "Carole." I asked my mother why she let me go through life not spelling my name right. She said people never got the "e" on the end and she just let it slide. But why was I Carole with an "e," I wanted to know? My mother said when she was close to giving birth to me in December, Christmas carols were playing on the radio and her favorite screen actress was Carole Lombard, who was married to Clark Gable. Mama decided to name me for Christmas and a movie star. A year after I was born Lombard, after appearing at a World War II bond rally, was killed in a plane crash at age thirty-three. I meet women my age all the time who are named "Carol with an 'e.' They said their mothers loved Lombard, too. She must have really been something.

In the fall of 1954, I was thirteen years old and off to Chicago's Hyde Park High School, at the time considered one of the best high schools in the city. I didn't appreciate the significance but in May of that year, the Supreme Court ruled in Brown v. Topeka Board of Education that "separate but equal" schools were unconstitutional. Civil rights lawyers such as Thurgood Marshall, William Coleman, and others successfully argued before the high court that schools in the South were separate, but by no means equal. It was the beginning of the legal assault on southern states' laws segregating whites and blacks.

At my high school, the student population was about seventy percent white, mostly Jewish, and thirty percent black. It was located in a "white flight" community. By the time I graduated four years later, the racial makeup was sixty percent black to forty percent white. In 2004, I went back to visit my old high school and it is now 99.6 percent black and 94 percent of the students live below the poverty line. It is now a school with some of the lowest test scores in the city.

Before I entered Hyde Park High my academic achievement already had been recognized. I was chosen from my elementary school to be part of an educational experiment. I wonder now if the Brown decision had anything to do with it.

The project picked twenty-five of the top students from the four feeder elementary schools and all were placed in the same classes to take required courses for college preparation. Since only one of the schools was predominantly Negro--mine--three black girls were chosen for the experiment: Anna Kimbrough, Helen Ivey, and Carole Simpson. We were working class kids thrust into a daily school situation with affluent and better-educated Jews.

In our special class, we were encouraged to question our teachers, and what they taught. We were told to not necessarily believe everything we heard people say. "Put on your thinking caps." Now I appreciate the fact that they were teaching us critical thinking skills. Certainly, good tools for a journalist.

At this point in my education, my parents, who could no longer help me with my homework, had two standing orders: to be a "good girl" and not bring home any C's on my report card. I think I got two C's in high school and I had to have for my parents a damn good explanation.

I watched the white students in my class. They joined all kinds of activities, so I did, too: student government, drama club, the choir, and the school newspaper. I signed up for as many extracurricular activities as I could handle, because I worked after school three days a week and on Saturdays at the local branch of the Chicago Public Library.

We "special students" were also urged to become school leaders. We three colored girls each thought of ourselves as "different" from the other kids, not just because of our skin color. We didn't have poodle skirts with crinolines and several pairs of school shoes. Nor did we have gold circle pins and pearl necklaces to wear with our sweaters. We had never seen girls our age with their own jewelry. There was, I think, more snobbery than discrimination against us but none of the kids chose to sit next to us, so we wound up together in the back of every classroom. We felt intimidated by our loquacious classmates whose fathers were doctors or lawyers, their mothers schoolteachers or society women.

In my junior year I joined the staff of *The Hyde Parker*, the school newspaper. That was after a teacher told me that I wrote well and should be on the staff. The editor assigned me a column, called "Home

Room News." Each week I visited each of the homerooms to find out who was doing what, when, where and why. I didn't know then I was using the "5 W's," the fundamental rules of reporting that I would later use for decades as a broadcast correspondent. I loved asking questions and finding out things before everyone else did and then putting them in writing under my byline. It wasn't long before I decided I wanted to be a newspaper reporter.

By my senior year, I decided I must be a journalist. A guidance counselor was not supportive. She conceded that I was a good writer but thought if I wanted to go to college I should become an English teacher. She asked me if I knew of any colored women who were reporters. I didn't know about Ida B. Wells, Frances Murphy, and Ethel Payne. I couldn't name anybody, but I also couldn't name any white women who were reporters. The only ones I could think of were in the Sunday comics, Brenda Starr and Lois Lane. Comic strip characters were my only role models. I didn't mention to the counselor their names.

Never mind what she said. When I graduated I would go to journalism school. My parents always assumed I would go to college. They had been putting away what little extra money they had to help pay for my college, but they had decided I would be a teacher, a stable and fairly well paying career for a young colored woman.

One evening the sparks flew when I walked into the living room to tell my mother and father I wanted to study journalism in college.

"Study what?" my father asked.

"A journalist, Daddy. You know, a newspaper reporter. I want to write and report on all the things that are going on in Chicago, or in other places, even maybe around the world. I want to write news stories, like you read in the *Tribune*."

My mother quickly asserted, "You're going to be a school teacher. I've never heard of journalism. They aren't going to hire a Negro girl to work for *The Chicago Tribune*, except maybe to sweep up. Are you crazy?"

Little did I know, this would be the first of many "No's" I would hear as I struggled in my early years to become a journalist. I never expected this reaction. I argued that I didn't want to teach. I wanted to do something different, something exciting.

Young college-bound women black and white in the 1960's had few career choices open to them other than teaching, nursing, and social work. In retrospect, I should not have been upset with my parents. They were concerned and loving, but they had never said "No" to me on big issues.

The argument went on for a couple of hours. My parents' concerns were about racial discrimination, about wasting money on an education in a field in which I probably couldn't get a job because I was a black female. They were also worried about my safety in a profession that could be dangerous. They came up with a compromise. If I would go to the Chicago Teachers College and get a teaching degree first, then I could pursue "this journalism thing" and pay for it myself. They just wanted to make sure I had something to fall back on so I could take care of myself and not have to depend on a husband. There were black men who deserted their families back then, too.

My arguments, I admit, were not nearly as compelling. I had the equivalent of a teenage temper tantrum. I wanted to be a journalist because I wanted to be a journalist. I had been a good student, a good girl, and my parents should let me do what I want. I would make it. They would see. Nothing was resolved and I went to bed, the first of many nights I would weep in my pillow because I wanted to be a journalist.

Only as an adult did I realize that I had great parents who didn't, couldn't go to college but wanted their daughters to have the opportunities they never had. After several days of my petulance, they called me into the living room and told me I had been a wonderful daughter who had made them proud and if being a reporter were how I wanted to spend my life's work, they would support me. I think it was Daddy who pressed the decision. He knew what it was like not being able to pursue his dream of becoming an architect.

Joy of joys, I could go to college and major in journalism. I started sending out letters requesting catalogues and applications. There was really only one university I wanted to attend, Northwestern in Evanston, Illinois. At the time the Medill School of Journalism was one of the best.

I sent off my application with the transcript of my grades, descriptions of all my extracurricular activities, my newspaper clips, teacher recommendations, and an essay on what I wanted to do with my life. I thought it was an impressive package. I was confident I had fulfilled all the requirements for admission to Northwestern.

A few weeks later I was invited by the Admissions Office to come for an interview. Dressed in my sister's best hand-me-downs (our mother made all of our clothes), I was excited and confident that I would do well during the interview.

A middle-aged man invited me to take a seat in his office. He remarked that my application was "very nice." Without asking me any questions about it, he said he was going to level with me. If I made it through journalism school I wouldn't be able to get a job at a major newspaper, but maybe at "Ebony" magazine, or *The Chicago Defender.*" I told him I didn't want to work at a Negro publication, I wanted to work for *The Chicago Tribune* or *The Chicago Sun Times.* His face eased into a patronizing smile.

"You're a Negro and you're a female," he said, "and I just think Northwestern would be a waste of your time because nobody at those publications is going to hire you."

"Why not?" I timidly asked, fearing the answer.

The admissions officer replied flippantly, "That's just the way things are. You should go to Chicago Teachers College and become a nice English teacher."

Did my parents call him? I was shocked he said the same things as my parents and the guidance counselor told me. Here it was the second loud, "No." The admissions counselor said, "Thank you for coming, Miss Simpson." I managed a strained smile.

As I left my stomach began to churn. I knew what I would be hearing from Northwestern. The night of that interview my pillow was wet again. Was it possible that despite my strong application, my good grades, my school activities, that Northwestern, my dream school, would reject me because of my color and sex? I knew there were problems of racial discrimination in the South, but I was in Chicago, in Illinois. This couldn't happen here. I had done everything right, except being born a white male. My disappointment turned into anger.

A few weeks later I got the one-page letter from the Admissions Office. It began, "We regret to inform you..." The third "No." The official version.

While I was working as a Chicago television reporter I taught a course at Northwestern for three years. I loved telling my students I wasn't good enough to go there, but I was good enough to teach there. I was even a finalist in the 1990's search for a new dean for the Medill School of Journalism.

After seeing the rejection letter, I was ashamed to show it to my parents. I became more determined than ever to prove everybody wrong. I would show them. I would be a journalist and a damned good one. I wasn't going to let "No's" stop me. I would use them like vitamin pills to give me the strength to wage my struggle to reach my goals. That struggle would continue for forty years.

There were other universities. I applied to the University of Illinois, Navy Pier in Chicago, and got accepted by the in-state public university. The school had to take me. After two years of core courses I wanted to move away from home and experience life on a real college campus. I transferred to the University of Michigan to major in journalism in 1960.

As I did in high school, I became involved in many extracurricular activities: president of my sorority, Delta Sigma Theta; member of the

Pan-Hellenic Council; a star of the Junior Girls Play; an usher at the classical concerts at Hill Auditorium; and a reporter for *The Michigan Daily*. The editor was Tom Hayden who became a famous anti-war activist, the husband of Jane Fonda during her "Hanoi Jane" days, and a California State Assemblyman. Who could know that seven years after receiving assignments from him, I would be reporting on his tumultuous federal trial in which he and seven other leftists were charged with crossing state lines to incite a riot during the 1968 Democratic National Convention in Chicago?

The spring before my graduation I registered with Michigan's Placement Bureau, which helped students find jobs. I was the only student of color among the 60 graduating seniors and I was the only one who couldn't find a job. I went to all the interviews on campus for newspaper jobs. I got the same story from every employer. I had three strikes against me. STRIKE ONE: COLORED; STRIKE TWO: WOMAN; STRIKE THREE: INEXPERIENCED. Why was inexperience a strike against me? My fellow students weren't told that and they were just as inexperienced as I. No, No, and No for me. Three big vitamin pills.

Three strikes. I'm out? Wet pillow time. I wondered if I had been too stubborn. I thought about my parents' concerns, the words of the high school guidance counselor and the Northwestern admissions counselor, and now the newspaper recruiters. It was wrong. It wasn't fair. It was illegal. It was racist. It was sexist. It was un-American. I was furious. I graduated with no job. I returned home from Ann Arbor and went to work at the Chicago Public Library, shelving and checking out books. It was an after school job I started as a sophomore and it was where I worked every summer through college. I was humiliated. With my B.A. degree in Journalism from the University of Michigan I had the same job I started when I was 15 years old.

Thank heavens, my parents didn't say, "We told you so." My mother's suggestion was to turn to prayer. I had been raised in the

Lutheran Church. But my youthful indignation believed prayer wouldn't change my color or my gender, or the prejudice of white people. More determined than ever, I kept telling myself that I had done everything right. I was prepared. They said I would never be a journalist. I said to myself, I will show them. I will show them all.

FROM THE URBAN NORTH
TO THE RURAL SOUTH

Professor Wesley Maurer was chair of the University of Michigan Journalism Department, and when he found out I was the only graduating senior who couldn't find a job, he called me at home. He said he felt terrible about my situation because I had been a very good student. He promised to work all summer trying to find a position for me somewhere. He said he owed me that.

"It may not be Chicago, Carole. The job could be in a small town in the Upper Peninsula of Michigan," he told me.

"I don't care, sir," I replied. "I'll go anywhere."

Professor Maurer called me in August to say that he had lined up an internship for me at a college. My responsibilities were to run the public relations office writing press releases, teaching a course in journalism, and advising the student newspaper. I would also gain credits towards a Master's Degree in Journalism at the University of Michigan. He said they were expecting me in a month.

I wanted to leap through the phone and hug my portly, bespectacled professor. I was so excited. A job at last, not as a newspaper reporter, but I could write and teach and work towards my Master's degree. It occurred to me that he hadn't told me which college and where. I asked.

"Well, Carole, it's Tuskegee Institute in Alabama," he said with a tinge of doubt in his voice. He must have anticipated my reaction.

Alabama? The South? It was 1962, seven years after Rosa Parks refused to give up her seat on a bus and Dr. Martin Luther King led the Montgomery boycott against segregated public transportation. (Montgomery was only thirty miles from Tuskegee, Alabama.) In the early 1960's the civil rights movement was moving into high gear challenging segregation laws across the southern states with: sit-ins at white lunch counters; blacks and whites making freedom rides on Greyhound buses from the North to southern cities: blacks refusing to sit in segregated seats, use segregated restrooms, or eat in segregated diners. Alabama Governor George Wallace "stood in the school house door" to block the integration of the University of Alabama. I remembered seeing on television his vociferous vow: "Segregation today. Segregation tomorrow. Segregation forever!"

The Rev. Martin Luther King, Junior, and his "lieutenants for justice" were getting arrested regularly and civil rights demonstrators were being beaten and killed. My chilling experiences in Georgia flooded to mind. The South was scary. Could I really work there under the laws of segregation?

I guess there was a huge pause in my telephone conversation with Professor Maurer because he asked, "Carole, are you there? What do you think?"

I told him I wasn't thrilled with the location but I wanted the job. I was twenty-one years old and I had to start somewhere, and this was my only option. Besides, I could experience firsthand what it was like to live and work in the segregated South.

Professor Maurer said he would draw up some papers and I should plan to be in Tuskegee the week before classes began in September. I hung up the phone happy but apprehensive.

My mother was sewing in the dining room. I told her enthusiastically that the University of Michigan had called and I had a job. She put down her sewing and said, "Give me a hug. You did it."

NewsLady

"There's just one little problem, Mama. It's in Tuskegee, Alabama."

"Oh no, baby," she said. "I don't want you going to Alabama. You could get killed. You know how dangerous it is down there now."

"But Mama, I told my professor I would take the job," I explained. "I've got to go."

My father was none too happy either when he heard the news. But they agreed I was a grown woman and it was time for me to make my own decisions. They believed they had done a good job of preparing me for life. They said they trusted my "good head" and expressed their faith that I would be under God's protection.

My mother uttered an expression that I use to this day with my own children: "Let go. Let God."

I can now appreciate my mother's angst. She cried over my leaving home and over where I was going. My father later told me that for the two years I was in Alabama, she was constantly worried about me.

After packing up my few worldly possessions, my parents took me to O'Hare Airport, and after many hugs and my mother's tears, I boarded the plane for Atlanta, my first airplane trip. After landing I had to transfer to a flimsy little puddle jumper to Columbus, Georgia, where I rented a car to drive the eighty miles to Tuskegee, Alabama. During the car trip I had cold sweats and heart palpitations. I was so afraid something would happen and I wouldn't know how to act. Poppa's admonition that I not talk to white people came quickly to mind. God forbid I get a flat tire on the rural two-lane highway leading to Tuskegee, a small predominantly black town with a population of five thousand.

Before I left Chicago I found out what I could about Tuskegee Institute and learned it was founded by a former slave, Booker T. Washington, who established the Normal School in 1881, when he was only twenty-five years old. It was set up to educate teachers, but Washington later decided that Negroes would make more progress if they studied the skilled trades. His school offered black boys masonry, carpentry, and agriculture. Over the years Washington established 5000 small schools across the South to train black tradesmen, which brought him national renown. He dined at the White House with President Theodore Roosevelt and counted among his greatest benefactors some of the white captains of industry.

But Washington was criticized by scholars like W.E.B. DuBois, a Harvard University graduate and founder of the National Association for the Advancement of Colored People, the NAACP. He believed colored people should learn business, engineering, architecture and the humanities to compete on a more level playing field with white college graduates. DuBois wrote that Washington was too cozy with the white power structure and called him, "The Great Accommodator," in other words, an "Uncle Tom."

I also learned that the most famous faculty member ever at Tuskegee was George Washington Carver of peanut fame. Also born a slave, he became an expert in agriculture and taught ex-slaves how to farm, believing it was an important road to self-sufficiency. He was a civil rights activist, scientist, inventor and poet, but he became best known for his advocacy of crop rotation. He discovered 300 uses for peanuts, hundreds more for soybeans, pecans and sweet potatoes. He became a national celebrity.

During World War Two, the now-famous Tuskegee Airmen trained on the Tuskegee Army Air Field near the campus, becoming the first black military pilots in history. At the end of the war, the Airmen were credited with shooting down 109 Luftwaffe German aircraft in air battles over Europe.

By the time I was hired by Tuskegee, it had gone from a school specializing in the industrial arts to a real college offering degrees in business, engineering, architecture, liberal arts, nursing, agriculture, and veterinary medicine.

All of this fact-finding made me feel better about working at Tuskegee. The institution was historic. Having grown up in integrated neighborhoods in Chicago and going to integrated schools, I was looking forward to living an all-black experience. I soon learned I wasn't ready for it.

The southern accents were so thick, I could scarcely understand what people were saying to me. I was always asking, "Excuse me. Could you say that again?" I also didn't know I was expected to speak to everyone who spoke to me. I grew up in Chicago. My mother taught me not to speak to people I didn't know. But in the South, if you don't speak up, you're stuck up.

My fair complexion contrasted with the darker skin stones of the majority of students and faculty and created another problem. Some darker-skinned people felt inferior and envious of lighter-skinned Negroes. This attitude dates back to the "house niggers" and "field niggers" of slavery times. Spike Lee comically portrayed the rivalry in his movie "School Daze." After making a few friends, they clued me in on how to behave. They shared what they heard people saying about me: "A stuck-up, high-yellow, blow-hair from the North. She talks and acts like she's better than everybody else."

That was so untrue. I had plenty of dark-skinned relatives. I never thought much about my color. It never really came up in the North. I quickly changed my ways. If a stranger spoke, and said, "How do you do?" I immediately responded with a smile and a "Fine. How are you today?" In a few months, I got used to the accent, and soon I sounded like the people of Tuskegee. I've always had an ear for language and can imitate whatever accent I hear around me. By the time I left Alabama I was saying, "Hey, y'all" and "Thahnk yeww" with the best of them.

One of my biggest shocks was the quality of the students. I taught an introductory course in journalism and if I had been insensitive I would have thought the freshmen and sophomores in my class were dumb, stupid, and ignorant. When they turned in my writing assignments, it was the rare surprise to find a complete sentence or a sensible thought. The papers were filled with misspellings. They looked like the papers of ten-year-olds.

Then I remembered that these college students had gone to black segregated high schools in Alabama, which were notoriously inadequate and nowhere near equal with white schools, despite the Brown decision. The black educational system had dilapidated facilities, outdated books and materials, and ill-trained teachers. How could I expect better of the students?

I apologized to them for the D's and F's I felt I had to give them on their papers and decided that I would have to set aside the journalism and teach basic grammar. What are the subject, verb, and predicate of a sentence? I felt so sorry for how segregation had shortchanged these students, who had good minds but lacked the most basic academic skills.

During the two years I was at Tuskegee, from 1962 to 1964, all hell was breaking loose in Alabama and neighboring states. The civil rights movement was gathering more and more steam but violence stalked the protestors wherever they took direct action. Very few students participated in the demonstrations in nearby Montgomery. I wondered why. Several students told me they had worked so hard to get to college that they didn't want to risk getting arrested and stopping their education. They said their parents also wanted them to stay in school and told them to let others do the protesting. I also learned from news reports that many of the civil rights activists were white college students who came from major universities in the North. The whites felt they could always go back to school after they put their bodies on the line to fight segregation. I had respect for both sets of students.

While I was learning about racial hatred and segregation, I also learned what could happen to a fairly attractive 21-year-old working for an older, married man. I don't think the phrase sexual harassment had reached the lexicon yet.

My boss, who oversaw my work and also graded me for my Michigan internship, was a wonderful mentor and a man whose intelligence I admired. He also seemed to genuinely care about my success in the job and my graduate education. However, over time our working relationship changed. He began leaving his house after dinner, returning to his office to call me at my room in the women's dormitory. At first he wanted to talk to me about projects, which we could have done when we were both in our offices. He was, I thought, the happily married father of four children.

The conversations turned into chitchat about my social life on campus and his wife and children. One day at work he asked me to come to his office that night at 8 o'clock to discuss my internship. It was time for him to submit a grade to the University of Michigan. I thought he really wanted to talk about it.

I entered the old Victorian house, which served as the Office of Development, climbed the creaky stairs to the second floor and knocked on his door. There was no one else in the darkened building. He let me in and I noticed he was in elegant casual dress and had the strong aroma of a men's cologne. He literally snatched me across the threshold and caught me in a strong embrace and tried to kiss me. I pulled away but he was too muscular for me to escape his tight hold. As I swung my face from side to side to avoid his lips, he was licking my face. My boss, twice my age, breathlessly uttered, "I need you. I want you."

I was totally shocked and hurt. I pleaded, "Dr. Jones, (not his real name) don't…" But he forced me down on the sofa in his office and I fought him, hitting and kicking. I was afraid he was going to rape me. He tore my dress, revealing my bra and naked shoulders. His hands were all over me, up and down my legs to my crotch. My first instinct was to scream, but I knew no one would hear me.

My mother's admonition came to mind: "Do whatever it takes to protect yourself." If I played the crying and weak woman I could be sexually assaulted. But if I took control of the situation I may be able to avoid an unsavory outcome. Thank you again, Mama.

In the empty hope that someone might hear me, I shouted in a loud, angry voice, "Stop it. You stop it right now." I sounded like a stern school marm. I followed with, "Are you crazy? What are you doing? Are you trying to rape me?" He released his grip on my shoulders and rolled off the sofa onto the floor moaning softly.

I wanted to run from his office and the building as quickly as I could. But I saw now that I had the upper hand. I smoothed my clothes about me and began to lecture my boss. I told him that he should be ashamed of himself. He had a wife and family. I said that until that night I had great respect for him and now it was lost. I told him I was not attracted to him sexually at all.

This big strong man was reduced to sobbing on the floor, begging my forgiveness. He apologized profusely and said he couldn't help how he felt about me. I warned him that if he ever tried something like this again, I would report it to the President of the University.

At twenty-one, I had learned how important it was to take charge of a situation and use it to my advantage. After that disturbing night my boss and I managed to resume a professional relationship but I continued to see the special looks he gave me. I was afraid this problem would cause him to grade me more harshly on my internship. Thank God, he didn't. But I was never again comfortable in his presence.

On the college campus, just miles from the violence perpetrated by racist whites against civil rights activists, I felt safe. It's when I left the campus to shop for groceries or clothes that my anxiety grew. I went to Montgomery to buy cooler summer clothes at the one department store. It was hot down there. I picked out three dresses and asked a white clerk where I could try them on. She said I would have to go downstairs to the colored fitting room. She pointed and said. "All the coloreds have to try on in that room, the men, ladies, and kids."

I read the sign, "Colored Fitting Room." I turned that phrase around in my head. Instantly I was transported back to the Great Smoky Mountains National Park and the "Coloreds Only" sign on the dirty water spigot. I couldn't do it. How could "they" treat my people with so little respect? I refused to use the "Colored Fitting Room."

I held the dresses up to my body and tried to imagine how I would look in them and I folded them around my body to see if they would fit. I was so disheartened by what I was doing that I put all the dresses back. I couldn't buy them under these circumstances. On my way out I saw a pretty straw hat, perfect for the hot Alabama sun. Without thinking, I plopped it on my head. A startled clerk told me to take off the hat because coloreds aren't allowed to try them on. I finally found my voice and asked her why not. She said the grease from "you'alls hair" just ruins the hats for "other people." What made her think I had "grease" in my hair? So black women had to guess whether a hat would be flattering. I flushed with embarrassment, rushed to the exit, got in my car and headed back to Tuskegee. I never went there again and resorted to ordering from catalogues or asking my mother to send clothing from stores in Chicago.

One night I was asked on a date to the movies. There was one small theatre in Tuskegee. I asked my escort if it were segregated. He replied, "Of course, it is."

"How segregated?" I asked him.

"Well, the first floor seats are reserved for whites," he explained. "We have to sit in the balcony. And if you want some popcorn or candy we'll have to buy it in town and take it with us, 'cause we're not allowed on the first floor where the concession stand is."

"Thanks, but no thanks," I told him. "I just can't." Instead, we had some French fries and Cokes at the black diner near campus and took a walk. Some date. I disliked that guy from that night on. It wasn't his fault. I just projected that segregated movie theatre on him and the very sight of him was a painful reminder of how people were so accepting of the discrimination.

While walking to my office one morning, a group of white teenagers were hanging out of car windows, and as they slowed down and came alongside me I heard, "Hey, you black bitch. You want to fuck? How big is your pussy?"

I started walking faster as they kept my pace with their car. I was flushed and my cheeks hotter than I have ever felt them. I was afraid of those boys. Would they grab me and assault me? When I ignored their repeated taunts about my moral character and color, they gave up and sped away probably to harass some other black female. God, I hated those racist white boys.

A year into my two-year internship at Tuskegee I learned a lot about living under segregation. I knew there were reporters covering Dr. King's non-violent crusade, and I so wanted to be among them. But they were, for the most part, white male journalists. I wanted to tell the story to the American public from a black perspective. Those white reporters had never gone through the rejection and prejudice I had faced. I felt I could bring another dimension to the story which would help white Americans better comprehend why black people were fighting so hard to end segregation.

While at Tuskegee I wanted to join the civil rights movement. I was bitter about the suffering, the brutality, and the white hatred that my people endured. There were laws that should have protected us from second-class citizenship. I could get my head cracked open and be one more of the thousands of casualties of the struggle, but I decided I could do more by becoming a journalist. I decided that telling the stories of oppressed peoples fairly, objectively, and accurately was my destiny. Someday.

TAKE ME BACK TO CHICAGO

After two years at Tuskegee I was anxious to get back on track to becoming a working journalist. I also wanted to get out of the South. The struggle against segregation was becoming more widespread and more violent. I reasoned that if I got another degree in journalism that I would become a more attractive candidate for a newspaper job. I applied to several colleges and chose the University of Iowa because I was offered a good-paying internship writing stories for the *RTNDA Bulletin*, the trade publication for the Radio-Television News Directors Association. That opportunity sparked an interest in broadcasting. I still wanted to work in print until the only course that fit into my class schedule was a Radio-TV Workshop.

Students learned to write for broadcast and our work appeared on a closed circuit campus TV show and on the commercial radio station owned by the University. I had never heard a woman broadcast news but I auditioned. Before I took to the microphone, the station manager said no women had become newscasters because their voices were "so thin." Men's voices, he said, were more suitable for delivering the news.

Thank heavens for my acting experience throughout high school and college. I held the pages of the five-minute newscast I had written, dropped my voice into a lower range, projected the words from my diaphragm, and delivered them with my best articulation. The station

41

manager was in awe of what he called my "pipes." He said he was anxious to get me on the air as soon as possible. I still had to learn how to pace the stories and how to count myself down by the clock to get off the air on time. Once I mastered those radio skills I was ready.

In the fall of 1964, I became the first woman to broadcast news on WSUI, Iowa City. Word spread quickly and people wanted to hear this new broadcaster. I received rave reviews and people would tune in to listen to my newscasts. It didn't take long for me to start favoring broadcasting over print.

I particularly liked the fact that as a broadcaster I could still go out and cover stories but with a tape recorder instead of a pad and pencil. I could bring back my audiotape and my personal impressions from an event and craft a news story, writing around the sound bites from people I interviewed. The most fun of all was sitting in front of the microphone and reading my stories directly to the public, using my voice intonations and pauses for emphasis. I learned the power of the human voice, my voice, to evoke reactions from the public. Radio is an intimate medium and I told my stories as if I were talking to just one individual. It worked. My broadcast journalism professor said I <u>could</u> be a print reporter, but that I had a unique talent for broadcasting. He told me to consider radio <u>and</u> television, even though I had never seen a person of color doing the news on TV.

I decided I would be happy doing news reporting in any medium as long as I could finally practice the profession I had been preparing for such a long time. Shy of my master's thesis, I left Iowa and returned to Chicago and the love and support of my parents. It was the summer of 1965 and I planned to spend it finding a job. I went on interviews for jobs at newspapers, the wire services, radio stations, and traveled to St. Louis, Cleveland, and a number of news outlets in Chicago. They said they would get back to me. I waited.

On August 11, 1965, it seemed as though everything was going to change in this country. The violence that accompanied protests in the South broke out unexpectedly and horrifically in Watts, a poor black suburb of Los Angeles. Embittered Negroes in the North, who lacked jobs and decent housing, saw that non-violent protests in the South did little to help them. The Watts riots lasted six days leaving thirty-two dead, more than a thousand people injured, and more than 3000 arrested. The burning, looting and killing were precipitated by the arrest of a black man by two white policemen, the kind of incident that became the most popular recipe for unrest in Northern cities across the nation.

All of a sudden I started hearing back from the news organizations, which had kept me waiting for job offers most of the summer. Watts woke up the news media. Editors and news directors realized they might be on the brink of a second American Revolution or Civil War. In Watts, black activists refused to talk to white journalists, who were left to report only the views of the police and city officials. The major group responsible for the violence, disadvantaged blacks, would not answer questions like: "What do you people want? "Why are you burning your own neighborhoods?" They refused to answer such questions from white reporters. Some of the ad hoc leaders even said they would only talk to black reporters. Most of the major news organizations didn't have any. That started the scramble to find them.

There were many black journalists who, like me, had been having trouble finding jobs. But now our color had become an advantage, not a hindrance. We were being scooped up by news organizations which needed black reporters to get inside ghetto communities and tell the stories which might explain the urban uprisings.

I turned down several job offers to take a reporting job at WCFL Radio in Chicago. While it was a 100-thousand-watt rock and roll Top 40 powerhouse, the station also had a large and widely respected news department. I was thrilled. I had gotten a job at last, in one of the best news towns in the country, and I was home.

My first day on the job I was introduced to some of the most famous disc jockeys in the city, but of more consequence, the thirteen white men I would be working with in the News Department. They did not hide their resentment that a colored woman without any previous commercial broadcasting experience got hired in what at the time was the second biggest radio market in the country. Although I was more educated than any of the men, I knew I was going to have to work hard to win their respect. Most had been doing radio news for a long time. I would need to make friends out of a bunch of guys who appeared at first glance to be potential enemies. They whispered among themselves—so loudly I could hear—that I had no business being hired in Chicago. I had come straight from school and a campus radio station. They didn't hide their resentment.

When I became the first woman to broadcast news in Chicago in 1965, I <u>became</u> news. The press attention was more than my colleagues could bear. Who ever heard of a woman delivering the news, much less a colored one?

In the beginning, the news director assigned me the so-called "women's stories": celebrities in town, childcare conferences, gala openings of new movies, beauty pageant contestants, health news and baby animals, lots of baby animals. Both Brookfield and Lincoln Park Zoos are in the Chicago area, so every time an animal gave birth I was there to capture the "blessed event." If anything happened involving black people, I was first up. My male colleagues didn't like going to slum neighborhoods. In fact, they were afraid. I also was the station's movie reviewer. This is not what I expected. I wanted to cover Mayor Richard J. Daley's City Hall, the Chicago mob murders, the politics, the fires, and the disasters. My education prepared me for that kind of reporting. For the first of what would be many times, a news executive told me, "You're not ready." What I heard was, "You're not good enough." It became one of those "No's" I refused to accept, which compelled me to work harder.

My mother stepped in again with her frequent words of wisdom. When I expressed my frustration about not being allowed to cover the "big stories", she told me what many young black people probably heard from their parents.

"Because you are colored, you're going to have to work twice as hard as everybody else and you'll still get only half the credit." At that time my mother, who had never worked outside the home, didn't know how much my gender played a role, as well.

The men had it in for me at WCFL. Among their efforts to derail the "colored woman who didn't belong" were things like: the assignment editor sending me to a news conference that occurred an hour before I showed up; sending me to the wrong address for an interview; or sticking me on the stupid stories that would never make air, like a neighborhood cherry pie-making contest. All the better to make me look incompetent to my news director. He would demand to know why I missed stories or came up with ridiculous ones. I was reduced to sputtering, "but that's what they told me to do." I learned to check everything out before I headed into the streets to cover a story. These things would not happen to me again.

There were times I would come back from covering stories and my interview tapes turned up missing. I couldn't put together my reports without the tapes. I could deal with some of the foolishness but not the day my tempestuous news director threw a heavy Smith and Corona typewriter at me. I was trying to explain to him why I couldn't get the parents of a murdered teenage girl to grant me an interview. I dodged the typewriter, which smashed into the wall and crashed to the floor. I ran from the room. I was really frightened. But I didn't want to go to our boss and report the incident and have everyone think I couldn't take it. Silly me. I was so young. It never occurred to me that I could have charged this violent man with attempted assault by what I considered a potentially deadly weapon. In my later years, an incident like this would not go unchallenged. I would learn my rights and exercise them.

I kept pressuring my boss to let me cover the stories which led the newscasts, the stories that were the most important, that were not just interesting but had real consequences for our listeners. Because I had done well with the "fluff" pieces, he began to relent, but only when a man wasn't available.

My male colleagues gave me the most difficult trial under fire when I got my own newscast, a daily five-minute show at 9 o'clock in the morning. I had to write the news stories, pick the sound bites and reports I would use, and make sure they timed out exactly to five minutes. I would give the broadcast engineer my script and the cartridges containing the sound clips. I then went into the small on-air news studio, settled into my seat and adjusted the microphone. I would then mentally prepare myself, focusing on my delivery so I wouldn't fluff any words and could deliver a newscast that would demonstrate women could read the news as well as men.

During my first weeks in the broadcast booth and, mind you, while I was on the air, one guy pushed the heavy door open. You're not supposed to come into the studio and disturb an anchor on the air unless there is breaking news or a story needs a correction. But the door was opened so that I could see my male colleague's big white buttocks. He had pulled down his pants and "mooned" me while I was reading news about American deaths in Vietnam.

Another day one of my male co-workers threw a huge rubber tarantula on the desk while I was again on the air live. Then there was the time one of them came into the booth, walked behind me, and snatched the unread pages of my script off the table. What are you supposed to do when you have to fill a five-minute news hole and three of the minutes are being held out of reach over your head? You think fast, that's what you do. I picked up the pages I had already read and started reading them again, "Repeating our top story..." Since I had written the stories, I was familiar enough with the facts that I adlibbed a couple of them. I slowed my reading pace to the length of time I was to fill. Anyone listening probably had no idea something was amiss.

When I saw the naked butt, I could have stopped reading and

tried to suppress my shock. I could have screamed when that tarantula landed on the desk. I wanted to. And when my script was snatched I could have tried to snatch it back from that idiot, but I was live on the air. I couldn't stop. I had to keep going. Even though my head was steaming, none of these pranks prevented me from doing my job. Because of my anger and the knowledge that there was a white male conspiracy to wreck my fledgling career, I was better than ever considering the circumstances.

I returned to the newsroom to complain about the antics only to have the guys say I had no sense of humor. (I would hear this from men many times during my broadcast career.) They said were just having fun and that they haze all the new people. Maybe once for others, but it was over and over again for me. Fun they called it, at my expense and they hoped the expense of my career.

As hard as it was to work under the threat of one of these men derailing me, I learned a valuable lesson: to never lose my concentration. It served me well through years of live broadcasts and stupid men.

After I left radio and went to work for the NBC television station, WMAQ, I had to go into the studio one day to do a live report on a major criminal trial underway in Chicago. I had to stand to deliver my report, and while the artist's sketches of the courtroom scenes were on the screen, the anchorman got down on his knees, reached under my dress and used both hands to fondle my behind. Did I shriek? Did I mess up? No, my delivery was smooth because I had learned not to be distracted by what was going on around me and to me. Thanks to those shenanigans from my early radio days, I was able to finish any live report, whether I was talking in the midst of gunshots, surrounded by riot police beating back protestors, or walking in a minefield in Angola.

So, all of their efforts to mess me up made me a stronger broadcaster. Throughout my career nothing has been able to interrupt my concentration thanks to the men who conspired to make my work unbearable. No's again. During one of my news broadcasts at ABC in New York, a giant overhead studio light exploded, sounding like a loud gunshot. We played back the tape and you could hear the "bang," and everyone marveled that I didn't flinch.

I felt constant pressure to represent my race and gender in the best possible way. I learned that affirmative action wouldn't guarantee my success, even though I consider myself an "affirmative action baby." I was coming along when the news media was under pressure to hire more women and minorities. Affirmative action may have gotten me in the door but I wouldn't have stayed if I didn't have the necessary skills.

To succeed in corporate America there is an expression that while coarse, nails it. "Your shit must be tight." What does that mean? Be at work early and leave late. Be dependable. Volunteer for the assignments no one else wants. Work weekends, and if necessary, cancel personal plans if asked to work. My stories had to be strong and well written. I had to be nice to people who weren't nice back. A sense of humor and a sense of the absurd also helped.

It is difficult for an employer to slam the door in your face if you are among the best. I have seen too many of my people blame every problem they have on racism. There's no doubt it exists, but one of the best ways to deal with it is to make sure your "shit is tight."

Why do I talk this way? I never cursed until I had to work with men. There is a lot of cursing in the workplace. I discovered I had to get down on their level and use curse words. If I said, "Would you please be quiet?" I was ignored. But when I said "Shut the fuck up!" I got their attention. Only when I used foul language would I be taken seriously. It's a sorry shame but that's how it is in many workplace environments.

I AM WOMAN

Throughout this period I was totally focused on my career, I did very little dating and found most of my suitors unsuitable for me. I was satisfied that I was making good progress in my career. Marriage and children were not on my mind, but after a year at WCFL, I felt it was getting time to move out of my parents' home and live on my own.

An old boyfriend, Jim Marshall, was living in San Jose, California, but we continued to remain in contact. We had been girlfriend and boyfriend at the University of Michigan, we became best friends while I was in Tuskegee, Iowa City, and then Chicago, and he was working as an engineer in Richland, Washington, and then California. There were frequent letters and phone calls for three years.

In August of 1965, three months after I started at WCFL, he called and said he was coming to his Alpha Phi Alpha fraternity convention in Chicago and he said he hoped we could have dinner or something. I was excited. I hadn't seen him since 1962 and I knew we would have fun because in college we always had fun. He was smart and humorous and we enjoyed many of the same pastimes, like going to movies, arguing politics, playing "Tag, You're It" like a couple of ten-year-olds. He was certainly more appealing than the guys I dated in Chicago.

Jim came to pick me up for a dinner date and I was amazed at his growth and maturity. He was an imposing six feet four inches and no longer dressed in his University of Michigan jacket, khaki pants, and beat up sneakers. He was now an engineer for General Electric and wearing a suit and tie. I was bowled over. My God, he's a real man, I thought, not the dopey student who dropped ice down my back and spit after our first kiss.

That week Jim spent more time with me than with his frat brothers at the convention. I have to admit I was smitten again. Clearly, he was too. I was a radio personality and still the drama queen he took so many pokes at in school. Yet he admitted I still turned him on. While we were at Michigan he talked of a serious relationship. I laughed it off. I was going to be a journalist and didn't have time for that. Now in Chicago, one romantic night parked near Lake Michigan, in view of Chicago's stunning night skyline, he told me that he had never stopped loving me when we both left Michigan. But I didn't love him in college; we were just a couple who went to football games, movies, and the rare meal in a campus hangout. This time I felt totally different. I was falling in love.

Jim had to return to California and I didn't want him to go. I even cried when he left. Our relationship had moved to the serious level. No more funny cards and trinkets; I started getting red roses, a pearl necklace, and real love letters.

He began looking for an engineering job in the Chicago area almost as soon as he got back to San Jose. He found a job doing nuclear reactor research at Argonne National Laboratory in Argonne, Illinois. In January of 1966 he moved to the Windy City, renting a kitchenette in a downtown residential hotel. He went to work in the day and pursued me relentlessly at night.

When I started my broadcasting career a year earlier, doing well at work was all I was concerned about. I wasn't worried about getting married, and certainly not about having babies. Jim really pushed me to marry him. After leaving Tuskegee and then graduate school at the University of Iowa, I moved back home with my parents. Jim expressed time and time again that it was time for me to get out on my own, permanently.

On a cold and wintry February night in 1966, Jim came to my house because I was in bed with the flu. As all of our conversations ended in those days, he asked again that night when we were going to get married. I hemmed and hawed, "I don't know. I'm sick. I don't want to talk about it now."

He jumped to his feet, said goodbye, and left my room. I knew he was really angry. In a hoarse voice I called to him, "Jim. Come back." No answer. I heard the front door slam. I was weak but I got out of bed, grabbed my robe, put on my slippers and dragged myself to the door. He was walking down the snowy sidewalk to his little red sports car. I went outside in the sub-freezing weather and called to him to come back. I must have been a sight, standing on the walk with no make-up, mussed up hair, and dressed in my robe and fluffy slippers. I called out, "Don't leave, Jim."

He turned around and asked in a stern voice, "Are you going to marry me or not?" I felt like a little child and timidly answered, "Uh, I guess so."

He came running back and we hugged. "Now, let's get you back in bed so we can set a date." He was so persistent.

It wasn't the romantic marriage proposal I dreamed of, with my "Prince Charming" on his knee holding a little velvet box in which a beautiful diamond ring sparkled. But in many ways, my real proposal was better, because it was so "us."

Seven months later we got married on the campus of the University of Chicago. We moved into a two-bedroom apartment in Hyde Park, the University neighborhood. Legally, I took my husband's name, but to the rest of the world, I was still Carole Simpson. I was working for WCFL Radio and my name was already established on the air as the first woman news broadcaster. My boss didn't want me to change my name to Carole Marshall. That was fine with me. The name sounded alien. I had been Simpson all my life and I was enough of a feminist that I didn't want to change my name to that of my husband. I would never be Mrs. James Marshall. That's what his mother called herself. His father was named James, too.

In the early years I was quite content with our life together with our Siamese cat, Pyewacket. We went out on a moment's notice and took trips when we felt like it. I wanted to be married but didn't care about having children. Then, after three years of marriage I woke up one morning and wanted a baby. Yes, there is a biological clock and mine went off without warning. I not only wanted a baby, I had to have a baby. Jim was not thrilled at the prospect, believing it would complicate our lives. Kids will do that, I knew. Still, I wanted to fulfill my female role as a child bearer.

Four years after we married I gave birth to Mallika Joy. While I was on maternity leave I enjoyed taking care of Malli, feeding her, singing to her, dancing with her, stimulating her tiny mind. Then after a couple of months I discovered that I wasn't talking to any grownups. News was happening and I wasn't covering it. I missed my job. As much as I loved my daughter, I knew that I would never be happy being a stay-at-home Mom. I have respect for women who make that choice. I take nothing away from them, but it wasn't for me. I still had the strong ambition to prove to people that I could be black and female, married with children, and still be able to excel in the workplace.

During my maternity leave I got the offer from WMAQ-TV, a powerful NBC-owned station, to join the staff as a general assignment reporter. The station was like a farm team for the network. Many top NBC News producers and reporters had to go through Chicago before moving on to bigger and better things at the network.

I loved radio because the public can hear your voice and the sounds of the news, but on television they can see and hear you. I knew that TV anchors and reporters were among the city's celebrities. That was of no consequence to me. I wanted the opportunity to tell a more compelling story by not just describing it for the audience but showing pictures of an event. I could say on the radio that, "the woman sobbed uncontrollably," but on television I could show her actually crying making the story have more impact.

During the interview with the news director I admitted I had only done TV while I was in college. I felt there was so much I had to learn. He responded that what he needed was a good reporter who could write and tell a story well.

"You already have mastered that," he said. "All we have to do is show you how to work with the pictures."

"But the makeup, hair and clothes. Don't I need to look good?" I asked. I never had to worry about that before. I didn't go out reporting for radio looking bad, but I knew that in television, appearance counts.

"That's nothing. We'll help you with all of that," he answered.

"But will I know how to write for TV?" He told me that radio had been the perfect preparation for television because I already knew how to write concise scripts written for the ear, and he said I didn't have to work on my voice because he thought I had one of the strongest broadcast voices he had heard. All I needed to learn, he said, was how to use pictures to enhance my storytelling and how to pick the film (yes, we were using film in the 1970's) that would illustrate the story most effectively.

I felt a lot better. The learning curve would not be as steep as it would be for a print reporter. I talked it over with my husband, who thought it was a great opportunity. I would be on one of the city's four stations, three of them owned by the big three commercial networks. I accepted the offer, called in my regrets to my friends at WBBM, and was set to report for duty in September.

My baby was a little more than three months old. In those days you didn't leave a child that young to go to work. When I reported to WMAQ-TV I was totally unprepared for the reactions from men and women when they found out I had a baby at home and wasn't taking care of her. I heard comments like:

"What kind of mother are you?"

"You must not love your baby."

"Is your work more important than your family?"

"Without you there, she may grow up to be a problem."

I tried to explain that my mother will care for her while I'm at work but that didn't mean anything to people who thought women worked only until they had children. They hadn't heard of women like me who truly loved their profession and hoped to make a contribution to society by communicating to the public the problems the city faced.

I was one of the females in the 1970's, the decade of the women's liberation movement, who was called a "Superwoman." It was not a compliment. It was a pejorative against women who wanted to have it all: marriage, children and a career. Working men can have small babies at home and nobody raises an eyebrow. Why not women?

My antennae had already been raised by racism and now I ran head first into sexism. Women can't.... Women aren't supposed to... Women belong... It made me furious.

At WMAQ I felt the sting of being both black and female. How did I get a top job at Channel Five? I wasn't that good, some employees whispered. She's only done radio and she abandoned her baby. She must not be a good mother. Her poor child.

What none of them knew is that I worked as hard at being a good mother as I did a good journalist. I bought all the books I could about raising children. I didn't rely on what they said, but was familiar with the latest literature and applied that knowledge to what came naturally to me. And of course, my mother had plenty of advice.

Since I was such a terrible mother, I must be a terrible person. I had to work with older white cameramen who didn't want to work with me. I had no TV experience and didn't know anything about putting together a picture story. I knew that to have a distinctive report, better than the competition's, I would need to get the best pictures. That meant the total cooperation of my TV crew, which consisted of the camera operator, a soundman, and a lighting man.

There were six different crews of predominantly white men, who would be assigned to work with all the reporters.

Every time I went out on a story I traveled in a station wagon with a crew of three men. How to get them to work with me and not against me? Since I had worked solely with men in radio, I learned some important things about men, in general. They need stroking; they need to be in charge; they need to feel they have to take care of the "weaker sex"; and they like food and drink. Those that work in technical fields don't appreciate the on-air college-educated people talking or looking down on them.

With those observations in mind I was very crafty dealing with my all male television crews by playing the dumb brunette. When we went out on a story, if it was winter, I brought cups of coffee down to the crew car; in summer, I brought soft drinks or lemonade. Sometimes I would double a batch of cookies and bring some for the crew and offer them in the car before we got out of the garage. Now how could you be nasty to someone who started the day with you in such a pleasant manner, even if she were an unqualified black woman?

When a story involved catching all the action, I had seen crews move like 150-year-old tortoises, slowing down intentionally as they were getting their gear together and so by the time they were ready, the "money" shots were over. Instead of saying to my crew, "Hurry up. Hurry up," I would calmly ask the gentlemen if it weren't too much to ask, could they get some specific shot I wanted which was taking place right now? They all hustled for me. Instead of ordering them to go up a hill (camera crews hated to climb up anything) to get a panoramic shot, I would say something like this: "I don't know, but what do you think? If you got up on that hill do you think you could get a wide shot that would show the whole area? I think the producer would like that shot. I don't know if it's possible, but what do you think?"

The cameraman would usually agree with my suggestion or make an even better one. Then he would tell the rest of the crew, "Let's get up on that mound and get a wide shot." It became his idea and he ordered the crew around.

When my stories aired, I always called to thank the cameramen for their excellent work and said that without them I wouldn't have been able to come up with such a good story. Stroke, stroke. Other reporters didn't do that, so I made them feel pride in their camera work and they became more anxious to work with me in the future.

It didn't work on some men. They weren't going to like me no matter what. On long drives to a news event they would ask questions about race and use crude language to talk about their sexual exploits, which I knew were designed to embarrass me and get me flustered. Call me a prude, but I didn't like to hear that kind of talk, and once those hateful guys found that out, they would do it all the time. Of course, it never occurred to me then to report them to management. I was so afraid that it would be used against me and other women to keep us out of the news business because they thought we could never "be one of the guys."

Playing dumb was onerous to me, but I did what I had to do to get the best story. (I just read how that sounds.) No, I never used sex to get my way. There are some places I just wouldn't go.

After I got comfortable with the rules of television, I decided I wanted the opportunity to anchor the news. In addition to the main newscasts at 5 and 10 p.m., there was the noon news and the weekend newscasts at 10 o'clock. Here are some of the excuses I heard about why I couldn't anchor:

> "White people don't like to hear black people deliver the news."
> "Women don't like to hear other women on the air."
> "Your enunciation is too perfect." (The black male reporter on staff was told he sounded too ethnic.)
> "You need to practice your delivery with a tape recorder at home, so you can relate better to the audience." (I

had been a broadcaster for six years and was already
being called "The Voice" by many in the city.

I wanted to know where I could find the market research that
came up with some of these conclusions. Well, of course, it didn't
exist. My news director said it was the "prevailing opinion." By whom?
He said, "by everybody." I think he meant everybody who was male.
I argued that it was ridiculous and we should test it and see if people
turn me off the news. That little experiment wouldn't occur for some
time.

All of my untoward experiences with men were occurring during
the time of the Women's Liberation Movement. I read about women
working at universities, at Fortune 500 companies, at law firms and
in blue and pink-collar jobs, all complaining about the treatment
they had to endure from some men in the workplace. Feminists were
determined to change things. And, by the way, "feminist" is not a bad
word. It simply means that a woman believes that men and women
should have equal rights. In the Seventies, women were getting "mad
as hell" and not going to take it anymore. As I heard about the slights,
insults, the sex discrimination and sexual harassment in fields across
the board, I started becoming radicalized too. Women had to speak
up. And so I did.

Historically, whites considered black women as "loose" or "easy."
Men I worked with apparently bought the myth and were always
"hitting on me" to a degree white women didn't experience. My white
female colleagues might get a come on like, "How about we grab a
drink after work tonight?"

To me they would say, "Why don't we get it on tonight?" or "I
could use a good lay. I'm up for it. Are you?"

They would talk about my legs. The conversation with one guy
began, "You have some great legs. Why don't you wrap them around
me?" And he would make a crude gesture.

I had one man at WMAQ stick his hand down my blouse and
touch my breasts. Another pulled down the long zipper on a dress I

was wearing in front of other people. These coarse actions and remarks always took place while we were trying to work, or at least while I was trying to work. It was a hostile work environment. But at that time there were no laws protecting women from sexual harassment on the job. When I had enough, I got up my nerve and I went to the news director to report the sexual remarks and gestures. I told him it was difficult to work with the particular men I discussed. I believed I would find a sympathetic ear. Wrong. It was my fault.

The boss asked me in a nice way if I were flaunting myself around the men. "Of course not," I replied indignantly. "If you think I would be interested in any of them, you're out of your mind. Have you taken a good look at these guys? Besides, I'm happily married."

He smiled and countered that, "They're just playing around with you. You obviously don't have a sense of humor."

"No, I don't." Realizing nothing would be rectified in that office, I would have to handle this myself.

When I was working in Washington at a network, I was in the midst of writing a report and was looking for a good sound bite from Corazon Aquino, the first female president of the Philippines, who was visiting the United States. I was sitting with the tape editor while listening to her news conference. She described her love for her assassinated husband. She said the first time she met him he stole her heart, her mind, and her soul. My editor pipes up, "And my pussy."

I told him to shut up, that I didn't want to hear that kind of talk.

"Oh Carole," he said laughing, "Lighten up."

"No, you lighten up or I'll demand you be taken off this story."

We continued screening the tape and I found President Aquino utter the statement I wanted to work into the report. The producer was in another room and I wanted him to hear it. I shouted to him, "Dick, come. I found it. Come, Dick."

The editor said softly. "Come. Dick. I like the way that sounds. Dick. Come."

I jumped up from my seat and said, "That's it. You're finished."

He looked truly frightened. He never thought I would follow through and he literally begged me not to say anything. "I'm sorry, Carole. I didn't mean anything. I could lose my job." I found out later he was skating on thin ice with his supervisor for a variety of technical missteps.

I am generally a good-natured person but you can push me only so far and I blow up. Don't push me. I can get ugly and loud real fast, especially when I'm trying to get my work done. I also learned that while I never used curse words, to deal with men in the news business I would have to cuss.

My voice became an effective tool. I can speak so loudly and so forcefully that I could stop traffic at work. Of course, everyone heard the ruckus and wanted to know what happened to get "Carole so riled up." People would find out why some men became the victims of my verbal wrath, and eventually it would get back to management. I was never called in by any supervisor to discuss the problems I found degrading, humiliating and sexist, and I never heard that anyone I complained about was ever reprimanded. It was the price of being a woman in a white male-dominated workplace.

Women were encouraged that they would secure their rights when the Supreme Court ruled in the 1973 Roe v. Wade case, which made abortion legal. A woman could control her reproduction. By the mid-1970's women were filing lawsuits against companies and individuals on charges of sexual harassment and sex discrimination. Men were upset. Again. They had gone through black demands for equality and now here come the women. They feared that their jobs were in jeopardy if the courts ruled that women should have equal access to employment opportunities. The men still thought women were supposed to stay home and take care of the families. Many men didn't realize that hundreds of thousands of women were widowed, divorced, or abandoned by men and had to work to become the family breadwinners. They didn't want to be stuck in low paying waitress, retail clerk, and secretarial jobs. Women wanted to become fire fighters, police officers, airline pilots, astronauts, chefs, forest rangers. Every job available in any field had a woman who wanted it. Ambitions were soaring as women sought to get into the trade unions, into career tracks in the business world, and into the executive suites of corporations. Women began running for political office, realizing that their voices and votes could change laws to benefit women.

Women's organizations formed to urge Congress to pass the Equal Rights Amendment to the Constitution. The words "woman", "she", and "her" are not mentioned anywhere in the document which governs the United States of America.

Because of my problems at work as a black and as a woman, I was determined that in my profession, I would speak out against prejudice, stereotyping, and discrimination. That meant using my voice to assist other employees as well as speaking out against racist and sexist reporting. I felt it was my obligation to the blacks I met in the South and to the women I worked with, both of whom were not considered "as good as white men."

During this period of my career I developed my female "roar" for equal opportunity and equal rights for women and minorities. I had found this non-broadcast voice, which I would use to benefit others. I always felt I was on the side of right.

DR. MARTIN LUTHER KING
GIVES ME A BOOST

Thanks to Dr. Martin Luther King I made my first mark in journalism in Chicago. In 1966, four months after the riots in Watts, California, he announced from Georgia that he was going to bring his non-violent civil rights campaign to Chicago, but he gave no reason. Nearly everyone in America was befuddled by the news. Why would he come North? There were no segregation laws in Illinois. Of course, I was excited that the great black leader would be making national news in my city. I wanted that story.

The national and all the Chicago media were trying to find out what Dr. King was guarding so closely. Public interest continued to heighten. In early January, the journalists following him in the South reported that the civil rights leader and a group of his closest aides had boarded a plane in Atlanta bound for Chicago. The flight would take about two and a half hours.

I literally begged my news director to let me cover his arrival at O'Hare to try and find out what the Chicago campaign was all about. Okay, he said, and he reminded me we were in a highly competitive situation with other Chicago media. "If it's to be gotten, I will get it," I said too boastfully.

I joined throngs of reporters and camera crews at the gate where the Atlanta passengers were to arrive. No Dr. King. Flight attendants told us he had been whisked out the back of the plane to a waiting motorcade on the tarmac to avoid the press. We all shouted, "Where did he go?" As if they knew.

I knew I had to find his hotel. Most of my more experienced colleagues headed downtown to look for him at one of the major hotels. Dr. King was usually put up in the best hotels when he came North to make a speech or receive an award. But it made sense to me that he wouldn't go that far since he was being so secretive. There were several hotels near the airport. I went to each one and asked the desk clerks stupidly, "Is Dr. King registered here?" Of course, they all denied it.

There was something about one of the hotels that piqued my interest. It just seemed to have more activity going on, although I didn't see any black faces, or extra security. It was just my gut feeling. I sneaked past the front desk to get to the elevators leading to the twelve floors of the hotel. I got in one of them and pushed the button for the second floor. The doors opened and I looked up and down the corridor. Fortunately it was a rectangular hotel so there were no hallways leading off the main corridor. Nothing was going on. I stopped at each floor, repeating the exercise. Three, four, five, six. Then lucky seven.

The doors opened and at one end of the long corridor, I saw six or seven black men chatting at the end of the hallway. I squinted to see if one of them were Dr. King. I couldn't tell, but I got off the elevator. It was about 7:30 p.m., and if I hurried I could get a story on the 8 o'clock newscast. I set up my heavy, clunky reel-to-reel tape recorder, plugged in the microphone, hoisted it on my shoulder and headed toward the group of men. One of them walked forward to block my path. He said, "Can I help you, young lady?"

"Uh, yes. I'm Carole Simpson from WCFL Radio and I'd like to interview Dr. King." Oh, my naiveté.

"Dr. King is resting and he's not granting any interviews. He's holding a news conference at 10 o'clock in the morning. You can ask your questions there," he said with finality.

"But I can't wait that long," I pressed. "I have to get the story now."

"Well, you won't," he said. Another "No."

"Then I'll wait here," I told him. "Dr. King might change his mind."

I got back on the elevator and went to a pay telephone in the lobby and called the news editor on duty. I reported that I had found where Dr. King was staying and that I didn't see any other reporters around. I told him his aides said he wouldn't give me an interview. I also gave him the news about the press conference the next morning. I surprised myself when I said I was going to stay on his floor of hotel all night if I had to, that I was determined to get the exclusive. I told him I would call when I had something. "Good girl," he offered. Just as an aside, if I had been a man, I doubt he would have said, "Good boy."

The hotel gift shop was still open. I bought some newspapers, some cheese and peanut butter crackers, and a Hershey bar. I stopped on a random floor and got a Coke out of a vending machine. Armed with my provisions I headed back to the seventh floor and plunked everything down right at the edge of the bank of elevators. Dr. King would have to get past me to leave the hotel and I was prepared for a long wait. It was winter so I had a big coat I sat on to soften my makeshift seat on the marble floor.

I kept one eye on my reading material and the other on the end of the hallway to my left. At around eleven, one of the men came over to me and said, "Why don't you go home, miss? You're not going to get anything from Dr. King tonight."

I stared up at his kindly face and said, "Thank you, sir, but I'm going to stay until I can talk to Dr. King." I figured I was still ahead of the rest of the press corps by having him a few hundred yards away from me.

The comings and goings from the row of guest rooms at the end of the hall continued until well after midnight. I would later learn the names of the men I saw: The Rev. Ralph Abernathy, The Rev.

Andrew Young, The Rev. C.T. Vivian, and The Rev. Hosea Williams. I had seen them all on television, arms interlocked with one another, Dr. King at the center, marching through Birmingham and Selma, Alabama, and Albany, Georgia. I also recognized the civil rights leader in Chicago, Al Raby. This was going to be big.

The night seemed like an eternity. At 3 a.m., I was tired and sleepy and wanted to go home. But I didn't risk nodding off. I was starting to feel a little foolish. I read the horoscopes, did the crossword puzzles, even read the sports. I ran out of things to do to keep me awake.

Shortly after 7 a.m. (I had become an inveterate clock-watcher by this time) there were stirrings at the end of the corridor. Doors began to open and men were chatting in the hall. One of them approached me and said, "You really stayed all night?"

"I have to get a word with Dr. King," I responded with sleep in my eyes and my muscles aching. By now, I concluded an interview was out of the question. The man told me Dr. King would be going down to breakfast shortly. My opportunity had come. The sleepiness and exhaustion dissipated quickly.

I tried to straighten myself up, pressing out the wrinkles in my skirt, taking a brush to my hair, and applying some lipstick without a mirror. This was about to be the biggest moment of my life as a journalist. Dr. King was an iconic figure, a rock star, the most important black man in America and the moral conscience of the nation. He had won the Nobel Peace Prize at age thirty-five. I was in Tuskegee, Alabama, when he delivered his historic "I Have a Dream" speech on the steps of the Lincoln Memorial during the 1963 March on Washington. Living in Alabama at the time, I hung onto every eloquent phrase, which I'm not sure I would have done if I were still living in Chicago. I now had an appreciation for how much degradation and injustice segregation was inflicting on my people in the South.

Dr. King came out of his hotel room. His male contingent filed behind him. My heart swelled. Don't blow this, Carole, I said to myself. He walked closer to the elevator bank that had been my temporary home for twelve hours. He was shorter than I expected, not much taller than my 5 feet 7 inches. But he was a towering figure. I was in complete awe.

He spoke first. "Are you the nice young lady I've been hearing about? You spent the night here?" he questioned.

I stuttered, "Y-y-yes, sir. And it is my greatest pleasure to meet you." He extended his large hand and gave my much smaller one a firm shake.

"Dr. King, I hate to bother you on your way to breakfast but I've been waiting to find out what your crusade in Chicago is all about." My words tumbled out. "I'm the only Negro female reporter in Chicago and it would really help my career if I could find out before the rest of the reporters. Please tell me Dr. King, please?"

He leaned his face toward mine and whispered in my ear: "I am here to challenge the authority of Mayor Daley on the issue of fair housing. This city, as far as housing is concerned, is the most segregated in the nation." He turned his face away and in his cultured southern accent he said in a friendly voice, "Now don't you tell anybody, ya' hear?"

For a moment I was taken aback and then he winked. I took that to mean, "It's yours."

"Oh, Dr. King, thank you so much."

As he got into the elevator, he looked back at me and said, "I admire your perseverance, young lady. Good luck."

I felt as if I had been blessed. But I quickly recovered my composure to call my news desk. I screamed into the phone that I had just talked to Dr. King and I know why he's here. The news editor didn't want to wait until the 8 a.m. newscast. He went straight to the morning disc jockey and said we've got a scoop from Carole Simpson on Dr. King's mission. "Can we break into programming and I'll put her on the air with you." The deejay quickly accepted the offer.

I hadn't written anything. I would have to just tell what happened. And I did, somewhat breathlessly. Things happened so quickly. For the 8:30 newscast, I was live again. The Mutual Broadcasting Company, which my station was affiliated with, put me on the national network. I was heard on radio stations all across the country, my first national exposure.

The wire services, the Associated Press and United Press International, picked up the story, which began, "WCFL Radio in Chicago reports..." Those wires went directly into newspaper, radio and TV offices across the nation. I later heard that many newspapers were skeptical of the story. Who is Carole Simpson? She works for a rock station. How can we trust her reporting?

That didn't seem to matter to their bosses, who started running reports that Dr. King will announce at press conference this morning that he will mount a campaign against Chicago's segregated housing, taking on the political machine of Mayor Richard J. Daley.

I got back to WCFL from the airport hotel at about 9 o'clock, and walked into the newsroom to applause. The news editor said "we" had beaten the entire Chicago press corps. Get that. "We." I had a lot to do with it, but it was still too distasteful for the guys to congratulate me directly.

Unwashed and still in my wrinkled clothes I went to Dr. King's news conference and one of those nice hotels he usually stayed in. I beamed when he made his announcement. I had gotten it right. At age twenty-four, I had trumped all the national veterans on the Dr. King beat. During the news conference they eyed me warily. During the question and answer period, I caught Dr. King's eye. He smiled and I gave him a baby "Hi" motion with my hand.

With his whisper in my ear, Dr. Martin Luther King literally made my career. With an exclusive on one of the biggest stories in the nation, I was now a force to be reckoned with inside Chicago's prestigious journalism corps. Without my scoop it may have taken much longer to attract the attention of the Chicago media establishment.

To press his point about Chicago housing, Dr. King moved into an apartment in the Lawndale community, one of the city's poorest, to launch his anti-housing discrimination protests in some of the all white neighborhoods of Chicago. I continued to be the reporter on the King beat in Chicago and went where he went to demonstrate and hold rallies. White violence had followed him North. He was hit by a rock thrown in Gage Park, a middle class neighborhood on the Southwest side, whose residents vowed blacks would never move in. He later remarked that he was more frightened in Chicago than in any of his marches in the South. Chicago proved that racial hatred was not confined to states below the Mason-Dixon Line.

BLACK, FEMALE AND PREGNANT

I finally won the begrudging respect of my male colleagues at WCFL. They started calling me a "good lady reporter." But I was working for the day when they would call me a good reporter who happened to be a lady. Soon I was relieved of the "women's stories" and was on near equal footing with the men as far as story assignments were concerned. I started getting the major stories, too. Remember however, I was working twice as hard as they were. I still had much to prove. I happened upon news events when I was off duty and started covering them without being asked. My news director began to acknowledge that I was one of his top reporters.

On the night of July 14, 1966, a year after I started my broadcasting career, the city was rocked by the mass murder of eight student nurses who worked at South Chicago Community Hospital. Their strangled, stabbed, smothered and raped bodies were discovered the following morning in the blood splattered dormitory townhouse they shared. There had been one survivor who rolled back and forth under two beds, confusing the killer's count of how many nurses there were. It saved her from the fate of her roommates. After the screams and noise stopped, she untangled herself from the ropes used to tie her up, pushed out a window screen in a second floor bedroom, and started screaming out the window, "They're all dead."

The gangly 24-year-old drifter who had forced his way into the house with a gun, a butcher knife, a rope, and murder on his mind, is now listed among America's most notorious mass killers: Richard Speck.

Like every newsroom in the city, we scrambled to cover elements of the story. There were so many angles: the police investigation, the one survivor, the victims' identities, and the manhunt for the killer. Well, I believe I got the women's angle this time, but it was fine with me. I wanted to tell the stories of the murdered nurses and humanize them. I went to the neighborhood and the hospital to find people who knew the young women, who were all in their early twenties. At the hospital, the doctors and other nurses who worked with them characterized them all as young women dedicated to helping the sick. Neighbors said they were pretty, pleasant and friendly. Among the eight victims were two Filipino women. The lone survivor, Corazon Amurao, was also from the Philippines.

Because Amurao had seen the murderer's face and the infamous "Born to Raise Hell" tattoo on his arm, she was able to provide a police sketch artist a good likeness of the life-long loser, distinguishable by his blond pompadour and droopy pock-marked face. Forty-eight hours after the killing spree, Speck was arrested when his attempted suicide failed and he wound up in a hospital. The doctor treating him saw the infamous tattoo and called the police. Later, the FBI identified Speck's fingerprint, which placed him in the townhouse of murder.

This was another national story. I was assigned to cover the trial. The court decided Speck could not get a fair hearing in Chicago, so the venue was changed to the home of Caterpillar Tractor, Peoria, Illinois, located 130 miles southwest of Chicago.

Jury selection began in February of 1967, just five months after Jim and I got married. I had to report to Peoria and spend every week there for the duration, covering the trial. The reporters had to stay in a tacky motel, which was still one of Peoria's best. It was a good distance to Chicago so I remained there over the weekends and Jim would drive down from Chicago on Friday nights and leave on Monday mornings so we could spend time together. Little did we know how long the trial would last.

Impaneling a jury to try Speck took two months. It was difficult to seat impartial jurors. Many said they thought he was guilty and should be executed. I sat in the first couple of rows in the spectator section where seats were allocated to the press. Richard Speck's chair faced the judge's bench, but the first day of the trial I saw his head turn towards me and his dull and empty blue eyes were staring right through me. It was terrifying. The hair on my neck rose. What could he be thinking? Does he want to kill me? It really gave me the creeps. Every day it would happen. The other reporters saw it, too. We had a chance to talk with the Sheriff about the defendant's prison routine and I asked him why he kept staring at me. The Sheriff said Speck thought I was Filipino and might have been the nurse who survived. He said he told the accused murderer that I was a reporter. But Speck was still fascinated with me, thinking I was reporting news for the press in the Philippines.

The Cook County Public Defender offered a lame defense, first that Speck wasn't there, then that he had a mental disorder, and finally that he was under the influence of drugs and alcohol and didn't know what he was doing. Any hope for him was lost when the surviving nurse, Amurao, took the stand and described how all the girls were tied up in a circle on the floor of one of the bedrooms. How Speck, over six hours or more, took each nurse to another part of the house and executed his bag of horrors on them. One by one, they were led to slaughter.

Speck's fate was sealed when the prosecutor asked Amurao if she saw the man who killed her friends in the courtroom. She stood, left the witness stand and walked over to Speck, and with her finger just inches from his face, she said in loud strong voice, "This is the man." It was a dramatic and chilling moment.

I managed another Chicago scoop on the trial verdict. Two other WCFL reporters and an engineer came down for the verdict and set up outside the courthouse so I could report live when the decision was handed down. We all relaxed thinking the jury would take at least a few hours to deliberate. Reporters wandered off. Thankfully, my crew and I didn't. The jury was back in forty-nine minutes with eight verdicts pronouncing Speck guilty of first-degree murder. I will never forget one last chilling glance from Speck as he was led from the courthouse in handcuffs. Before many reporters could return to the courthouse, the court session was over, and I was already reporting the verdict to my station and the Mutual Broadcasting Network's national audience. It was another proud day for WCFL Radio.

A few days later, I got a call from the news director of WMAQ-TV, one of NBC's owned and operated stations. The news director told me he admired my work and wanted me to come in for an audition. Television? I hadn't done television. I told my radio boss, who was now a friend, that Channel Five was interested in me. He advised me that while that was a good thing, I should not jump to television before spending another couple of years honing my skills in radio. He said once I was a household name, WMAQ would still be interested and I could command more money and responsibilities. What my news director said made sense, despite my suspicion that he was operating in his own self-interest rather than mine. He offered me a healthy raise as incentive to stay. I believed I was still not paid as well as the men. But I <u>had</u> only been on the air for two years. The television offer was really tempting, but in the nicest way possible, I told WMAQ thanks, but that I thought I had more to learn in radio before I moved to television.

WCFL became known in news circles as the station that has a woman doing news. I was being used so frequently that my name was getting out. People heard me, but they didn't see me. I found out they thought I was white. I showed up to cover stories and would introduce myself as "Carole Simpson, from WCFL Radio."

The typical reaction was a long, incredulous, "Noooo." Then some version of, "What's your name again?"

"Carole Simpson," I would repeat.

"That's impossible," more than a few said with wide-eyed wonder.

"Why impossible?" I queried.

"Because you're colored," one man said, who should have known better. "I never heard anybody colored talk like you. Did you have to take special speech lessons, or do you do something special with your tongue and lips?"

Seething, I explained that I sounded just like my mother and sister, and no, I didn't have to do anything special to sound the way I did on the air. I grew up talking the way I sounded.

Remarks like that would have been laughable if they didn't illustrate the stereotypes whites had of people of color, even in my hometown. Now I really was Chicago's curiosity. I was a woman and a Negro. But I was still in demand.

In 1968, after Dr. Martin Luther King was assassinated on a Memphis motel balcony, Chicago's West Side went up in flames, 125 fires. The riots left eleven people dead, all blacks, and more than 500 injured. It was an emotional and trying experience to cover that story. I was in tears half the night of April 4th because Dr. King, the savior of poor and oppressed black people and my benefactor, had been killed. I found my anger rise as people in a church memorial service I had been assigned to cover shouted their outrage at white America, vowing revenge on the white power structure. Those who argued for calm and prayer were shouted down as appeasers and cowards.

After being up all night with my husband by my side, he had to go to work and I went to the City Hall press conference the following morning when Mayor Daley announced he was asking the Governor to deploy the National Guard and asking President Lyndon Johnson to send in Army troops to help the city's police force quell the rioting. Then the Mayor uttered the now infamous order that is still chilling. He said he had given the police orders to "shoot to kill arsonists" and "shoot to maim looters." We in the press corps couldn't believe it. The people setting fires were criminal, of course, but did they deserve to be shot on sight? And the looters all appeared to be kids and teenagers. Maim them for life? It was an out-of-this-world moment.

Racial tensions were heightened by the riots, and the race story was pushing aside news about the Vietnam War, consuming more space in the newspapers and more airtime on radio and television. WBBM Radio contacted me. It was the first station in Chicago to change to a twenty-four hour, all news format. The station wanted me, and I wanted it. No longer would I be working for a rock and roll station, but a station so serious about news it was broadcast around the clock, and it was owned by CBS, generally considered the top news network.

After three years, it was "Goodbye" WCFL and "Hello" WBBM, which offered me more money and the title of Special Correspondent. I was to report four days a week and anchor four hours of news from 4 p.m. to 8 p.m. on Saturdays. Not the greatest time slot to build an audience, but a good opportunity to polish my anchoring skills and continue reporting some of the fateful events of 1968, the worst year of civil strife in America many could ever remember. Rich were against poor, white against black, old against young, hawks against doves, all against the background of the most unpopular war in American history.

One of the biggest stories of the year was the event surrounding the Democratic National Convention during the week of August 26th. Leftist groups, civil rights organizations, urban guerillas, Black Panthers, other black power groups, and a large contingent of anti-war activists converged on Chicago to disrupt the convention and showcase their causes. Vice President Hubert Humphrey was slated to secure the Democratic nomination for President for a run against former Vice President Richard Nixon. Tens of thousands of protestors arrived a few days before the Convention promising to shut down the city and practicing techniques to thwart the police. Most of it was showboating, like threatening to poison the city's water supply, nominating a pig for president, and promising to prevent the Democrats from holding an orderly convention. Those were exactly the kinds of taunts and threats that made Mayor Daley angrily dig in his heels. No outsiders were coming to his city and wreak havoc. This was his city. He took preventive actions, which nearly amounted to martial law. Permits were denied for demonstrations anywhere near the Amphitheatre where the Convention was to be held. So the protestors, who slept in city parks, used the city's beautiful green spaces as staging grounds. Grant Park was across the street from the Conrad Hilton Hotel, the Democratic Party's Headquarters Hotel.

I was one of the reporters from WBBM who covered the protestors in Lincoln Park, where they rallied and held press conferences. In all previous confrontations with police, reporters would usually stay behind police lines as police and provocateurs went at each other. One night the "crazies," as the police called them, had formed a large group of several hundred and began advancing on a line of police in full riot gear. The protestors began throwing rocks at the police and injured some of them, but the police fought back with tear gas and used their billy clubs, which cracked heads, arms and legs. Then the most remarkable thing happened. The police turned around, away from the crowd, and began beating members of the press corps. A reporter and a television cameraman were seriously injured. Photographers trying to capture this unheard of police behavior discovered that the officers had removed their badges so they couldn't be identified. We all started running away from the police. I fell and sprained my ankle and just lay still until the herd went running by to another area of the park. Some fellow reporters helped me limp to a busy street where I caught a cab to a nearby hospital. That ankle has never been right since, a constant reminder of the 1968 Democratic Convention. I was told to stay off my feet, but how?

Chicago was under siege. One of the most chilling sights I ever saw was the parade of tanks and personnel carriers rumbling down the street in front of my apartment. They were loaded with uniformed armed soldiers with bayonets at the ready. Would this lead to civil war? Would the troops shoot the protestors?

What happened the third night was later called "The Battle of Michigan Avenue." Violence against white Americans had never been seen on live national television. It occurred in front of the Hilton Hotel and was later described by a special investigating commission as a "police riot." It's amazing no one was killed as police swung their batons against what appeared to be as many as 5000 mostly peaceful protestors of all ages and colors trying to march to the convention, which Mayor Daley vowed would never happen. It was shocking to see the police attack citizens trying to exercise their rights to free speech and assembly guaranteed by the First Amendment to the Constitution. The more radical protestors threw rocks and stink bombs. The police responded with tear gas that not only irritated the eyes but also caused violent vomiting.

I don't want to give the mistaken impression that the protestors were blameless for the bloody confrontation. Some of the fringe groups did fight back against the police. There was provocation, but most would agree it was not enough to justify the police brutality. Nearly 600 people were arrested; one hundred demonstrators were injured, as well as one hundred nineteen police officers.

In March of 1969, a federal grand jury handed down indictments against eight leaders of the Chicago protests, charging them with conspiracy and crossing state lines to incite riots. The defendants were anti-war activists David Dellinger, Tom Hayden, Rennie Davis, John Froines and Lee Weiner; Black Panther Party Chairman Bobby Seale; and Yippies Abbie Hoffman and Jerry Rubin, the clown princes of the "week that was." The protestors collectively became known as the "Chicago Eight."

Their trial began in September of 1969, and WBBM assigned me to cover. My reports would also air on the four other CBS owned radio stations in Los Angeles, St. Louis, Washington, DC, and New York City. This was a big break; however, I was three months' pregnant with my first child and the trial was expected to last several months. I wondered how I would do it, but I was determined my pregnancy would not rob me of this big story and this big opportunity.

During the early days of the trial, Bobby Seale wanted the trial delayed so his personal attorney could represent him. Presiding Judge Julius Hoffman refused. Seale then wanted to represent himself. The Judge denied that request. Seale responded by calling the Judge "a fascist dog" and a "pig." Every time the Judge would try to proceed with opening statements, Seale would jump up in the courtroom and shout, "I object." In fact, he objected to nearly everything said by Judge or the lawyers representing the other defendants. It was more than the 74-year-old judge could stomach. He ordered the federal marshals to handcuff Seale to his chair so he couldn't stand. That didn't stop his disrespectful outbursts. Judge Hoffman then ordered him gagged. It was another terrible spectacle to see an American protesting denial of his right to represent himself, bound and gagged. It was determined the gag wasn't thick enough because Seale's angry murmurings were still audible. The marshals carried him in his chair out of the courtroom and a few minutes later carried him back. Seale's head was swathed with a thick wad of cloth that went around his head and bulged over his mouth. It was a ridiculous spectacle that to many sullied the federal justice system.

It was during all this courtroom drama that I had a serious bout of morning sickness. I alternated runs to the telephone to report Seale's latest actions with runs to the Ladies Room to throw up. For days I was so sick. God forbid I call my news director to say I was too ill to cover the trial because I was pregnant. If I missed a day, I knew I would be permanently replaced. I also never wanted my femaleness to get in the way of my ability to get the job done. So I continued to work when I felt ill.

Bobby Seale was eventually severed from the rest of his co-defendants to be tried alone at a subsequent time. The Chicago Eight became the Chicago Seven, and the trial became even more of a circus: the recalcitrant judge, whose disdain for the defendants was unmistakable, was an unrelenting practitioner of the rule of law. But here he was butting heads with Yippies Hoffman and Rubin, who came to court one day wearing judicial robes to make a mockery of the trial. It was impossible to count how many times Judge Hoffman found the seven defendants and their lawyers in contempt of court.

As the case and the months wore on, my abdomen got bigger and bigger as my baby grew inside me. It became harder to sit on a hard chair for six or seven hours each day. My feet were swollen and there was nowhere to prop them up. People were not used to seeing a pregnant woman working. The courtroom personnel were concerned about me and kept asking, "Should you be doing this in your condition?"

"Of course," I replied, thinking of the pioneer women and the slave women who delivered their babies while working in the fields.

They also weren't used to a woman who was married and kept her maiden name. My husband was Marshall, but I kept Simpson. At the time it was not about feminism, but about my name having been established on the Chicago airwaves and my bosses not wanting me to change it. Lots of people back then thought I was a rebel. Today people say I was a trailblazer.

The case went to the jury for deliberations, and because I was almost eight months' pregnant, WBBM put me up at a hotel close to the downtown federal courthouse so that when the verdict was handed down, I wouldn't have to worry about traveling from my home. Each day the press waited for word that the "jury has come back." It took four days before we heard the welcome news. I had been at the hotel and while the jury was out I started feeling nervous and anxious. I hadn't slept for several nights and was feeling sick when I took the call from my news director telling me to get to the courtroom. He told me that we needed to beat the competition. "We have to be first," he said in a commanding tone.

My boss explained that they had plans to make that happen. He had persuaded a Federal Courthouse employee down the hall from Judge Hoffman's courtroom to let us use his phone that morning. Once the jury was inside the courtroom, one of my colleagues would keep the line open to our studios. At the other end of the phone was an engineer who, with the flick of his finger, could put me on the air of all the CBS radio stations simultaneously. The news director said all I had to do was get to the phone and report the news. "First, first, first," he kept saying.

I told him I would do the best I could, but I was not going to risk a premature delivery trying to be first. I got to the courthouse, found the office with the phone, and made my way back to the courtroom. This was an international story and there were roughly fifty reporters inside the packed courtroom waiting for the verdict. I decided I wouldn't sit with the rest of the press corps in front. Instead I chose an end seat at the back of the room next to the door. I knew once we heard the verdict, there would be a mad dash to the telephones and in my very pregnant and ungainly condition, I didn't want to be knocked down.

The jury filed in and the verdicts were handed to the judge. He didn't look pleased. He handed the papers to the clerk to read aloud. I had my pad and pen ready to write it all down. All the Chicago Seven were found not guilty on the conspiracy charge, but five were found guilty of crossing state lines to incite riot, and two were found not guilty. A mixed verdict. I scribbled a report on my note pad. I was ready to go. The judge, however, decided to poll the jurors, asking each and every one of them if this were his or her verdict. That was going to take a while.

When the judge was about halfway through the polling, one of the deputy U.S. marshals got up and walked to the door next to my seat and pushed it open. To this day I don't know why, but I got up and followed right behind him. Other reporters saw me leave and began a stampede towards the back of the courtroom. As I learned later, Judge Hoffman saw yet another assault on the decorum of his court and he shouted, "Bolt that door." He said no one could leave until court was adjourned.

By that time I was gone. Straight to that courthouse office I hurried, took the phone and told the editor I had the verdict and was probably first. Within seconds I heard an announcer say, "We interrupt our programming to bring you the verdict in the Chicago Seven trial. Here's CBS reporter, Carole Simpson, at the Federal courthouse in Chicago. Carole, go ahead." I began my report.

I was on the air ten minutes before the rest of the reporters were released from court. CBS television went with my radio report on the network because its reporter was locked inside with everybody else. I was "first." Sick, but "first," just like my boss wanted. That evening I received flowers and champagne and telegrams of congratulations from CBS executives and my WBBM boss. It became a big joke in Chicago that the rest of the media was scooped, by a "black, pregnant woman." That seemed to prove a great deal to folks who wondered whether color, gender and physical condition were limiting. Give us a chance to prove what we can do.

After my third scoop I went on maternity leave and on May 24, 1970, I gave birth to an 8-pound, 4-ounce girl. Since my married name was Marshall, the other reporters covering the Chicago Seven trial wanted me to name the baby Ulysses Simpson Marshall, so the initials would make its name U. S. Marshall. They also suggested Deputy Marshall and Marshal Marshall. But Jim and I chose Mallika Joy Marshall. She was my joy.

While I was on maternity leave, I received a call with a job offer from the news director of WMAQ-TV, just as my WCFL Radio boss predicted. I had become a household name in Chicago and a respected member of the Chicago press corps. I couldn't believe the TV station actually wanted to hire me a second time. I had accomplished all I thought I could in radio and decided it may be time for me to make the switch. As the WMAQ news director told me, "You are definitely ready for television now." When my daughter was three and a half months old, I began my television career, which would last thirty-three years.

MS. SIMPSON GOES TO WASHINGTON

As much as I loved my job at WMAQ and living close to my family in Chicago, I believed that after spending seven years covering local news, I was ready to go national. My dream was to move to Washington, DC, become a correspondent for one of the major networks, and cover politics.

During this period there was pressure again on the news media to hire more minorities and women to avoid threatened lawsuits. I was already part of the NBC News family and considered ways I could achieve my goal at the Peacock network. I actually didn't have to do a thing. In the fall of 1972, only two years after I began my television career, I got a call from the Vice President of NBC News, Bob Mulholland. He was going to be in town and suggested we have lunch. News people know that means one of two things: either you're in trouble, or you're getting a promotion.

We met at a downtown restaurant and Mulholland told me that the network had been monitoring my work on WMAQ and wanted to hire me as an NBC network correspondent. I knew that meant I would be covering news, not about my state and local region, but all the states, the whole country, the world even. It was hard to contain my excitement. But the offer came at a time my job satisfaction had never been higher. I was among the top reporters at my station, covering news stories during the week and anchoring the 10 o'clock news on Saturday nights. People recognized me everywhere I went, and I would get the good tables in restaurants and the best seats at the theater.

Mulholland asked what would make me happy, working in the Midwest Bureau of the network, located in Chicago, or moving to another bureau? I blurted out my desire to go to Washington. He said it might be possible. He would talk to other executives in New York and the Washington bureau chief to see if there were a slot I could fill there. I was ecstatic.

While I was waiting to hear from NBC I got devastating news. Mama, a woman who had never smoked in her life, was diagnosed with lung cancer. She had a terrible cough for a long time. I thought at first it was a bad cold and then later bronchitis. I never suspected anything so serious. When the coughing left her struggling to breathe, my father and I persuaded her to go to the doctor. After a series of tests, my father called to tell me the results. He was crying when he delivered the hated and shocking diagnosis. I had to hold myself together for him. I got the call at work and I didn't want to be seen crying in the newsroom. However, when I got home I wanted to take a shower. In the stall, the fact that she had lung cancer hit me like a punch in the stomach. I slid down the wall and collapsed on the tile floor, water spilling over me while I cried for what seemed a half hour. My husband and 2-year-old daughter could not get me out of the shower. I had to get the tears out so that I would be strong enough to help my mother undergo the necessary medical procedures doctors had laid out for her.

Mama and I had our share of disputes over the years--as do all mothers and daughters--but the thought of losing her was unthinkable. My friend, my counselor, my teacher, my critic, and my role model was about to begin the fight of her life and the odds were against her. With a demanding career and a toddler to rear, I put both aside temporarily and became concentrated on my mother's care and treatment.

Mulholland called from New York to say that I would be welcome in the Washington Bureau of NBC News. He said my boss at WMAQ had been notified, "So when can you move?"

With virtually all my attention focused on my mother's illness, I had forgotten about my network offer. I told Mulholland about her serious disease and told him I couldn't possibly leave Chicago now. He wanted to know when I could be in Washington because they really could use someone there right away. I saw my dream job slipping away. I responded that I didn't know what was going to happen to my mother or when. I said I hoped he understood, but I would have to decline the job. That was difficult. But, my Mama. I couldn't leave now. My mother was dying.

Over a two-year period, she suffered a debasing struggle against the disease. She had radiation that left her chest burned almost black. Still she cycled downward. The cancer had metastasized to her brain. More radiation. She lost her beautiful hair and was a near vegetable for the last nine months of what you could hardly describe as a life. This vital, strong, humorous, and pleasantly plump woman was eventually down to about seventy pounds. By the time she died on March 18, 1974, she bore no resemblance to herself. My father was grief-stricken but I was grateful she was finally out of her misery. She was sixty-four years old and I was thirty-two. Not a day goes by now that I don't think of her. I pass a mirror and see her fleetingly in my face. She remains with me.

I took a week off from work to help my father pick through her belongings to give to relatives, and I helped him to wrap up her few affairs. The very day I returned to Channel Five, Mulholland called and expressed his sympathies (how did he know?) and told me that the job in Washington was still open and waiting for me. After two years? I really thought there would never be a second chance. I told him I would have to talk with my husband, who had a job at Argonne National Laboratory and was finishing his MBA at the University of Chicago. It was a big decision. Would my husband give up his career and allow me to uproot our family to follow my dream career?

We had a major discussion. I wanted Jim to know how lucky I was to get another opportunity to go to Washington. I could stay in Chicago and be happy, I said, but if I did, all my life I would wonder what I could have done, what I could have been, if I had gone to Washington. I promised him that if he ever had a job offer he couldn't refuse that would require me to pull up stakes and move with him, I would do it. And I meant it.

While we were mulling a decision, trouble was brewing for me at WMAQ. I was called into News Director Ed Planer's office. He told me he had some bad news. I was going to be replaced as weekend anchor by a man that the network was interested in making a network anchor. They wanted him to get some experience at a major station. He was from Poughkeepsie, New York. It didn't matter that my show, with Greg Gumbel as the sports anchor, was the top-rated weekend show. I was out.

The decision about moving was now very easy. I didn't want to stay in Chicago after being bounced as an anchor. My husband said that if we waited six months, allowing him to finish his degree, we could move to Washington. He was planning to leave the engineering field, so instead of looking for another job in Chicago with his new MBA, he said he could surely find one in Washington. During the six months it took to complete his degree, I became an NBC network correspondent and worked out of the Midwest Bureau located in the same offices of WMAQ, in the massive Merchandise Mart building. I was doing a lot of agriculture stories throughout the fourteen-state Midwest region and getting them on the Nightly News anchored by David Brinkley and John Chancellor.

When everyone found out I was moving, they started calling me a rebel again. Not only did I keep my maiden name, have a baby and go back to work in three months, but now I was "forcing" my husband to leave his career and move with me to Washington. *The Chicago Daily News* did a story about us and Jim was called "a tag-along husband." His family was not pleased.

The network paid for the move from Chicago to Washington. Leaving my hometown to start all over again in another city was traumatic. My daughter was only four years old, but thank God, our housekeeper agreed to come with us. By the time we relocated, my husband had found a job as a systems analyst at a growing management consulting firm in Arlington, Virginia, which developed computer systems for corporations and the federal government. I had been worried he wouldn't find a satisfying job and would regret the move. Thankfully, he was happy with his new position.

I fell in love with Washington as soon as we flew in from Chicago, and as we descended to National Airport, I could see the spectacular views of the U. S. Capitol, the Washington Monument, and the Lincoln and Jefferson Memorials. I couldn't believe that the young black girl from the South Side of Chicago who wanted to be a reporter had left her male co-workers behind, made it to the network, and now to the most important news city in the world. An estimated 5000 reporters from around the nation and the globe covered Washington, DC, and I was soon to be among them.

My first day at NBC News was September 1, 1974. Some employees welcomed me; others kept their distance. I was the first black woman to work for the network in its biggest and most important bureau. Catherine Mackin had been the first woman. Gordon Graham, the first black man. Both intimated that they had once had their share of gender and racial problems, but when I arrived they were doing well.

Despite my stellar record in Chicago, I was not assigned to cover the White House, or Congress, or the State Department. My beat was the Department of Health, Education and Welfare, which today is the Department of Health and Human Services. I was not particularly happy with my assignment because it seemed I was being typecast. The black woman would be the best person to cover issues about health care, children, welfare for the poor, Social Security, the elderly, and public schools. Nine years after I began reporting in Chicago, it seemed as if I were back on my first broadcasting job and covering "women's issues." I felt then and in Washington that if I worked hard enough, I would be able to cover Congress and the White House.

I had much to learn about working as a reporter in the nation's capital. Getting to know the issues and the public information officers at the government's biggest Cabinet Departments was a huge undertaking. I sent letters, wandered halls, spoke to random employees, researched topics, and took press secretaries to lunch. I did all the things you have to do to develop sources and keep track of developing stories. Now I was competing with CBS, ABC, *The Washington Post* and *The New York Times*, and hundreds of other news operations.

Reporters are judged at the networks on whether they can break a story before anyone else, and coming up with good story ideas. I knew it would be a while before I got an exclusive story, but I could propose stories. The routine was to write up an idea, submit it to a producer in Washington for "NBC Nightly News," and then to the executive producer of the show in New York. The same procedure was true for getting stories on the "Today Show."

Since so few people were friendly to me, I had no trouble focusing on my work, submitting ideas for stories nearly every day. New York didn't bite. I would get back replies like, "Thanks, but no thanks," or "Been there, done that." I'm sure all reporters get rejections on story ideas, but every single one?

After nine months, friends and family in Chicago started asking why they didn't see me on the air. I had to be honest. I didn't know. The assignment desk had taken to sending me out to do interviews for other correspondents' stories. That's something anybody could do in the Bureau. I was going backwards. I was so unhappy. I couldn't let my husband know I wanted to move back to Chicago. Things just weren't working out between NBC and me. I made inquiries about why I couldn't get a story on the air, and a top producer in Washington told me that my ideas weren't strong enough for the national news. He acted as if I was a beginning reporter. Out of the Midwest Bureau I had appeared on "Nightly News" several times. New York had accepted those stories. I pointed out to him a couple of instances in which I had proposed stories to NBC and saw them later reported in prestigious newspapers such as the *Post* or the *Times*. I stiffened my back and said, "They were strong enough for them." He dismissed me with a flick of his hand. He was a man with a short temper. I admit I was afraid of him and what he could do to me professionally.

Suddenly it hit me. I was being told "no" again. It was time for me to stand up for myself. I was not going to allow NBC to make me feel I was incompetent. I suspected somebody was up to something. I vowed to identify the person or persons responsible. I watched closely to see how other correspondents were treated and how they were able to get their stories on "Nightly News."

While my private investigation was ongoing, I received a call from Pat Thompson, a reporter I worked with in Chicago and one of my best friends. She told me she had been vacationing in Europe and stopped by the London Bureau of NBC to see our former Chicago news director who was now the bureau chief there. During their chat, Pat said she asked him why I wasn't showing up on "Nightly News." He told her that according to the grapevine I had moved to Washington and "got lazy."

Into the telephone I blasted her ears with, "WHAT??!!??"

"Slow down, Carole," she shouted back. "I told him that you said you couldn't pay to get stories on the air. It wasn't your fault because you said you were trying everything to appear on 'Nightly News'."

"Exactly, Pat," I said more calmly. But I was so angry. I thanked her for letting me know. If you have no clue of what's being said about you, how do you combat the misconceptions? I had a lot of investigative work to do.

This was so upsetting because the network's "grapevine" was so entwined and long that it had crossed the Atlantic Ocean. I felt everybody in the company, in locations in America and around the world, had probably heard that I was "lazy."

The premise was ludicrous. My dream had been to work in Washington for a network. I wanted to make it to the top of the profession. Why would I come to NBC and stop working hard? How or why would anyone say I had gotten lazy? To me that was a racial epithet. Black people--to ignorant people--don't want to work, are stupid and unqualified. A black woman was even worse. That's why there was discrimination. To them I didn't deserve a high-paying job, much less a glamorous one.

I thought about the weeks I spent trying to get up to speed on my beat and the scores of story ideas I had submitted which generated no interest. I was more determined than ever to uncover who put this lie onto the NBC "grapevine." Immediate action was required. I called every one I knew at the network. Many of them I had worked with in Chicago and they knew me and my work. To every person I reached I asked if they had heard that I "had gotten lazy." To a person, they had. I wanted to know if they knew who was spreading the malicious rumor. Of course, nobody knew. I went on to point out that it was untrue and ridiculous. I reminded them of how hard I worked when we had worked together. I asked each of them to do me the favor of knocking down the rumor whenever they heard it and telling people about my work ethic. I also shared with them that I thought someone was out to get me.

I concluded that some of these white men I called might help; most would not. There was nothing in it for them to go to bat for the black female correspondent at the network. My reputation had been so sullied that I made up my mind I had to quit NBC News, even though I had signed a four-year contract. I told Jim I had to leave the job and I said we didn't have to move back to Chicago because I was confident I could find another job in DC, even if it were at a local station.

This was the beginning of the time I decided I would speak up for myself and not ever take for granted that my work spoke for itself. No longer would I take verbal abuse or emotional abuse from anybody in the news business. I was as educated, as prepared, and as capable as anyone in that Bureau. I would not let others' negative vibes mess with my psyche, raising doubts in my own mind about my capabilities. If they get to your head, you're finished. I saw it happen to some other correspondents.

With my firm decision to get out of my contract, I went to Don Meaney, the Washington bureau chief, and told him that I couldn't take it anymore and I wanted to break my contract.

"Carole, what do you mean?" Meaney asked. He was clearly taken aback.

I gave him the whole story about not being able to get on the air for the nine months I had been working there, about the "grapevine" saying I was lazy, about how hard I had worked to get stories on the air, and about my suspicion that people were conspiring to make me fail, and about how much I hated my situation. He said I shouldn't be hasty. He would have a talk with the executives in New York and the show producers and try to find out what the problem was. I told him he could do all the talking he wanted to, but I wanted "outta there." Then the *coup de grace*: "I may have to go public, because I believe I've been singled out for this treatment because I'm a black female."

"Oh no, Carole. It's nothing like that. What would make you think something as awful as that?" he asked, looking really worried now.

"Well, Don, you tell me. I am the only black female correspondent and I am the only correspondent who can't get on the air. What do you think, Don?" I continued. "Could it have something to do with my sex and color?"

This is the first time I learned that--for the networks--bad publicity is as bad as bad ratings. I would use that knowledge often in what continued for many years to be a struggle to survive and thrive in network television.

89

I left Meaney's office with his promising me to get on the telephone right away to New York. I went home that evening and at about 9 p.m. the phone rang. It was an NBC senior vice president calling from New York. He related how important I was to the network and he didn't think there was any way I would be allowed to get out of my contract. He told me that I should expect an immediate change; that from now on I would be appearing on the network. Just don't leave. This will all work out, he assured. I said to myself, "We'll see."

Within the hour, I got another call, this one from the Washington assignment desk. I was told I would be covering a hearing on Capitol Hill the next day and that "Nightly News" already had ordered a story for tomorrow night's broadcast. The assignment editor nonchalantly gave me all the times and room numbers, the crew and producer.

Sure enough, that next day I made my first appearance on NBC "Nightly News" from Washington. It had been so long I had almost forgotten what to do. Not really, doing television is like riding a bicycle. After the show aired, I got a call from the executive producer telling me, "Nice spot. We hope to be seeing more of you."

Just like that. Nine months of hell and all of a sudden I am doing "nice" spots with a guarantee of more airtime. The NBC News executives had clearly laid down the law and people had to comply. Oh, to have such power. So simple. A call here, a call there, and I'm on national television, the only black female correspondent on any network. Again, I became an oddity. The viewing audience, especially black Americans, was thrilled. My fan base started with my people and spread to women, young people, and eventually the core network news audience, white older Americans.

As for my agent provocateur, it took me two years to identify him. After the Republican National Convention in Kansas City in 1976, NBC threw a "wrap party" for all the reporters and technicians who had worked to televise the proceedings. For the umpteenth time, I wasn't happy with my assignment which was covering the Black Republicans, but it got me to the convention and eventually onto the floor to see all the hoopla over the nomination of incumbent President Gerald Ford.

The wrap party was a huge affair, with plenty of food, drink, and live music. It's a great way to unwind after the long hours of working the convention. I was having a great time, but a lot of people were drinking too much. Among them was a "Nightly News" producer in Washington. He was so drunk that I doubt he remembers what he did and said to me. I was with a group of people laughing at some joke, when I felt a hand pull the back of the collar on my dress and I was literally dragged away from the group. Looking angry, this man threw me against a fence. He put his hands around my body, pinning me to the wall, his face inches from mine. I tried to push him away but couldn't. He reeked of alcohol.

"Simpson," he began, "who the fuck do you think you are?"

"What are you talking about? And get out of my face."

"You think because you're black and you're a woman you can get anything you want," he said in a nasty tone. "And you slut, you don't deserve it. You're nothing. Do you hear me? You're fuckin' nothing."

The alcohol had clearly given him the courage to verbalize what he had been thinking about me from the day I arrived in Washington. I saw my chance to nail him.

"Interesting, that you think I'm nothing. Would you also say I'm lazy? Have you told people I'm lazy?" I asked.

"Yeah, you're lazy. All you fuckin' people are lazy." Case solved. I was seething. This was the creep who had made my life miserable, who had spread the word that I was not doing anything. NBC management had ordered him to start using me on the air. He resented it and no doubt hated me more for his being chastened by New York. He had insulted me and my people. I was no longer afraid of him. My neck stiffened, and my back, too.

To get him to understand I had to resort to gutter language: "And you are a fucking asshole. Don't you ever talk to me that way again, and get your fucking, stinking body away from me. Maybe everybody

91

here would like to hear the bullshit you just said to me. You tiny little man," I added. It was the ultimate sting to a male of shorter stature.

My filthy language must have sobered him up a bit. He removed his hands and backed away. Oddly, he started shucking and jiving saying he was only kidding. "Don't you have a sense of humor, Simpson?"

"No, I don't!" I scurried away from him but was proud I had stood up to him. Later in my career I would do that again and again as I tangled with racist and sexist men.

After that night my relations with that producer remained strained for years, but we still had to work together. He may not remember the incident in Kansas City, but I never will forget it. It demonstrated to me that talent and hard work have nothing to do with your success in a business where one person can bring you down. This guy started a vicious rumor and it changed people's perception of me and that perception became reality. That wouldn't happen to me again.

Four years after starting at NBC News, I was assigned to cover Congress, to my delight. This was what I had been waiting for, the chance to cover an important beat and politics. It was a thrill every day. But it would not last.

THE NBC PUSH TO ABC

Despite the consistently low public approval ratings for Congress, I loved being the congressional correspondent for NBC News. It was my dream job in Washington and it took me four years to get the assignment. It was a heady experience. Instead of going to my office, I reported to the Capitol every morning that Congress was in session. The building is so spectacular inside with its murals and historic paintings, the grandeur of the Rotunda and historical figures circling Statuary Hall. I was working in locales where the laws of our national history were enacted. I became a true patriot. I saw democracy up close and personal, but I also saw gridlock, scandal and corruption. I reported on Congress grappling with issues foreign and domestic: from reducing the trade deficit to welfare reform, to ending violence against women. I covered Senator Ted Kennedy's first attempts to pass universal health care.

After nearly four years of pounding the painfully hard marble floors of the magnificent Capitol and riding the underground tram to the members' office buildings, I was hitting my stride. I knew the Democratic and Republican leaders, a good number of Senators and Representatives, legislative aides, and press secretaries. I was covering the people's business as it was conducted or not conducted by their elected representatives. I was the eyes and ears of the public, working in the interest of the American people. I was proud of what I did for a living because of its importance to a democratic society.

I was so enthralled with congressional responsibilities that I considered moving back to Chicago and running for office to represent the First Congressional District, the seat held at the time by Representative Gus Savage. I told Barbara Walters about my ambition and she said, "Are you crazy? Do you want to be one of 435 members of Congress or reach millions of people every night with your insight into the news affecting their lives?" Well, if you put it that way...

Sid Davis, our Washington bureau chief, called to tell me to come to his office the next day instead of going to Capitol Hill. I knew it was not a good sign. It turns out he wanted to give me the official word that I would no longer be covering Congress. He said the network wanted to replace me with someone else.

"Sid, what happened? Did I do anything wrong?" I was puzzled.

"Not really," he replied. "It's a New York decision. They want to hire this certain guy and the beat he wants is Congress."

"So what happens to me?" I asked.

Davis said sheepishly that I might be covering the Department of Energy.

My body seemed to cave in on itself. "You can't be serious. You want me to go from Capitol Hill to the non-news making Energy Department?"

Sid responded, "That's the edict from New York."

If that were the edict from New York, then I would have to go there and make a case for myself. Davis obviously had not. I never could depend on anyone else to go to bat for me. I never had mentors or "godfathers" at any of the places I worked. I was always on my own.

A former network news president was hired to run NBC News. Things began to change dramatically. He decided that our correspondent bench was not as strong as the one he built at his former network. Slowly, he began hiring his people away to take over the plum jobs at NBC. I was not one of "his" correspondents.

During a special meeting with the new president, requested by the black employees of the NBC Washington Bureau, I took one of the leadership positions. Minority employees wanted to raise the issue of fair employment. They felt they were not getting the same opportunities as white employees. If you looked at the ones who got promoted and the ones who got stuck in the same old job, the complaints rang true. The meeting didn't go well. He listened but did not agree with our charges. Both he and we left the meeting disgruntled. I am certain he took note of my vocal stand against racial discrimination.

After my disheartening talk with Davis about my future at NBC, I called the president's office and made an appointment to see him the next day. I flew to New York and was ushered into his office. Instead of inviting me to sit with him in his comfy conversation area, he sat behind his desk and I sat in front of his desk, which caused a wide expanse between us. He clearly wanted to maintain a power advantage and a lot of distance from me. I would have normally made some small talk before getting to the matter at hand, but his gruff tone and body language said to me, "Get on with it, so you can get the hell out of my office."

I told him I was shocked that I was losing the congressional beat. I thought I had done a good job, was popular with the viewers and maintained good sources on Capitol Hill. I acknowledged that if he thought there were someone who was more experienced than I, he had every right to hire him, but why was I going to the Energy Department? Couldn't he have come up with an assignment which didn't appear as though I was being demoted?

Without batting an eye he said, "You're not as good as you think you are. We need more heft on Capitol Hill."

More heft? That sounded like a masculine term. A respected political reporter got the job. I had no beef with him. I knew I was competitive with my counterparts at the other networks. But in television, nobody cares what you think or what you want, especially if, "You're just a black female." I was powerless to change his mind. I was hearing another "No," again.

I felt like a child, when I asked "What will I do now?"

The network president gave me no quarter. He said he really didn't care what happened to me, or what I wanted to do. It was of no consequence to the network. He said he made decisions in the interest of NBC News not Carole Simpson. He told me that the Energy Department was about my speed. His offer would grant me a new contract but with just a cost of living increase. He said if I didn't like the assignment maybe I should go somewhere else. He was showing me the door.

For one of the few times in my life, I was speechless. I had no comebacks. I was fighting back tears. I would not, could not let him see me cry. "I see," I said, and gathered my things and walked out of his office, literally reeling. I don't think the meeting lasted any longer than three or four minutes.

NBC News had been my "home" for twelve years: four in Chicago, and eight years at the network in Washington. I substituted for the once climbing star Jessica Savitch on the NBC weekend news. I was on NBC in primetime, anchoring one-minute NBC News Updates. Hadn't I proved my abilities as a reporter and an anchor? I guess not. Before leaving this man's office, I decided my long love affair with the NBC peacock was over.

I don't remember what happened next, but I must have left Rockefeller Center in a daze. When I came to, I was in Saks Fifth Avenue a few blocks away, walking up and down the aisles on the first floor. I don't remember how I got there or what the heck I was doing. I recalled the devastating conversation. Somebody was saying "No" to me again. I started getting angry over the denigration of my work by the news president. I would use that to re-energize myself. I was being told I did not have the wherewithal to cover a beat as important as the Congress. Nobody tells me I'm not good at my job. I knew better.

I don't want to sound cocky, but when you're on television you have to have confidence in yourself or you're going to always remain a journeyman reporter. You have to know that you can go on camera and do anything, anytime, anywhere, and do it well. I made sure I would maintain an edge by working on my skills through the years. At home I would listen to news stories done by other correspondents at NBC, ABC and CBS, then judge their ability to move and interest the audience. I worked hard on writing well for broadcast. I practiced adjusting my voice for sad stories, happy stories, and difficult stories to understand, such as the federal budget.

To try and speak directly to a viewer, I always wrote for my mother. She hadn't finished high school but she was intelligent and interested in the news. If I could make her understand, empathize, or smile, then I knew I was successful. She died in 1974, but she was the viewer I was always trying to reach. And when I delivered the news, I didn't narrate a script. I told her the story in a conversational style but with an authoritative voice to demonstrate to her I knew what I was talking about. I don't think anyone knows how hard I worked to perfect my craft. "Not as good as I think I am." I would not be taken down. "I am as good as I think I am," I told myself.

I found a couple of public telephones in Saks with a Manhattan directory. I started looking up the names of the talent agencies I had heard about from other correspondents. I never had an agent before, but I realized I needed someone to "shop me around" for another job. I could no longer stay at NBC with a top executive who disliked my work and me.

I had no change to make my phone calls. I bought a fairly inexpensive bottle of cologne and requested from the clerk at least four quarters in change. I returned to the telephone bank, put my coat and purse on the floor, and took out a note pad and pen. I started calling Arthur Geller, ICM (International Creative Management), and finally N.S. Bienstock. It was the only agency that said I could be seen that afternoon.

The appointment was scheduled for 2 p.m., but it was only noon.

How to kill the time? I went into a coffee shop, bought a *New York Times*, ordered coffee and read. I probably went through the newspaper three times. Fortunately no one in the shop asked me to give up my booth. It was a short distance to Columbus Circle, where Bienstock was located. I found a Ladies Room and re-applied my makeup and walked to the building. I found the office suite well appointed and the staff friendly. "Would you like some coffee," the receptionist asked. "No, thank you. I've had way too much already."

I was told Stuart Witt would be seeing me. It turns out he was a lawyer who had negotiated contracts for CBS News and had been working as a talent agent for ten years, specializing in news personnel. He ended up working as my agent for twenty years and remains a close friend.

An assistant led me back to his office cluttered with broadcasting memorabilia and walls stacked high with videotapes. He greeted me dressed in a tie and rolled up shirtsleeves. He was extremely pleasant (what a change). He said he was happy to meet me, and that he admired my work on NBC. Well, that was all I needed for the waterworks to start. I was hearing him say he admired my work after my boss had just said, in effect, that I was mediocre at best.

Stu wondered what caused my outburst and I told him. He was so reassuring. He told me not to worry. He'd get me out of NBC and into another job where I would be appreciated. He took notes as I gave him a rudimentary work history. Stu promised to call in a few days because he said he was going to work on my case right away. I think it was the tears. That's another important thing I learned about men. Crying makes some of them feel uncomfortable and empathetic; others feel superior and more powerful. My tears moved Stu.

Within five days, Stu called and said that ABC's Washington Bureau Chief would be calling me to set up a dinner. He told me "ABC is very, very interested in you."

"Thank you, Stu, thank you." Every day at NBC was miserable now that I didn't spend my time at the Capitol. I had to go into the office and show everybody how involved I had become in studying the nation's energy problems, but none of the shows wanted any of my suggested stories. I may as well have been reporting from Outer Mongolia.

ABC? When ABC Sports President Roone Arledge took over the News Division as well, he had a seemingly unlimited budget and raided the other two networks for what he considered to be the best correspondents and anchors. From NBC he acquired celebrities like Barbara Walters and David Brinkley, as well as lowly me. Diane Sawyer was later lured from CBS. He made Max Robinson the first black network anchorman, sharing duties with Frank Reynolds and Peter Jennings.

Thanks to Stu's deft discussions, ABC did not know I wanted to leave NBC, nor that I had lost the congressional beat. At dinner the bureau chief did a strong selling job, saying ABC was anxious for me to come aboard. He said the network wanted me as a correspondent for "Nightline" or the White House. Wow! My color and gender may have played a role in ABC's strong interest, but I also had the experience and the skills. I had a graduate education in journalism, nine years of local news, and eight years of network television experience.

Playing hard to get, I told him I would have to think about his offer and have my agent get back to him. I sounded like a correspondent who had used agents all the time. Stu had taught me tricks that would allow him to negotiate a contract for more money and perks than ABC may want to give me.

My dinner was in October of 1981. I notified NBC that I had an offer from ABC but NBC was not willing to match it. So I was free. On January 4, 1982, I moved to the downtown Washington Bureau of ABC News. That first day I had a guided tour of the seven-story bureau, introducing me to people at each of the ABC programs in radio, the crews, editors and assignment editors. I had been reporting in Washington for years, so many of the employees knew who I was and heartily welcomed me.

I settled into a large office equipped with everything a reporter needed, including a sofa on which to catch a nap during long news days and nights. I had signed a three-year contract making twice the money NBC was going to pay me with hefty annual raises built in, a guarantee that I would be based in the Washington Bureau, five weeks of vacation, and the contract was no cut. I was guaranteed the money and three years of employment. It was a good deal.

I was anxious to find out where I was going to be working, at "Nightline" or the White House. The bureau chief said the company was still working that out and until I got a permanent "home" I would be a general assignment reporter. Silly me. Why did I ever think ABC management would actually put me in the White House, the most coveted beat in Washington, or on "Nightline," the most coveted broadcast in the bureau? Stu and I concluded we had made the mistake of not getting spelled out in the contract exactly what my assignment would be. But I figured I'd do a lot of different stories, which I enjoyed, and best of all I was away from NBC.

Just a week and a half after I started at ABC, I got a piece of a major story, the crash of the Air Florida jetliner during a blizzard in morning rush hour. The ice buildup on the wings kept the aircraft from lifting, and it first crashed into the 14th Street Bridge and then plunged into the frozen Potomac River. Seventy-eight people were killed, including four motorists crushed in their vehicles on the bridge.

Correspondents and TV crews were dispatched immediately. We had to walk three miles to the crash scene from our bureau because the snow was too deep for driving, too deep for walking, too. We were exhausted. I was sent to the Bridge to cover the recovery operation. The sight of the mangled cars with their dead motorists still inside was horrifying, as was the tail of the jetliner jutting up from the river. I ended up spending every day for almost a week in the bitter cold, reporting from the bridge the hazardous recovery of the passengers. Divers went underwater to hook equipment to rows of seats in the broken plane. It's not possible to adequately describe the awful sight of a row of three seats being hauled upside down, dripping with water, holding the frozen corpses still strapped in by their seat belts.

My first story at ABC left me with nightmares. Not an auspicious beginning.

Three months after I started my new job, my phone rang off the hook. The calls were from dozens of friends from NBC. The NBC President, my nemesis, had been fired and the new regime, which included some of my ardent fans, wanted me back. One of my friends said that people were dancing in the halls singing, "Ding Dong, the witch is dead." Tom Pettit, who had been a correspondent, was named Vice President of News. His call was not to be believed. He said that NBC would give me whatever I wanted to come back "home." I could write my own ticket.

"Doggone it, Tom," I said sadly, "I signed a no cut contract and if I try to break it, I'm sure ABC would take me to court."

Tom, somewhat of a free spirit, said, "Hell, let 'em take you to court."

I reminded him of the time, cost and hassle, and I said regretfully, "I can't do it, Tom. I wish I could, but I can't."

"All right," Tom said. "But remember, you are loved."

It was a wonderful conversation, just what I needed to boost my spirits. I was not the only NBC staffer to suffer the wrath of the now ex-president. Everybody felt he finally got what he deserved. I recalled one of my mother's old bromides: "God doesn't like ugly."

I thought the grass would be greener at ABC, but I found out it was not. Perhaps it was the nature of the business clashing with my nature. I had become a strong advocate of minorities and women in the broadcast industry. So much so that I established scholarships for minorities and women with the Radio Television News Directors Association, at my alma mater, the University of Michigan, with the National Association of Black Journalists, and at a private high school in Washington, DC.

It was matter of putting my money where my mouth was. Over

twenty-two years I have supported the education of at least fifty of my scholarship winners. I wanted to make a difference and when I look at where those young people are today, I know that I did.

However, at ABC I would find the biggest challenge to equal opportunity I had ever seen.

ABC NEWSWOMEN VS. ABC NEWSMEN

Thanks to the brilliant and legendary television producer Roone Arledge, I made my escape from NBC. Roone wanted me to be part of his buildup of the News Division the other networks derisively called the "Almost Broadcasting Company." A few years later the joke was over. ABC had taken over as the top rated news network.

Roone ran ABC Sports for many years and revolutionized sports coverage by inventing slow motion and stop action. He was at the pinnacle of success in sports programming. But he trained his sights on the News Division. He had a masters' degree in journalism from Columbia University and was able to convince ABC executives that he could continue to run Sports while at the same time making the News Division the best in network television. He would later give up ABC Sports to concentrate on news.

ABC corporate management gave Roone what he said he needed: money. His philosophy was that to make money you had to spend money. He went on a hiring spree at the other networks, able to dangle large sums of money in the faces of talent he wanted to front his news programs. I was a beneficiary, as were so many others. He sought the best camera operators, producers, editors and writers. In a few years ABC News was not only first in news, but it also won all of the highest broadcasting awards for its news programming. I like to think that I made a small contribution.

Roone gave the staff an *esprit de corps*. We were encouraged to beat the other networks with scoops and exclusives. We were expected to have the best video, the best writing, the best production and direction. If our competitors took a charter plane to get to a story, we hired two to get more feet on the ground. If they had two reporters on a story, we would have four. It was great. I craved the adrenaline rush I got when I was on a big story and trying to beat the pants off NBC and CBS.

As a result the work at ABC was fun and challenging; however, I discovered that many women and minorities felt there was a hostile work environment. In the Washington Bureau there were seven women correspondents, but none of us had a top spot on a major beat. Men covered the White House, Congress, the State Department, the Pentagon, the Supreme Court, and national security. We women served in backup positions on those beats or we covered the federal agencies: the Food and Drug Administration; the National Institutes of Health; Housing and Urban Development; HEW. And then, of course, the occasional Kennedy Center Honors gala, the White House Easter Egg Roll, the sexual misadventures of the National Zoo's first panda couple, Ling-Ling and Hsing-Hsing, and if we were lucky, we might catch a breaking story involving political scandal, or fires and murders in the District of Columbia.

One of the things I thought would make my time at ABC more pleasant was the fact that there were six other women correspondents in the Washington Bureau: Susan King, Ann Compton, Bettina Gregory, Rita Flynn, Sheilah Kast, and Kathleen Sullivan. Counting women from the other network bureaus, there were a total of sixteen female correspondents. That may sound on the surface fairly good. But given the fact that there were sixty-five men, our number was pathetic. The other networks were not much better.

I reached out to the other women in the Bureau, trying to be friendly, stopping by their offices to chat. Some were distant to the new girl on the block. They weren't interested in being my new best friends. I determined that management was pitting women against each other. Divide and conquer. A story I thought I was going to cover would be given to another woman, and vice versa. So the women, instead of competing with the men, were in conflict with each other for assignments. Women saw other women, not men, as the competition to their getting more airtime.

When I was working at NBC, the female producers and writers and 3 correspondents would get together from time to time to have drinks or dinner. We talked about news, and gossip, and women's stuff. I wanted to get something like that going at ABC. I felt we needed to unite to improve our status.

I talked with Susan King about it and she agreed we women were getting a raw deal at ABC, and we should get to know each other better and talk about it. She decided to have a dinner at her house. She invited the correspondents, some producers, and desk editors. There were about twenty of us and Susan arranged for us to sit at one long table. We introduced ourselves, because as I said, women hadn't been talking to each other, except for the occasional "Good morning." After the salad, chicken and walnut casserole, and glasses of water or wine, we began talking and laughing at stories about ordering breast creams when we were teenagers, our parents' idiosyncrasies, and bad blind dates. I contributed one about the guy I agreed to go to a dance with who only had one arm. The matchmaker hadn't told me. I didn't know what to do with my hands while we were dancing. To make matters worse, he wanted to dance every dance.

As the night wore on and the wine kept pouring, our conversation took on a serious tone. We started talking about ABC News: the unfairness, the sexual discrimination and harassment, the lack of promotions, the glass ceiling, and the men who perpetrated the indignities. The women correspondents learned that we were being pitted against each other in such a way as to create envy among us.

Bettina Gregory pointed out that she had been called early one winter morning to go to the Washington Monument where a man had pulled up a truck, strapped himself with dynamite, and was threatening to blow up the national landmark. All day long she reported from the scene without food or a break, gathering interviews from law enforcement officials who feared that the guy, at any moment, would blow up himself and the Monument. When it was time for a story to be written and produced for the evening newscast, she said she thought she was going to be relieved at the site so she could return to the bureau to do the story. She was told to continue to stay at her location and they would get someone else, a man, to do the piece for "World News Tonight" who would use all of her video and interviews. Bettina had worked the story all day, and a man who had not been anywhere near the scene reported the story for the evening news.

The anger in the room was palpable. There were similar stories, in which female producers and editors were moved aside for men when the big stories developed. The women correspondents discovered that we had similar trouble with a top producer of "World News Tonight." Correspondents wrote their scripts for a story they covered and had to take them to him for approval before they went to the New York broadcast producers. By the time I submitted a script, I had written and rewritten several drafts before I got it the way I wanted and the way I thought New York wanted it. On several occasions this man read my scripts at the rim, where many of the program's other producers sat. One time he balled up my script and made a hook shot with it into the trash basket. Another time he slowly tore my script into halves, quarters, eighths and sixteenths, if he could, and threw them into the air so I could watch the pieces flutter to the ground. The first time it happened, I was shocked and asked what was wrong with it. He said flippantly, "Start over." No suggestions. No specific criticism. Nothing.

Women seemed to be singled out for this ridicule. I knew he was trying to screw with our minds and I personally refused to be intimidated. The next time he destroyed a script of mine I told him, "Okay, that's the best I can do. Have somebody else write it. Or maybe you should do it?" I left the big open room and went back to my office. Within a few minutes, my phone rang and he told me to bring him another copy of my script.

I refused to let him get to me. But some of the other women weren't as sassy. They lost confidence in their ability to write a good script and developed writer's block on deadline. They were so afraid to take their scripts to him.

It was almost midnight and Susan asked if we wanted to get together again. Everyone eagerly agreed. We discovered we had a common problem, the sex discrimination that seemed to pervade the News Division, and we should do something about it. I have to admit some women started to fall away from the group not wanting to be involved with something that might become serious.

It really ticked me off that women were still struggling in journalism. The correspondents were women in their late thirties and early forties who had extensive experience and had paid their dues by working their way up to producer and correspondent jobs at a major commercial network news operation. They had the same qualifications as the men: college degrees, local news experience, reporting and writing skills, and ambition. For those of us on air, there were the additional worries about hair, makeup, and wardrobe, because the men were often more critical of our looks than our storytelling. All the guys had to do was wear a suit and tie and dab on a little pancake makeup. They could be short and bald, wearing glasses or bearded. The public didn't seem to care, nor did our supervisors.

We formalized our newswomen gatherings to once a month, sometimes a Saturday breakfast and sometimes a night at a restaurant, but our most productive discussions occurred in our various private homes where we could really let loose. We also were forming friendships. Word spread all over the company that the women in the Washington Bureau were holding "secret meetings." Everybody wanted to know why. We would answer, "No reason in particular." It was a good strategic move to generate buzz. After a year, we decided none of our problems would be solved until the women of ABC News made demands on management to solve them.

In 1984, our core group of fourteen women decided we needed to meet with Roone Arledge and other top management but not until we had done some in-depth reporting on ABC News programs. We weren't going to confront them with whining about our not being given the good assignments or promotions to the executive ranks. We would present them with hard facts that could not be denied.

We gave ourselves specific areas to investigate. We wanted to find out if there was a disparity in men's and women's salaries; we wanted to find out the number of appearances by men, women and minorities on every ABC News program: "World News Tonight," "Good Morning America," "Nightline," "This Week with David Brinkley," and "20/20." We wanted the numbers of women executives, correspondents, bureau chiefs, senior and executive producers.

For three months we worked. Each woman had an area to investigate. We did a content analysis of all the shows during a three-month period and found out women represented twenty percent of the correspondents, but reported only six percent of the stories. We found out women producers were making, on average, 30-thousand dollars a year less than men producers. That was a shocker. There were no women vice presidents, no bureau chiefs, no foreign correspondents, no executive producers, no senior producers, and no assignment editors. Other than Barbara Walters on "20/20" and Kathleen Sullivan doing the short news segments on "Good Morning America," no woman was anchoring any of the main news broadcasts. It was our group's belief that if women were part of the decision-making process, we wouldn't be slighted. We decided the promotion of women to the executive suite was critical.

Since women in our society are the majority of the population we thought it was unconscionable for ABC to broadcast news shows produced from the perspective of all white, middle-aged, upper middle class men. For the most part, they lived in places such as affluent

Westchester County, took the train into the city, and spent their days in their offices at 47 W. 66th Street, New York's tony Upper West Side. During the workweek they scarcely ever came into contact with "real people with real problems." They put together shows that interested them. That's the way it had always been done. Not anymore, if the ABC Newswomen were successful.

How did we get our information? Just as we did as reporters. We developed sources with other women who worked in the personnel and business affairs offices and had access to proprietary records. If the women made charges of sex discrimination, we wanted to be confident that we had the facts.

Once we gathered all of our information, we realized that things were so bad that we could sue ABC News. Some of the women wanted to consult an attorney right away. I was, I hope, a voice of reason suggesting that we first go through channels. Give Roone Arledge and his managers a chance to remedy the situation before we considered a lawsuit. The discussion to sue or not sue was heated. But I had many women on my side and we prevailed. First, we should confront them with the facts, and if they refused to change the corporate culture that worked against women, then we could take them to court.

By this time, everybody in the company was trying to figure out what the women were up to. They suspected it was something serious, but we remained silent, heightening the tension between men and women.

Our next task was to get a meeting with top management. But how did we do that? It was April of 1985. Out of the blue, all of the women correspondents received invitations to come to New York to lunch with ABC executives and later that night attend a gala dinner in honor of Barbara Walters who was receiving the highest award of the American Women in Radio and Television.

Now wasn't that a coincidence? Rumors were swirling about a "female cabal" in Washington and we get this lovely invitation from Roone Arledge. Was management trying to make "nice-nice" to the ladies? Whatever the cause, the newswomen knew this was an opportunity to make our case. On May 8, we would put it all on the line.

We had three weeks to finalize the presentations we would make on that fateful day. It was decided that someone had to do the talking. Several of the most active women were afraid to be in the spotlight on this one. They were worried it would hurt their careers. We all knew that was a good possibility.

I was not afraid. I was tired of women being treated as the weaker sex. As a woman of color, I got signals all the time that I just wasn't as good as a white male, a black male, or a white woman. I was at the bottom of that totem pole. I was determined to make a difference for the women and minorities who came behind me. If I got the chance to use all my interpersonal and rhetorical skills to make cogent arguments on behalf of the women of ABC News, I didn't really care if it hurt or helped me. I wasn't thinking about me, for once. I needed to show the dozen or so white men who ran the company that what they were doing was not only unfair, but also possibly illegal. I got the unanimous vote to be the spokeswoman.

I wanted to be able to make a formal presentation of our findings, so I took all the data the women had gathered and gave it to my husband, who was now the financial vice president of a computer services company. He spent many evenings analyzing the data and creating pie charts, graphs, and spreadsheets of data on his computer. He printed up what turned out to be a twenty-page document that we could present to management with all the facts backing up our contentions.

In the meantime, I worked on my oral presentation. I have the ability to use my voice in a deep, authoritative tone or in a high and childish one. My acting experience from high school and college taught me how to use my facial expressions and body language for maximum impact. I wanted to employ both. I wouldn't be the angry, hysterical woman the men may have expected to hear, but a woman possessing warmth and strength of purpose. I wrote an eight-minute talk and memorized it. Thank you, Drama Club. Without having to read a speech or look at notes, I could deliver my remarks in an extemporaneous style. I was intent on blowing the men away. They would see a side of me they probably never imagined existed.

Getting ready for the meeting also meant looking good. I went shopping at Nieman Marcus and spent what seemed like hours looking for the perfect outfit. Something feminine but business-like. I bought a 500-dollar, two-piece robin's egg blue silk dress with a beautiful pattern of cameos in black, white and gold. I found the perfect cameo earrings and for good measure I added a new pair of black patent leather pumps. I have to admit, with my hair freshly done, the physical appearance would be professional and polished.

The night before we flew to New York, the Washington women had an after-hours meeting at the office to finalize our plans. We learned that we had to make our play at the luncheon. Roone Arledge would be there with all his vice presidents, the executive producers of all the news programs and of course, Barbara Walters. We decided that I would have to seize the moment to speak, if it didn't occur naturally. I assured everybody that if somebody said, "Pass the salt," I would jump to my feet and say, "Speaking of salt. Women are the salt of ABC News." Everybody laughed and that broke the nervous tension we all felt. Two years of meetings and research came down to the next day. My biggest concern was that my colleagues would let me shoot the opening salvo and not support me by speaking up. They assured me they would have my back. I wasn't altogether persuaded when I left the session. Roone Arledge was a formidable presence.

The next morning I packed a bag with my luncheon dress, my evening gown and other essentials for the overnight stay in New York. At the airport I met some of the other women waiting for the 8:30 a.m. Delta shuttle. We had a great time on the plane, laughing, maybe a bit too loudly. We were joking and having fun to settle our nerves. Our reservations were at the Westbury Hotel, which allowed us to check into our rooms when we arrived. We were expected at a reception at noon and lunch would begin at 12:30. I got to my room and hung up my clothes and all of a sudden I was struck with paroxysms of fear. I was having a panic attack. I couldn't remember my speech. I didn't know how I got myself in this fix. I didn't want to do it. I was in a fetal position on the bed when I called Rita and Sheilah and told them I couldn't go through with it.

They must have bounded from their rooms immediately because the knocks on my door came so quickly. I opened the door. "Carole, what's wrong?" they asked in unison.

"I don't know. All of a sudden I can't remember what I'm supposed to say, what I'm supposed to do. I'm terrified."

They tried to talk me down, but I heard none of it. I was almost hyperventilating. There was talk of a paper bag. No bags in the room. There was talk of Valium, but none of us had any. Then, I believe it was Rita who said, "We need to get some wine in her." Sheilah pointed out it was 10:45 in the morning and the bar wasn't open.

Rita said, "I'll find some." She called room service. "I need a bottle of wine right away in room, whatever it was." Someone apparently told her that you couldn't get wine at that time of day. Rita replied, "This is an emergency. Get me your supervisor."

I don't know how she did it. But a few minutes later a waiter arrived with a bottle of warm white wine and two wine glasses. My friends got the bottle open, poured a glass and pushed it into my face. "Drink, Carole."

"Why?"

"Just drink," they ordered.

I took a few sips of the unappetizing warm wine. Sheilah and Rita coached me through my presentation. They reminded me to squirrel away our documents under my place at the table and after getting everyone's attention, pull them out and pass them around to all the executives. They didn't know what I had memorized but they recounted the major points I would be making. I took more sips of the wine that didn't taste nearly as bad as the first ones. They comforted me when they said my memory would come back as soon as I got in the luncheon and all my faculties would be sharp.

"Keep drinking, Carole." I could feel myself becoming more relaxed. Somebody looked at the time. We had to change and get to the reception at ABC corporate headquarters on the Avenue of the Americas.

By the time we met in the hotel lobby to grab a cab to the reception, I was looking rather spiffy and feeling in control of myself again. I remembered my speech and I was ready. As for how much wine it took? Just one glass.

We took the elevator to the penthouse where we Washington correspondents met up with the women from the bureaus in New York, Atlanta, Chicago and Los Angeles. There were sixteen of us. Earlier, we had alerted the outliers by phone what we had been up to and that it was all going to hit the fan at the luncheon.

"We're gonna eat 'em for lunch," someone said.

The other women agreed our issues were their issues, and they indicated on the spot their willingness to support whatever action we proposed.

Like good little girls we were right on time. We found out that we were going through a short receiving line. Leonard Goldenson, the boss of all bosses, was there. He created the ABC Television network. He was a legend. It was very special that he wanted to meet us. He was an elegant and polite older man, who remarked that we all "looked so pretty," and he took special note of my blue silk dress. Other than Barbara, I don't think he had ever seen any of us on his air. The entertainment division was the moneymaker and he had come from Paramount Pictures. The News Division was responsible for only ten percent of the network's programming. But for Barbara and the women of News, he said he was happy to be there.

After congratulating Barbara Walters on her honor, Goldenson bid his *Adieu*. Now there was time to mingle with our bosses. I don't know if any of my fellow women felt it, but I did. The men seemed to know something big was going to happen. I now believe they had moles reporting on the Washington women's comings and goings for a year. I sensed that they had been tipped off and were ready for us. We went into the luncheon. It turned out that with one or two exceptions, the women were sitting on one side of the long table and the executives were sitting on the other. Planned? I think so.

The food was expensive and fancy, but I could only poke at the salad. I can't eat before I speak. I find my brain dulls. Others ate heartily and there was pleasant chitchat along both sides of the table. I waited for my moment but couldn't find it. During dessert Roone got up to talk about this wonderful occasion of having the ABC women there to support Barbara Walters, and her big award and all she's done for women...trailblazer...role model...proud. I do not denigrate Barbara because she was deserving of all of Roone's accolades. But he went on and on. All of us respected her. She worked hard and made a name for herself. We just wanted to be able to do the same.

Barbara stood up to thank Roone for the tribute and thanked him for making all she did on ABC possible...innovator...brilliant...made her first woman anchor of evening news...genius. Then she thanked the women for coming and said she was sorry she had to run, but she had a story to finish for "20/20." She said she would see us later that night at the dinner, and she quickly left the room.

"Go Carole!" I told myself and then I literally jumped to my feet. It was now or never. I turned to Roone and thanked him on behalf of my women colleagues for inviting us to share this day with Barbara, who was an inspiration to us all. In a little stalling action I asked everyone to raise their glass in a toast to "Barbara, the best." That gave me a few moments to get my thoughts in order.

Surprisingly, none of the men got up from the table after my toast.

I reached under the table and got the documents and started passing them around while I said that there were many talented women in the room who aspire to the heights Barbara achieved at ABC

News. Then I began my memorized remarks, which sounded like a well-organized extemporaneous talk. I pointed out that we women believed that it was probably not conspiratorial, but at ABC News it seemed sex discrimination was institutionalized. With the documents in front of each executive, I pointed out the statistics showing women were not well represented on the shows or throughout the ranks. The men examined the charts while I spoke. I said the women believed the news we presented to the public was wrong-headed because white males called all the shots, without female input. That I said, with the broadest smile, is not right.

Roone didn't take his eyes off me. As I talked on and on, his face got red. All his life his genes prevented him from concealing his shyness, his embarrassment, and his anger. He didn't seem mad at me, just riveted by my remarks. The other top managers didn't expect the power of our data and the facts we uncovered. I reported the numbers of jobs in which women were not represented in the company and I laid out the salary disparity for producers. As the room got quieter my voice got stronger. I didn't miss a beat. The words came easily. I commanded the room.

My talk lasted about ten minutes and then I invited the other women around the table to offer any comments they may want to add. Thank God, almost every one of them had something to say. They took over the discussion. Under my breath, I was saying, "Go, girls, go." I got the attention but I could have done nothing without the support of my ABC "sisters." That's how I thought of them now that we had put in so much time together in common purpose to improve conditions for all women at ABC News.

I asked Roone if he had any response. He shook his head and said, "I never thought about it. I really never thought about it." I believe he was being honest. He came to News from years in Sports and he was a man's man. He liked being surrounded by other men. He was an avid golfer and his top execs joined him on the links. He loved to talk about sports and I don't think the women I worked with wanted to spend time talking about the intricacies of a Giants football play that won the team some important game. Most of us couldn't.

My hijacking of the lunch occurred at about 2:15. Our discussions with management lasted until after 5 o'clock with the men getting in on the action. There were angry and conciliatory moments. The back and forth may have gone on longer, but we had to get back to the hotel and change for Barbara's dinner at 6 o'clock.

The meeting concluded with Roone promising more talks between a committee of newswomen and a committee of his executives. Advantage, women.

As I was preparing to leave the room, Roone came over to congratulate me on the presentation. I told him the women all helped me with the documents and the presentation. But then Roone said something I had heard so many times from white people. He said, "You are so articulate." I thanked him, but then he said, "I can't believe how articulate you are." The third time he said that to me I got peeved. "Roone, why are you surprised? You hired me for my ability to speak, didn't you?" He replied, "Oh yes, of course. But you are really articulate."

Making my way back to the hotel, I wondered if he would tell a white woman, or a white man, that they were articulate. No. It's something reserved for black people who can enunciate clearly and speak with authority. Gen. Colin Powell, the former chairman of the Joint Chiefs of Staff, was always being described as "articulate." Why wouldn't he be, and why wouldn't I?

NEWSLADY TO ANCHORLADY

It was clear ABC News wanted to avoid a lawsuit filed by its women because it was in the process of being purchased by Capital Cities, Incorporated, a successful media company that owned newspapers, magazines and several television stations. I received word through a secret intermediary from Cap Cities that we women should continue our actions because the soon-to-be parent company wanted to see how ABC dealt with us. I was assured that the issues we raised were valid and would be addressed no matter what. That was gratifying news. In subsequent meetings with top management, the ABC newswomen put forth a list of recommendations to end sex discrimination. They were actually demands, but we didn't use that word. It seems everybody in top management was angry with us, except Roone Arledge.

There were five "recommendations." We were adamant about getting a pay equity study, conducted by an outside agency, to investigate the disparity between male and female producers' salaries. We wanted Arledge to create a new position among his top managers for a person who would recruit more women and minorities, and oversee career development and advancement. Perhaps the most controversial demand was that Arledge make his executives' pay raises contingent on their success in diversifying their staffs and promoting qualified women. We also asked the company for a formal employee evaluation process, so that women, minorities, and all employees would be told by their supervisors about their strengths, weaknesses, and what they needed to do to progress in their careers. Finally, we wanted quarterly meetings of the joint committee of women and managers to assess whether progress was being made.

We got almost everything we wanted. The biggest success was the pay equity study, which concluded that there was an enormous inequality between the salaries of the men and women who produce the news broadcasts. ABC tried to explain to us that it was not discriminatory because most men came from outside the company and had agents who negotiated their high salaries, while most women came from inside the company, did not have agents, and were subject to a company rule that provided only a ten percent pay raise upon their promotion to a higher level job. They wanted us to know that it wasn't discrimination, just company policy. We had to remind our bosses that while it may not be *de jure* discrimination, it certainly was *de facto* discrimination. We would not be satisfied until there was pay equity.

After the study was completed, the company came back to us and said, based on the report, they decided to average the highs and lows of producer salaries and raise the salaries of all producers to that average. That meant that forty-five of the women producers and fifteen of the men got pay increases. The annual cost to the company was an estimated quarter of a million dollars.

A former woman producer was named to the newly created position of Director of Talent Recruitment and Career Development. We were promised employee evaluations but that took more years than it should have to get off the ground. We had our joint committee meetings not every three months, but every six months. Tying executives' pay raises to their acting affirmatively was soundly rejected. That was no surprise, but it was also the hammer we thought should be held over the heads of top managers that would produce real results. Money talks. It always has.

At one of our meetings with management in New York, a producer and I traveled from Washington. We were very disappointed with the results of the session because the vice president we met said at one point: "I'm not here to sing nursery rhymes with you women."

We thought that was a sexist comment. We were no more interested in nursery rhymes than he. This was serious. We left the meeting talking about "Little Miss Muffet," and "The Old Woman Who Lived in a Shoe." We started laughing at ourselves and decided that since this man was so demeaning to us, we needed to shop. We went into an elegant boutique on W. 57th Street and bought clothes designed by Tomatsu. An orange suit cost me 800 dollars. My producer was charged twelve-hundred for a skirt, blouse and belt. A costly disagreement. At LaGuardia waiting for our shuttle back to Washington, we bought one of those giant Hershey bars and ate all of it. See what happens when women get angry? They shop and get fat.

In the two years we were working on the recommendations, the fortunes of women began to improve dramatically. Within a month of our May meeting, Roone promoted his special assistant, Joanna Bistany, to vice president, the first woman to be housed in a big office on the executive floor. In subsequent months a woman was assigned to run the national assignment desk—a powerful position because that person chooses who is assigned to stories, including the big ones that guaranteed airtime.

Step by step, we got two women foreign correspondents, a bureau chief in Los Angeles, and some reporters got better beats in Washington. Female senior producers were added to shows like "Nightline," "Good Morning America," "20/20," and the flagship broadcast, "World News Tonight with Peter Jennings." Cokie Roberts became a regular commentator on "This Week with David Brinkley." But some of us did not benefit, the most outspoken ones like me who were continuing to prod management for change.

By this time, the women of ABC News had become news. TV columnists across the nation were seeking interviews with us and writing about our anti-discrimination campaign. Women at the other networks told us that they were getting better treatment because of the publicity about ABC. Nothing good happened to me. I continued my regular assignment, covering Vice President George Bush, and the occasional White House story.

While still at NBC, I covered Bush's 1980 campaign for president, which he lost to Ronald Reagan, but became Reagan's Vice President. After the assassination attempt on President Reagan in 1981, I was assigned to keep close tabs on his vice president. There was fear that Reagan's age and gunshot wound might lead to an untimely death. They wanted to have a reporter that knew Bush and his inner circle in case he were to suddenly become president. When I joined ABC I was the Bush expert among the correspondents, so the powers-that-be decided it would be a good idea to keep me in that position.

The Bush assignment didn't get me on the air very much, but I did get to see twenty-seven foreign countries with the Vice President. We were in nearly all the European countries, Jordan, Israel, Egypt, Poland, and several African countries suffering drought: Mali, Niger, and Sudan. We went to China and Ecuador. With Bush I traveled to places I might never have seen in my life. Of course, on the foreign trips, which usually took only a handful of reporters along, I got to know Mrs. Barbara Bush, his close friends, his top staff, and Secret Service contingent. I developed some good sources. My coverage of Vice President Bush continued through the presidential primaries in 1988. On the campaign trail I saw almost every mile of Iowa and New Hampshire, most of Texas, Pennsylvania, Michigan, and Ohio, and we made stops in nearly every other state, with the exception of Alaska.

Traditionally, the reporter that covers the winning candidate in a presidential election becomes the White House correspondent. Bush was expected to be a shoo-in and I was secretly getting excited about becoming the first black woman to become the senior White House correspondent for a major network. CBS's Ed Bradley had broken the bar for black males.

In early June, after all the primary elections, I returned to the Washington Bureau after making a trip to Houston where Bush would rest and get ready for the Republican convention. I could rest, too, after the long slog across America during that primary season. I went into work and walked through the lobby and one of the female security guards asked: "Carole, how come you're not covering Bush anymore?"

"What are you talking about?" A sock in the stomach.

"It's in today's *Washington Post*," she replied. "You wanna see it?"

"No thanks. I'll read it upstairs."

As I rode the elevator to the fourth floor, I was thinking to myself: What the hell is going on? They wouldn't. They couldn't do this to me. They didn't have the decency to tell me? It's in the paper? What does it say? I know this is payback for my speaking out.

On the way to my office I snatched a *Post* from the stack of papers on the floor. I was steaming when I opened my office door. I threw my purse and jacket on the sofa, then settled in my chair with the paper. I went immediately to the Style Section and rifled through it to find the TV Column by John Carmody.

There it was. A small headline above the story read something like, "Simpson Out, Hume In." It was an item that stated something like: "Carole Simpson is being replaced on the George Bush presidential campaign. Brit Hume takes over the job, which includes coverage of the Republican National Convention and the general election campaign in the fall. When the next president takes office, Hume will become ABC's senior White House correspondent. There's been no decision about Simpson's future."

I was boiling. I grabbed the phone and called the vice president of newsgathering, who was someone in top management I believed was a friend. I felt he owed me some answers. He said hello and I just started in.

"Why didn't you talk to me? You know I know more than Brit Hume about George Bush. Eight years I've covered him. If he wins, and we know he will, I should be White House correspondent. But are you now changing the rules of the game when it comes to me?"

"Calm down, Carole," he said. "Talk to Joanna Bistany." She was the first female vice president, who I believe got her job because of the newswomen's confrontation with top management.

"I don't want to talk to her," I told Bob. "I want to talk to you. I'm really mad."

"I know you are. But hang up and Joanna will call you back right away," he promised.

"But, but…" I sputtered.

"Just hang up, Carole." I hung up.

Now what does she have to say? She can't argue that Brit is more qualified than I am to cover George Bush. Nobody can.

My phone rang. "Hello, Joanna," I answered tartly.

"Carole. Why didn't you call me back? I left messages for you all over the place last night. I didn't want you to read about our decision in Carmody's column," she explained hurriedly.

"That's funny. I don't know where you left them, because I never got a message. And I did read about your decision in the paper and I am royally pissed," I said rudely.

"Well, you shouldn't be," she said. "I am calling you with great news."

"Oh, really now," I spat out.

"Just listen. Instead of covering Bush, we want you be a weekend anchor, Saturday nights. Isn't that great? You'll be an anchor."

At that point I didn't care about anchoring. I wanted to be the White House correspondent, I thought I had paid my dues, and it was my dream to reach the most prestigious reporting job in American journalism. It wasn't fair.

Joanna argued that I could do minute-thirty-second stories from the White House two or three times a week, but instead I would have a thirty-minute program all to myself. She said I would start the following weekend. "We're going to give you a substantial raise because you will be an anchor. Now what's better for you?"

It was sounding better. I was suspicious, however, that New York would let me anchor for maybe a year and then demote me to, say, the energy beat. If management had decided last night I would get an anchor gig, why didn't somebody tell the TV Column about it, instead of letting Carmody write that my future was "uncertain." This was a huge embarrassment for me among the journalism community. It sounded like I had done a poor job covering Bush. Then my thoughts turned to the current anchor on Saturdays. It was Barry Serafin, one of Roone Arledge's steals from CBS and my neighbor across the hall. He had one of the greatest broadcast voices on the air and he was a hell of a correspondent. How would he feel about being replaced by me? Joanna said that was not my worry.

"You should be excited." Just accept this "gift," she was saying.

"I won't be excited until you call the *Post* and tell them about my new assignment and they print it tomorrow," I told Joanna.

"We'll try to do that," she replied. "But Carole, this is going to be great for you. During the week you'll report for 'World News Tonight,' and Paul Friedman (the executive producer) wants you to cover a new beat doing stories about the family and social issues." I listened closely. "You get the best of both worlds, reporting during the week, anchoring on the weekend. Now girl, get with the program and stop being upset. Be happy."

It began to sink in and it was the best job I could imagine. But why did I get it? I later found out that Roone Arledge wanted Brit Hume to cover the White House. There was rumor that it had been written into Brit's contract, which he told me was not true. I suspect that despite how articulate I was, Roone wanted more "heft" at the White House, like my former NBC president wanted more "heft" on Capitol Hill. White men just have more of that quality than a black woman.

I suspect my "gift" was to shut me up about losing the White House beat. Management didn't want to read any stories about the head of the ABC Newswomen's group being bounced from a job she was the best qualified to handle. I had quickly developed a reputation at the News Division of not being a "team player." I was not supposed to bite the hand that fed me, even if some of its practices were possibly unlawful. I was a troublemaker, a loose cannon. There were men and women at many levels of ABC who didn't appreciate my taking the company to task. I was just too "uppity."

My correspondent colleagues all thought they knew why I got the anchor job that began in June of 1988. To them I got it because of affirmative action and my big mouth.

Anchoring was not new to me. In 1965 at WCFL in Chicago, my first broadcast job, I wrote and delivered the five-minute 9 o'clock morning newscast and then hit the streets as a reporter. At WBBM in 1968, I co-anchored a four-hour block of news on the weekends. At WMAQ-TV in 1971, I anchored the 10 o'clock newscast on Saturday nights. At both the NBC and ABC networks, I also anchored the one-minute updates in prime time.

My first year at the anchor desk passed. I was waiting for someone to tell me it was over. But then I held on to the second...the fifth...the tenth. All the way to the fifteenth year. In cities with large minority populations like San Francisco, Seattle, Oklahoma City, Houston, Detroit, Chicago, New York and Washington, the news directors of those ABC stations told me I "killed" the competition.

Every time I was on live TV, I realized I was representing women and African Americans. I had to show America that we could be excellent. I felt I had to have an authoritative voice that was, yes, articulate. I had to have a lovely wardrobe. That didn't mean expensive; I couldn't afford it. I had to find reasonably priced suits that complemented my coloring and gave me a professional, put-together look. The make-up should be flawless and not a hair out of place. I wasn't a beautiful woman, so I had to make the most of what I had.

What I didn't know when I began anchoring weekends for ABC was that I would now have a make up artist and a hair stylist every week. What a relief. Other people could try to make me pretty. I had an executive producer, two senior producers, writers and young desk assistants to make the calls, do research, and run out for lunch or coffee. Our studio was always "hot" because we had to be at the ready in case important news broke so we could interrupt network programming for a "special report." On Saturdays, and later on Sunday nights, I was the face and voice of ABC News. It was a heavy responsibility and it kept me on my toes. I read six newspapers a day, two newsmagazines a week, and watched documentaries and other news broadcasts. At any moment I could be called upon to talk about a disaster, a plane crash, the death of someone famous, a Congressional action, or strife in other countries.

I loved reporting for work on the weekends. I arrived before 10 o'clock on weekend mornings. I sat in the conference room with the rest of the staff—coffee in hand—to listen to the executive producer conduct the conference call with our domestic and foreign bureau editors. Each would report on what they were covering in their territory that day and what stories they could offer for the evening news. In a half hour I would have a good idea of how the broadcast might look.

While the senior producers haggled over the rundown of stories and how much time would be allotted to them, I read the daily newspapers from New York and Washington, then read the stories on computer that the Associated Press and Reuters were running from the last twenty-four hours. I would sometimes find a story which I thought we should include in the broadcast, and the producer would assign a reporter to work it up into a television story. Sometimes I'd win; sometimes I'd lose. Producers prefer that anchors stay out of their business of crafting the newscast. They just want you to read it. But I always argued that it was my name, my voice, and my face on the broadcast, and I could not go on the air telling the American people news I wasn't confident was the best compilation of stories we could present. If something were wrong, people would say, "Carole Simpson said…" not the anonymous producer's name. It was the same with technical difficulties—bad lighting, buzzing sound, bad camera angles, or stories I would introduce that weren't there. The talk among viewers would be, "Carole Simpson really messed up." I wanted none of that.

By early afternoon, the executive producer would pass around the rundown of the night's show. It was discussed with me and the producers, who would be editing the reporters' stories, cutting video for voice-overs, or finding sound bites from newsmakers. It was a collaborative process.

All day long I sat at the rim with the producers and wrote as many of the stories as I could, because I knew my writing would be in my speaking style. I read the scripts that reporters sent in from the field and offered my suggestions while at the same time still keeping track of the day's news flow. If a Teleprompter were to break down, I wanted to make sure I could ad lib my way through the story with the salient facts.

At 4:30 p.m. my favorite part of the day came. I would go into the makeup room and change from casual clothes into my TV clothes, settle back in the comfy make up chair to have my hair done. It was so relaxing. Then the make up artist would start in on my face; concealing dark circles under my eyes, minimizing my double chin, and applying foundation and blush. The eyes were last. Mine are small and a little droopy, but by the time the make up was applied, my eyes had popped open and looked glamorous. That all took about an hour, during which time I could reflect on the newscast and try to release some of the tension that builds up when you're about to go live in front of millions of viewers. Once the makeup team signed off on my appearance, and I, too, was satisfied, it was time to go back to the rim and time each page of the script I would be reading. I also corrected some of the language to make it "Carolespeak," as my writers called it. I just tried to make the copy easier for the viewers to understand. That was an anchor's prerogative.

At 5:50, I went into the studio and walked onto the set, where technicians wired me up with a microphone and an earpiece through which the producer could talk to me during the broadcast. I adjusted my chair for maximum comfort, checked the order of the pages in the script, and spent a couple of minutes getting mentally prepared for my delivery while hair and makeup were putting on their finishing touches. I long ago lost my fear of the camera and doubts about my ability. But I still felt I was in a pressure cooker until I said, "For all of us at ABC News, have a good week, and good night."

Once I was off camera, I slumped in my chair and took deep breaths. It was over. I was exhausted. From sitting in a chair for a half hour and reading some pages? Nobody but another anchor can understand the mental exhaustion that comes from keeping track of things, maintaining presence and delivery. The hardest part was having the producer talk into my ear with instructions while I was continuing to read the script live.

Becoming a successful anchor means putting all those years of experience and knowledge together to present the public with news they both want to know and should know. And to be friendly about it. As I mentioned earlier in this book, I delivered news to my long dead mother and later, after his death, my father, too. I looked into the impersonal metal and glass camera lens and told my parents what had happened in the world that day. It gave me a style that many local anchorwomen have told me they tried to imitate. People often wrote fan letters from all over the country and overseas telling me they welcomed me into their homes every week and enjoyed hearing my voice and watching for my smiles.

My pronunciation was so precise that I won the Alexander Graham Bell Society's award from the hearing impaired for having the most lip-readable lips on television. I learned from a Japanese professor visiting Washington that my newscast, which was aired in Tokyo at 9 o'clock Monday mornings, was being used in classrooms to help students learn to speak English.

I may have initially gotten the anchor job for internal political reasons but I held onto the seat for 15 years. I kept the position not because I was black and female, but because I had the highest ratings, people liked me, and I was considered a good anchor. During the time I was weekend anchor, ABC refused to call the show, "World News Sunday with Carole Simpson" and despite my agent's entreaties, it was never written into my contract as one of my duties. Every year I worried I would lose the show. It was an effective way to keep the rebel off balance.

REPORTING ON "THE OTHER AMERICA"

In 1965, Michael Harrington wrote a small book called "The Other America" that had a major impact on United States social policy. Harrington acknowledged that the underclass had shortcomings but he blamed the existence of poverty in America on government failings and the indifference of the power elite. Harrington said that the problem did not arouse the consciences of decent Americans. I read that book when I was a young journalist and I never forgot it.

All I wanted to do was write, report, and be the kind of journalist who aroused the public conscience. I wanted to "afflict the comfortable and comfort the afflicted." Over a century ago that's how Chicago journalist Finley Peter Dunne characterized the role of newspapers. To me the mission was no more relevant then than it is now. The wealthy and the powerful have always been able to get their messages out and their stories told. The trials and tribulations of the poor, or the working class, are most frequently overlooked or underreported by the media. The poverty-stricken can't afford a public relations machine.

Most of my colleagues didn't particularly care for covering a beat where you spent most of your time in urban ghettos, migrant farm camps, Appalachian trailer parks, Mississippi Delta shacks, and the mean streets of crime-ridden inner cities across America. My colleagues wanted to hobnob with politicians, government officials, and business leaders, not social workers, gang members, street kids, or the sick and elderly. After covering government and politics, I knew the stories of the poor and downtrodden had to reach policy makers for their plight to improve. I wanted to give voice to the voiceless.

At first I resisted. For years I fought the stereotype that women are best covering human-interest stories. I pushed for the political beats, like everyone else in the Washington Bureau. Everybody wanted the plum of becoming White House correspondent. However, Paul Friedman, the executive producer of "World News Tonight with Peter Jennings," had a unique idea for a daily feature on the show. He chose five hot topics at the time that remain hot today: health and medicine, the environment, education, crime and drugs, and the family and social issues. He put together teams of some of the best correspondents and producers to work on a series of news reports called "The American Agenda." Our job was to take an issue and find places anywhere in the country where communities or institutions had developed successful programs to deal with the various issues. The purpose was to bring our audience some hope, instead of just a steady diet of bad news. It was Friedman's belief that if we spotlighted innovative solutions in some cities or towns, other areas of the country could try and replicate the programs, tailoring them to their local needs.

Over the six years that Agenda remained on the air, I worked with some of the best producers in the company: Robin Gradison, now at National Public Radio; A'Lelia Bundles, an author and lecturer; and one of my best friends, Rebecca Lipkin, who died of breast cancer at age forty-seven. The producers were responsible for helping find and research the stories, lining up the shoot, making travel arrangements, and hiring the crew. I had editorial responsibility. I would conduct the interviews, screen the tapes, and write and narrate the script. The producers would then put it all together with a talented tape editor to create the compelling stories we produced for the broadcast. Each of them contributed their best to help make my stories among the most interesting on the evening news.

I had been removed from covering the soon-to-be president George H.W. Bush, and had been given the weekend anchor chair. That's when Paul offered me the family and social issues beat. He convinced me that on these kinds of stories, because I was a woman and a minority, I probably would report rings around anybody else in the shop. "You're a natural," he said.

I reconciled myself to the fact that I could do the American Agenda assignment and do it well. The opportunity to do a four-minute piece on the evening news was also hard to turn down because most stories at the time were only a minute and a half to two minutes. It was also a chance to do in-depth reporting all over the country. I ended up my reporting news in 48 of the 50 states, missing only Montana and Alaska.

I am a people person. I had a reputation of getting people to talk to me who wouldn't talk to other reporters. I had the ability to make them comfortable by relating to them on some level. I would find something in their homes to admire, like their pets, or their collection of salt and peppershakers, or I would play peek-a-boo with their babies, or feign interest in their collection of duck art. I knew how to make ordinary people feel at ease. I could erase their anxiety about being in front of the lights and camera by just saying, "Forget about the camera. It isn't even here. Just look at me. You're just talking to me. We're having a chat, not a television interview." I wasn't a national correspondent or anchor for ABC News. I was just a nice lady. A nice "News Lady."

My subjects would often invite me and my crew--the camera operator, the sound person, and my producer--to sit down with them and share their Hamburger Helper-type dinners. My crew would always say, "Oh, no thank you." They would have none of it. But I felt obligated. While they were packing up the gear and the producer was labeling tapes, I was trying to eat the tuna macaroni casserole, or the Tater Tots and fish sticks. There was many a time I left homes with food sneaked into a napkin and later slipped into my pocket until I could get away from the house and find a trashcan. Most of the people were so nice and so willing to share their meager meals. Unfortunately, sometimes I forgot the food in my pocket and I would later smell it marinating my clothes.

The assignment turned out to be "the best of times." I reported, wrote, and edited during the week, and then anchored the weekend news. "The American Agenda" was a feature on the Jennings show for six years. During that time I did stories on the need for universal health care, crack mothers and their crack babies, rape, domestic violence, elderly abuse, homelessness, the effects of violence on children, adoption, the burnout of social workers, displaced homemakers, foster care, gang violence, heroin abuse, overscheduled children, the plight of caregivers, in vitro fertilization, the absence of women in heart studies, teen pregnancy, pediatric AIDS, welfare reform, immigration, prisoners with learning disabilities, high school dropouts, Third World conditions in Mississippi, hunger, the demise of the family farm. And those are just some of the topics.

It was difficult reporting. If you are an empathetic person, which I am, some of the people I covered I couldn't forget. From time to time, I would have to ask Friedman to give me a break because the stories were so depressing.

They were also good. I won almost every journalism award available for my trouble. What was also rewarding was the feedback we got from people wanting to help certain individuals I featured or from public officials wanting to know how to get more information on the solution-oriented programs we highlighted.

One of the haunting characters I met was a black woman, thirty-one years of age, whose four children were taken from her because of her crack addiction. Each of her kids had been born with crack in their systems. When I met her in Los Angeles, she was pregnant with her fifth child. She was very excited when I talked to her because she assured me she had been clean during this pregnancy and if the baby were born crack-free, she would get custody of her other children, who were in foster care.

During our interview I wanted to know how she began smoking crack. She said it all started when she was fourteen years old. She said she came home from school and her mother and father were fighting again. She tried to calm things down, but before she knew it, her father took a twelve-gauge sawed-off shotgun from behind a door and blew her mother's head off. She said she saw her mother's face and brains slide down the living room wall. She couldn't get the image out of her head and was tortured by it. She was a zombie. One day an older man in the neighborhood saw her and said he had something that would take her pain away. He lit his crack pipe and told her to "take a hit."

The image of her mother was erased immediately, she said. "I felt good for the first in my life." From then on, the young mother told me, she had to continue smoking crack to get rid of the vision. She became addicted almost immediately, and as so many addicts report, she never could achieve the euphoria of her first high, but was always trying to get it, to feel that good again.

I thought of myself at fourteen and guessed that if I had seen what she had seen, I, too, might have become an addict of some kind. How does anyone live with that without being mentally damaged forever? I could appreciate the saying that, "There but for the grace of God…" I didn't have parents who fought and had violent arguments, but what if I had? I understood how people wind up in horrible situations. Am I to judge her for taking drugs after such a traumatic event? I couldn't. In telling her story I tried to make the viewer understand the helplessness and hopelessness of many Americans who want to change their situations. I was sorry to report later that her fifth child was born with crack in his system and she lost him, along with the rest of her children, whom she loved. She just couldn't beat the crack addiction. And nobody really cared.

There was a story about a young mother in New Bedford,

Massachusetts, who was going to lose welfare benefits for her and her three children because of a new state law that guaranteed women benefits for only two years, after which they had to get a job. Even if they couldn't find work, their benefits were cut off. No health care, food stamps, or housing allowances. How do they live? Do we just write them off? Too bad. You lose.

The woman I profiled was a Portuguese immigrant who had been in the country since she was a child but didn't finish school. She could speak English but couldn't write it or read it. She was incapable of filling out a job application. The welfare department wanted her to get her GED, but she couldn't read. She tried getting hired at some of the lowest status jobs, at some of the lowest wages, but to no avail. What's a mother to do? I found many women on welfare that had been hiding their learning disabilities all their lives. Their families and friends told them they were dumb. That's why many of them hated school, got pregnant and dropped out. Wouldn't it be great if they had been identified early in their school years and been given special assistance to overcome their dyslexia?

I was teased around the office as being a "bleeding heart" or a "knee jerk liberal." After years of covering stories about people who were struggling to stay housed, clothed and fed in the richest nation on earth, my heart did "bleed" for them and I believed if they could have received assistance from the government and/or the private sector, then they might have been helped. That's just the way I thought.

In Salt Lake City, I did a story about the weekly family gatherings Mormons hold to stay informed about each other and maintain closeness with their children. It seemed to be a good idea for all families in an age when mothers and fathers and their children are all so busy they don't sit down together for dinner. They are like ships passing in the night. "Hi." "Bye."

It worked for many Mormon families because the majority of women didn't work outside their homes and were married to men making salaries well above average.

After I finished my interviews, I had tea with some of the women. They told me they thought it was "just awful" that women left their children in day care to go to work. No wonder, they agreed, there was so much delinquency and crime. One of the Mormons actually said, "A woman's place is in the home."

"What are mothers supposed to do," I asked them, "if the father deserts them and the children, or if the man became disabled and could not work, or God forbid, what if the father died? They have no choice but to find a job if they want to survive."

The Mormon women looked at me as if I were talking about sisters "from another planet." What I described was something they couldn't fathom. It was completely out of their realm of experience. I went on to recount some of the stories I had done about women who were struggling every day to make ends meet. I told them about the one out of five children in America who go to bed hungry every night.

This made me realize how and why conservatives believe the things they do. If you haven't visited poor people, seen how they live, heard what they think, and understood how they got into their predicaments, you could care less about them. Many conservatives who would cut off government support to the destitute claim to be Christians. They seem to have forgotten or ignored the words of Jesus re-told in Matthew 25:40: "In as much as ye did it to one of the least of these, my brethren, ye did it to me."

I tried to do compelling stories about "the least of these" to inform the public and make them care. If that made me a liberal, guilty as charged. Reporters are often accused of being liberal. I think liberal tendencies result because our jobs require us to cover both sides of an argument. You learn most things aren't black or white, but shades of gray. There are some things, however, that don't have another side. Who can make an argument that children should be hungry, or teenagers should become pregnant, or that forcible rape is acceptable?

In 1996, Disney purchased the ABC Television Network and things began to change dramatically. News wasn't that important to an entertainment company and budget cuts were imposed. Executives' attention was no longer fixated primarily on the excellence of the news broadcasts but on the ratings and ad revenue. The News Division became just another cost center for the corporation.

The news programs had been produced by professional journalists, based on their considered judgment of what the public needed and wanted to know. The typical viewers of the evening news were over fifty-five, college-educated and high income. But before long, focus groups and the number of "eyeballs" viewing news were driving its content. Preferred viewers were 18 to 49-year-olds, especially women. The primary emphasis was on attracting younger viewers.

Paul Friedman was promoted and "World News Tonight" was in the hands of his successor, who didn't like American Agenda and killed it. He had brought in focus groups of people to watch our newscasts. They were asked which stories they liked and didn't like, and what topics that most interested them. It turns out they didn't like stories that upset them, like those about the poor, the sick, and the homeless. The Congress and the environment weren't particularly interesting. They wanted to see more stories about health, business and feature stories about animals or interesting people. Celebrities? Probably.

Despite the fact that the American Agenda was no longer a feature, I thought that I would continue to cover stories on social issues. I wasn't getting any assignments, so I took a couple of days to research some topics and wrote up twenty stories ideas and submitted them to the new producer. I got them back and eighteen had been rejected with comments, like, "Not interested." "Thanks, but no thanks." "Already done." "No way." The other two, he suggested, were possible if I provided more details. More details made no difference. I didn't get to do any of the stories.

After the rejection notices I happened to be in New York and sought out the man who nixed them. The conversation ended with his telling me: "If I never see another story about public housing, it won't be soon enough for me."

My brand of storytelling was no longer welcome on the Jennings' show. But all the other beats continued to be covered. I suggested a new beat about aging baby boomers and how products and programs were being developed to reach the seventy-eight million of them. They were the majority of our audience, but even that beat was rejected. The top brass who wanted to attract the 18 to 49-year-olds didn't want our broadcast to have stories about people suffering failing eyesight and hair loss. If you ever look at one of the evening news shows on the major networks, you will see that most of the commercials are for the relief of arthritis, gas, incontinence, denture pain, and a variety of prescription medicines for depression, insomnia and erectile dysfunction. The advertisers knew who was watching the evening news, even if news executives didn't want to accept the fact.

No matter what I came up with in the way of stories, nothing was acceptable to "World News Tonight," even after my having been one of its "star" correspondents. It was clear I was being viewed in a different light. After all the awards and recognition for my work, I did not know this was the beginning of my decline as a news force at ABC.

The future NewsLady at 18 months

Doretha and Lytle Simpson (Mama and Daddy), 1930

Frank (Poppa) Wilbon, 1922

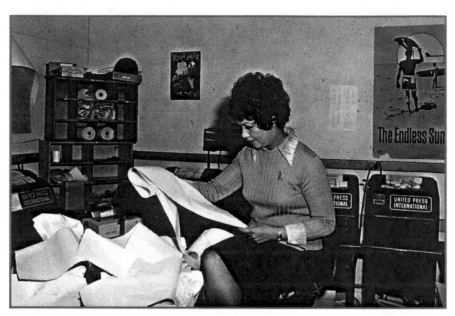

First broadcast news job, WCFL Radio Chicago, 1965

Live broadcast of President Richard Nixon's
arrival in Chicago for WMAQ-TV, 1972

Dr. Martin Luther King on the West Side of Chicago, 1966

Seven months pregnant at the Chicago 7
Conspiracy Trial for WBBM Radio, 1970

Anchoring NBC primetime News Updates, 1980

Covering event on White House South Lawn, 1986

The ABC News Anchor Lady, Washington Bureau, 1988
(ABC News Photography Department)

Reporting live from Johannesburg the release of Nelson
Mandela from a South African prison, 1990

African women journalists in Namibia attending
Carole Simpson Leadership Institute, 2000

Ethiopian boys at refugee camp in Sudan, 1986

Doorway to Nowhere, Goree Island, Senegal, 1997

Interviewing Vice President George Bush
aboard Air Force Two, 1987
(White House Photo)

As President of the Radio Television Correspondents
Association making toast to President Ronald Reagan, 1983

The 1992 Presidential Debate at the University of Richmond between President George Bush, Ross Perot and Governor Bill Clinton (Photo by Doug Burlein, University of Richmond Office of Communications)

ABC News President Roone Arledge, 1991

ABC Anchorman Peter Jennings, 1994

Senator Hillary Clinton before her run for President, 2007

President Bill Clinton and the ABC News Crew
on Air Force One, 1999

Mentoring New York City high school students, 2005

The family: Jim, Carole, Mallika and Adam, 1986

CRY, THE REVILED COUNTRY

For months in the late 1980's, I was the ABC Correspondent assigned to stand in the rain, snow, and scorching sun to cover the almost daily protests at the South African Embassy in Washington. Between 4 and 5 p.m.—in time for the evening news—a group of demonstrators would systematically flout police orders to confine their marches to an area no closer than 500 feet of the Embassy. They crossed the line and were all arrested.

Movie stars, entertainers, scholars, corporate officials, politicians, famous 1960's activists, and ordinary people would gather near the embassy with signs reading: "No more apartheid," "Free Mandela," "End Racism in South Africa." With signs aloft, they would walk in a circle in the designated protest area so that the waiting cameras and reporters could see their identities. While I wouldn't question their motives, because I believe all of them were strongly opposed to apartheid, it did become one of those "hip" things to do. The arrest of celebrities and "big" names would gain more media attention and public focus on the issue.

At some pre-determined signal the demonstrators would start moving into forbidden territory. Police paddy wagons and buses were already at the scene. A police official warned them they were in violation of the law. The activists continued their slow walk and the police hauled each one out of line, put him or her in a wagon or bus, and shuttled them off to Central Headquarters, where they were booked on misdemeanor charges and later released on their own recognizance. They would hold the inevitable press conference in time for the late news.

It was a daily morality play conducted by Americans who wanted to do their part in the international fight against South Africa's racist system of apartheid. The world could no longer countenance a country in which the fifteen percent white minority controlled the eighty-five percent non-white population with pass laws, rigid township rules, intimidation, political imprisonment, beatings and murder. In 1976, when black students rioted in protest of the requirement to abandon their tribal languages and learn their school lessons in Afrikaans, the white language derived from Dutch, the police put down the resistance with brutal violence, arrests, and even killing some schoolchildren.

The international community began turning its back on South Africa through the divestiture of investments in the country, termination of foreign business, economic sanctions, and political ostracism. The penalties against the government began to work. That's all I knew of the problems 10,000 miles away in South Africa: what I heard and read on the news. But soon I would find myself caught up in the violence and conflict there.

I was in Los Angeles on February 1st in 1990 covering a story about the mental development of crack babies when I got an urgent call from the television desk in Washington. I was sure it was to cover another story in California since I was already there. But it was far from that.

The assignment editor told me to finish up my shoot and get back to DC as soon as possible because I would be joining the "Nightline" team spending two weeks in South Africa. We would be covering the black and white sides of the story that would culminate in what was expected to be the release from prison of Nelson Mandela after twenty-seven years behind bars. I couldn't believe that I would be part of the coverage.

Mandela had become a mythic figure to people everywhere, the symbol of the struggle against apartheid. He had been a brilliant young lawyer of towering physical strength and a leader of the African National Congress who was tried in 1964 for his armed resistance to the South African government. Found guilty of treason, he was sentenced to life in prison. The decision to free Mandela was supposed to be seen as a demonstration by South African President F.W. De Klerk that his government was now willing to share power with the black majority.

I wondered why I was going with the "Nightline" staff. I worked for "World News Tonight with Peter Jennings."

Back in Washington, I talked with a "Nightline" senior producer who explained that they needed me to "round out" the coverage. That seemed odd. "Nightline" was always so insular in its coverage and had done a critically acclaimed and award-winning series from South Africa five years earlier. Why was I a last-minute addition?

I was then told that in truth Roone Arledge had looked at the roster of reporters and noted that there was no correspondent of color included. He was concerned about who was going to be best able to tell the black side of the apartheid story, perhaps the most important side? Hadn't it occurred to the "Nightline" staff that they had planned to go to South Africa to cover the end of white domination over blacks with an all-white reporting crew? Duh? Since "Nightline" had no black reporters working for the show, Roone ordered them to take me. I don't believe Ted Koppel was happy about it. He was used to calling all the shots on his show. He had also indicated to me that he didn't care for my work. I cared very much for his work, and told him so.

I was to leave the next day. I was so excited I could scarcely contain myself.

Pack. It's winter and cold here, so in the Southern Hemisphere, it must be summer and warm. Summer clothes. Casual and dress. Mostly casual for the townships. Sandals. Where the heck are my good walking sandals? Research. I need research. I called the desk and put in an urgent request for historical and current articles about South Africa. I could get it from the four other staffers I would be traveling with, the last of the team to travel there. We would have to fly to Frankfurt and then board South African Airways for the fourteen-hour trip to Johannesburg. More than twenty-four hours to get there. I'll die on the plane. Did I pack those sandals?

I couldn't sleep on any of the flights. I was a zombie when we circled Johannesburg for landing. I was shocked by what I saw below. It was a big city with bustling modern highways, power plants belching smoke, high rise buildings, and tall, purple jacaranda trees dotting sparkling green parks. It could have been Dallas or Houston. My mind had to switch gears quickly. Drop those preconceived notions. This is, dare I say, downright civilized. Of course, this was the view from the air, not at all what I would later encounter on the ground.

I had already done considerable world travel to exotic places and yet had never felt like I did when I arrived in Johannesburg. In baggage claim I suddenly felt like a "stranger in a strange land." White people were speaking Afrikaans, a difficult language to speak and listen to, and few signs were translated into English. No one was smiling. I already felt the tension.

As I walked through the gleaming airport terminal, the lobby centerpiece struck me: a stuffed zebra in a majestic galloping stance. I don't like hunting, especially if it is merely to display the kill. But I was fascinated by this taxidermist's masterpiece, amazed at the animal's magnificence and saddened, knowing that its very beauty had probably cost it its life.

I stopped to study it more closely. Nature had splayed its black and white stripes in the most striking pattern. It became, for me, a metaphor for South Africa. The stripes so deliberately and rigidly separated. Apartheid laws. The black stripes standing out more vividly on the hide. The majority black population. It had been killed and apartheid was killing South Africa. Poor Zebra. Poor South Africa.

My marching orders from Herb O'Connor, my "Nightline" producer in Johannesburg, were waiting at the Carleton Towers Hotel.

I was to drop off my bags and take a cab to Baragwanath Hospital on the edge of the city's largest black township, Soweto. Talk about hitting the ground running. I freshened up, changed clothes, filled my backpack, and went downstairs to exchange some U.S. dollars into South African rands.

Outside the hotel there was a black doorman who asked, "Your destination?" I read from my paper, struggling with the hospital's name. He recognized it immediately and hailed a waiting taxicab. The white driver said he wouldn't take me there. The doorman shooed him off and beckoned the next cab. That driver, also white, reluctantly agreed to take the fare.

We drove from the business district of Johannesburg onto a crowded highway that took us away from the high rises, past what I assumed were beautiful homes hidden behind thick, high walls with razor wire stretched across the top. The scenery and terrain began to deteriorate from green grass, flowers, and trees to scrubby brown hills and boulders as we made our way to the outskirts of the city where Soweto is located.

Johannesburg had a population of 500,000, but the black township had one and a half million residents living behind high fences in shacks, tin hovels, and the occasional wooden or brick houses. Rich or poor, doctor or professor, all black people had to live in a township. A foul, black reservation. Mandela's house was in Soweto. Of course, there were other townships surrounding Johannesburg as well.

The cab driver that had not spoken throughout the half-hour drive finally pointed ahead. I looked up and saw a sprawling complex in the middle of which was a six-story decrepit reddish-orange brick building. He pulled to the side of the highway and said "Out." Silly me, I asked, "Aren't you going to take me to the entrance of the hospital?" He replied with a clipped, "No. Too dangerous."

I argued that I would have to cross a median strip and the other two lanes of highway going in the opposite direction. He nodded. Was I going to argue with this guy? I don't think so. No tip for him either, I thought to myself, as if I could have figured out the exchange rate for the rand. For all I knew, I may have pushed into his hand fifty cents or fifty dollars.

I was afraid. I got out of the cab gingerly with cars whizzing by me and made my way to the grassy median. It would mean going down a steep decline into a filthy gully and making the steep climb up the other side where I found two lanes of traffic flying by. But you've got to do what you've got to do to get the story. It seemed like an eternity, but after about five minutes of gauging the traffic, when I saw a break in the flow, I darted as fast as I could across the highway. Thank God for my good walking sandals.

I breathed a sigh of relief but discovered that I was still outside the fenced hospital grounds. How in the world would I find an entrance from the middle of the highway? Fortunately, I only had to walk five or six blocks to find a rickety metal gate through which I slipped in.

My experiences so far should have knocked me into the realization that everything I tried to do in South Africa was going to be difficult. I made my way to the hospital lobby and asked the whereabouts of an American television crew that I was supposed to meet there. Someone found Herb, accompanied by the crew that came from our Rome Bureau, a white camerawoman and a black soundman. When I saw Herb, I hugged his six-foot-six inch frame as tightly as I could because I had finally found a friendly face. He was taken aback by my enthusiastic embrace and said with surprise, "Hellloo, Carole." Then he wanted to know what took me so long. I wanted to smack him. "If you only knew," I said with exasperation. "Later."

He told me we were doing a story on the health care situation for black Africans, while Jeff Greenfield was covering the white situation. Jeff and I would be doing similar contrasting stories over the next two weeks covering education, political power, the resistance and counter-resistance.

Herb said he and the crew had already been shooting cover footage of conditions at the hospital, which he said I wouldn't believe. With my being in South Africa for only two hours, I said I would believe. Sure enough, they were terrible.

The hospital was not just dingy, but filthy. The ceilings were cracked and the paint on the walls was peeling everywhere. Herb took me first to the "Cut Room" where people were lined up on benches in the hallway with blood-soaked rags and towels covering various body parts. Herb told me he learned from a doctor that because there was so much crime, there were always stabbings and slashings. The white South African government didn't allow black people to own guns so there were a small number of shootings, usually by police against what they would describe as "suspected" criminals.

People flocked to the "Cut Room" with their injuries, and it was nothing like our well-equipped emergency rooms. It was just an average-sized room with blood all over the floor from wounds that were simply sewn up. Bandages, gauze, alcohol wipes, and big spools of black thread were stacked high against a cracked wall. I avoided looking closely at the wounds the doctor was stitching.

In the maternity section, all the beds were full and as many as ten women were on pallets on the floor moaning in labor. That dirty, dirty floor.

It was time to interview the hospital director, a black woman doctor educated in England. She described in infinite detail how difficult it was to treat the people of Soweto with the small budget appropriated by the white government's health ministry. She said there were so many needless deaths because they didn't have the comparable staff, equipment, or facilities of the white hospitals.

She said that with so many people compacted in the comparatively small area of Soweto, and with high unemployment, grinding poverty, inhuman housing, young thugs running about, the lack of clean water and indoor plumbing, raw sewage running in the streets, and the refusal of the government to do anything about the wretched conditions, the township was a breeding ground for everything harmful and dangerous to human life. The worst thing I heard her say was that ninety percent of the women treated at the hospital from age one and older had been victims of sexual abuse. One-year-olds? That I couldn't believe, didn't want to believe.

I wanted to run screaming from that house of horrors. But it was my job to tell our American audience what damage had been done to a population of people after forty years of the strict enforcement of apartheid. A black life was worth nothing. It was a fierce unwillingness to accept that fact which got Nelson Mandela and many of his compatriots locked up in jail, all certain that the keys had been thrown away.

After finishing our shoot at the hospital, we took our videotapes back to the offices "Nightline" was renting from the South African Broadcasting Company (SABC). We worked there, writing and editing our television reports. The company was housed in a modern glass building with all the bells and whistles of any sophisticated television production facility in America. But there was another South African shocker. The television networks at SABC were segregated, too. There were two channels for whites, one broadcast in Afrikaans, another in English, and two channels for Blacks, one broadcast in Zulu, the other in English and other black South African dialects. You could see "The Fresh Prince of Bel-Air" on a black channel, but not on a white one. Shows on the white channels from the United States and other countries only showed white people.

Because of the time difference we worked 20-hour days, going into Soweto to do our reporting and back to SABC to ready our reports for broadcast on "Nightline" in the States. We visited schools with no books or chalk, housing with no plumbing and no food in refrigerators, political activists who still wanted to mount an armed resistance to rid the country of every Afrikaner. Everywhere we went, we had to play cat and mouse with the South African police. They would race up behind our car and slam on their brakes. They would turn up everywhere we went. A scary form of intimidation. I blamed my producer Herb for renting the conspicuous bright red Mercedes we drove. He claimed it was the only car the agency had left.

I was anxious to tell our audience all that I was learning about life for blacks under apartheid. I thought the plight of women was particularly harsh. Many had lost their husbands and sons to the freedom fight, and I am sure few people knew that more South African women had been imprisoned for political crimes than women in any other country in the world. Their prominent role in the struggle was virtually invisible to the outside world. The women's story had not been told. I wanted to tell it.

There was a library at SABC and I looked up "women" in several books on blacks. None of the books had a single notation in the indexes for "women" or "children." I persuaded the "Nightline" producers that it was a story we should do.

I began my reporting by approaching a group of women sitting on the ground in the major marketplace in downtown Johannesburg. A couple of them were selling a small number of fruits and vegetables; others were weaving baskets or doing bead work while selling their wares. I told them I was from America doing a story about South African women and what impact apartheid had on them.

"Why you care?" one woman said with resentment. "You colored."

Racial identities in South Africa were classified according to three categories: black, colored, and white. Coloreds were anybody not obviously black or white. So Asians, Indians, Middle Easterners, and mixed race people were classified as colored and didn't have to live in townships. They were forced to live in segregated neighborhoods but not the townships. They generally held better jobs than blacks and made more money.

I tried to explain that in the United States there was no distinction between lighter skinned and darker skinned black people. We were all black and all could face discrimination.

"Here," the woman spoke again, "you would be treated colored. Not be so bad for you."

I told them I had seen Alan Boesak, a light skinned anti-apartheid leader, who was my color but was considered black.

"Ah," she said. "His hair. Not colored."

I had read about this. The special government commission that had the ultimate say on questions of racial identity used hair as a final test.

The woman described the small pencil sized instrument used to test the hair. If they pulled out strands and the hair remained straight, you were classified white or colored, but if the hair bounced back to your head you were black, no matter your skin color. I assured her my hair was not straight but curly. "Not curly enough to be black." The women all laughed. Another piece of craziness I learned about the apartheid laws.

With constant urging on my part, they finally agreed to talk with me about being black and female in South Africa, even though to them, I was still "colored." They told me that most women usually lived with their children and elders. Their husbands were dead, in prison, or far away working in the gold and diamond mines where the women said, they were sure their husbands were consorting with other women and prostitutes. I could understand the explosion of HIV infections in the population after apartheid ended.

The women said their sons were skipping school to skip rocks at the South African police. Boys between the ages of ten and seventeen were called "The Young Lions," and they considered themselves integral to the struggle against apartheid. But their mothers said they were just as happy to be out of school and causing trouble in the townships. Only five percent of women were literate but not because they didn't want to learn. They couldn't go to school because they had to work for their families or work for white people's families to support their own. The hours were long and the wages low. They had to supplement their incomes with handicrafts sold to tourists, and eggs and produce bartered with other locals in the market.

I was so disturbed by their plight. How awful for them. Did they have hope for their daughters? "No, tis the way it tis."

"Wouldn't the end of apartheid make a difference?" "Why? T'ings do not change for us. We only women."

They told me that once the country gave rights to its black citizens, then maybe, long in the future, women would seek their own rights to be equal with men. The seriousness of the moment was broken when one woman said, "We all be dead by den." They burst into laughter again. How could they laugh about it? I decided we needed to concentrate on getting more pictures of women with their children, in their homes, and as an integral part of the movement.

Excitement had been building all week because it was expected that South African President F. W. De Klerk would have a news conference the next day to announce that he was releasing Mandela from prison.

On Friday afternoon a church service, sponsored by the African National Congress, was held to give thanks for the impending freedom of Mandela and to celebrate a new South Africa. It took place at the Anglican Cathedral in the center of Johannesburg. Nobel Peace Prize winner, Archbishop Desmond Tutu, head of the Anglican Church in South Africa, was officiating. Herb and I decided we could get good video of women and children attending the service, so we took our crew and mingled among the hundreds of exuberant white, colored, and black South Africans who had flocked to the cathedral.

It's difficult to describe the jubilation, excitement, and emotion that we felt in the church. South Africans have to be among the most musical people in the world; they all can sing. In every hymn they broke into song in four-part harmony, accompanied by drums. I found myself rocking to the rhythms and wishing I knew the words to the black South African anthem. The songs ended with fists shot into the air and enthusiastic shouts of "Amandla," "Amandla," Zulu for freedom. The women seemed just as militant as the men.

Archbishop Tutu offered his homily with his distinctive dramatic intonation, and the congregation wept openly as he described the lives lost in the past and the fervent hopes for a future of freedom and equality. A young girls' chorus—what more could I ask for—sang a hymn with their chins tilted skyward, sending their young pure voices to the rafters. And the women in the congregation wept. I would never know all of what these people had endured, but in that church I prayed that the change for which they had worked so long would come.

After the moving ceremony, Archbishop Tutu dismissed the congregation with something like, "...in the age to come have Life everlasting. Amen." During the recessional, the crowd began to chant and dance the "toi toi," the liberation dance of the people, which was widely performed during anti-apartheid activities. Young men stomped their feet loudly and thrust their legs into the air to unbelievable heights. Everyone exited the church doing the toi toi, happy and joyful. I made my own feeble attempts to try the moves. What none of us had realized during the church service was that the South African police had declared the church service an unauthorized and illegal gathering. In the cathedral?

As the hundreds of people exited the massive doors they found themselves surrounded in the church square by scores of South African police and their "yellow submarines," the name given to the long squat vehicles used to make mass arrests during "illegal" gatherings. They were parked on all sides of the cathedral.

I came out into the square as happy as anytime in my life, when all of a sudden the police charged the crowd. People running from the police propelled me forward and I began running, too. I couldn't understand what was happening and why. But everyone looked frightened. As I reached the edge of the street, a policeman wielding a rubber truncheon struck me from behind. The blow was across my kidneys. I fell to the pavement, groaning in pain. I am just grateful that was the only blow I received. Others around me were beaten on their heads with billy clubs and their scalps were split open and the blood flowed down their faces.

I lay on the ground, watching the violence all around me, afraid to move. If I got up, where would I go? I cringed when I saw a policeman dragging a woman, about seventy years old, by her ear down the street as she screamed, "I do not'ing. I do not'ing."

I had gotten separated from the rest of my ABC colleagues, but finally I looked up to see Herb and my camera crew. They lifted me up and guided me to a bench, where I sat gasping for breath. I was terrified, the most terrified I've been in my life. Again, Herb was my anchor in the storm. I was completely helpless in this God-forsaken nation where human rights were a joke. The melee continued all around us and other television crews took pictures of me crying in pain that were broadcast around the world. Journalists reported that a black American anchorwoman had been injured in the riot at the "violent demonstration" at the cathedral.

Herb arranged for our ABC bureau in Johannesburg to get a car to an area away from the trouble where I could be picked up and taken to a doctor. He and our crew helped me hobble as quickly as I could away from the violence. We reached the appointed pickup spot and they sat me down on another bench. It was at a bus stop. As upset as I was, I couldn't help noticing that all the white people who had been sitting there got up and moved with disdain on their faces, even though it was obvious I was injured. I looked up at the sign above us and discovered that I was sitting at a white bus stop, not the black stop further down the block where I belonged. What kind of people are these?

When the driver arrived, Herb and the crew stayed to cover the continuing riot while the driver took me to a private doctor who treated Americans. The doctor checked me out, found no bleeding from my kidneys and because I couldn't stop shaking, prescribed a tranquilizer for my fear and anxiety. I was to take it easy for a day or two. I remember leaving the office of this pleasant Jewish-

South African doctor saying I hated his country. He shrugged his shoulders.

ABC wanted me to anchor coverage of the events surrounding Mandela's release from prison the next morning from Johannesburg, with Koppel anchoring live from Cape Town. De Klerk's news conference was taking place on Saturday morning in the States and I still had back pain. So with puffy eyes from all the crying, and little makeup, I had to get in the anchor chair and do my job. I remember it seemed odd to me that ABC in New York wanted me to break in to a popular children's cartoon with a special report. No adults would be watching. Then I heard through my earpiece, "From ABC News, this is a special report. In Johannesburg, South Africa, here's ABC's Carole Simpson."

Assuming my "talking to children voice," I apologized to the kids for interrupting their program and told them to go get their parents to come to the television set because something important was about to happen that they might want to see. "Thank you, children." I always wondered if any kids did what I asked. I found out later from some parents that their kids did just that. "The lady on TV said you have to watch."

I opened the program but then threw it to Ted Koppel, who was in another live location in Cape Town. We covered De Klerk's news conference live, and as expected, he announced that the next day, Sunday, February 10, Nelson Mandela would be freed from prison. He called it a good-will gesture on the part of the South African government to help end the virtual civil war that had gripped the country. His words were delivered in his clipped South African accent in a manner not of victory, but of resignation.

After the broadcast, the "Nightline" team met and prepared our coverage for the momentous event the whole world would be watching the next day. This was a major international story and I would be part of it.

Again I would be in Jo'burg and Ted Koppel would be in Cape

Town with the major anchoring duties. I was the backup in case a satellite went down in Ted's location. To give context and analysis, the "Nightline" team had arranged to have an expert in the studio with me so that I could interview him from time to time when there were lulls in the action. He was the most popular journalist in the country, Allister Sparks, a white native South African, long-time reporter for *The Economist*, and, at the time he shared my studio, a correspondent for *The Washington Post*. We were both excited at the prospect of witnessing Mandela's release. It was good I had Sparks with me because I believe Ted and I were on the air for two hours filling time before the big moment came.

Our cameras stayed on a shot of the exterior of Victor-Verster prison for what seemed ages. When we finally saw the 71-year-old Mandela with his wife, Winnie, emerge from the prison overhang with wide smiles on their faces and their fists thrust triumphantly in the air, it was more than Allister could bear. I was glad Ted was doing the talking from Cape Town, because in Johannesburg, Mr. Sparks, a man in his 60's, collapsed in tears and I, with wet eyes, patted his back in an attempt to console him. He was a native of this country and had been covering the anti-apartheid struggle his entire life. I can only imagine what the moment was like for him. For me, it was the most moving of my career.

In later years I would make several trips to South Africa, and I now consider it one of my favorite countries on earth. Its beauty is unmatched. I have witnessed much of the progress that's been made but have also seen how much more remains to be done, especially for women and the fight against AIDS. To this day, South Africa leaves me torn, and when I think of the people there my heart aches for them: black, colored, and white.

IN TO AFRICA

When I covered the release of Nelson Mandela, South Africa was not the first country I had visited on the continent. With Vice President George Bush I traveled to Egypt, Niger, and the Sudan. It was during the drought in Ethiopia caused by the steady encroachment of the Sahara Desert into what were once fertile farming areas. What we saw in those countries were poverty, famine and death. African people are upset that coverage of their countries is most often about hungry people and wild animals. I understand what they mean, but the Ethiopian famine was a story that deserved the attention of the international community, because it could provide food and medical supplies.

In a Sudanese refugee camp, I huddled with George and Barbara Bush in tents where we saw new mothers who were so thin and malnourished that their milk had dried up. Their starving children were so weak they couldn't open their mouths wide enough to take a spoon of fortified mush. The mothers had to force feed them. One limp five-year-old boy was lifted onto a hanging scale. He weighed only seventeen pounds. Mrs. Bush cradled him in her arms and whispered to him. The Vice President wasn't as eager to touch the dying children, but he eventually held a baby and hoisted him into the air. The poor child probably had no idea what was happening to him.

One of the saddest sights I saw was a father digging deep into the sand on the outskirts of the camp. Standing above him was his grieving wife and on the ground a small white bundle. In it was the couple's four-year-old son. I stayed behind to watch this tragic scene. When the hole was big enough, the mother handed her dead child to her husband, who placed him gently into the makeshift grave. As he covered the body with sand, the mother gave out a primal scream, looked up to the sky, waving angry arms in the air. I wiped a tear. My own son was six years old. Later I learned that several people died each day, and the cemetery was sheltering the bodies of nearly 100 men, women, and children, a number that grew every day.

We were escorted to an area of the camp where the healthier boys and girls entertained us with a song. Their musical instruments were empty water cooler bottles, gas cans, and pots and pans. It sounded terrible but they were enthusiastic and so cute. Ethiopians are a beautiful people.

Because we were in Sudan, a Muslim country, American women were asked to wear skirts, preferably long. I wore a long, red shirtwaist dress, which unfortunately made me stand out. I was suddenly surrounded by ten little boys, ranging in age from, I'd say, five to nine years old. From their smiles, loud voices, and jumping around, you could tell they were well on their way to recovery. They were chanting something I couldn't understand. The camp director shooed them away from me. At a later stop, they showed up again, tugging at my dress this time, leaping and laughing and offering up that chant again. This time the camp director really gave them a talking to and ordered them to leave me alone. I wasn't the only woman or the only American woman touring the camp. Why me?

They didn't approach me again, but I could see them peeking through the tents everywhere I moved, grinning at me and making me laugh. I would shake my finger at them in mocking reprimand, and they burst into giggles of delight.

After four hours at the refugee camp, they told us to board the buses that would take us back to the airstrip and Air Force Two, the

Vice President's plane. The boys were now frantic, descending on me like the flies and mosquitoes that swirled inside the tents of death. I smiled at the boys and waved goodbye to them. Before I stepped onto the bus, I asked the camp director who the boys were, why they were all over me, and what they were chanting?

"All of them are orphans," the camp director told me, "and someone told them you were an African American woman. What you heard them shouting was Swahili for 'Adopt me. Please adopt me.'" My heart sank. I wish I could have adopted all of them. I took my seat on the bus and leaned out the window where they had all gathered with their skinny arms outstretched. I have never forgotten those boys and for years have wondered if they survived and what they are doing now. When I read stories about Darfur, I wonder if they are engaged in the conflict, now that they are men in their twenties.

Africa tugs the heartstrings.

After that trip my next direct encounter with African people was during a conference in Washington, DC. I am a founding member of the International Women's Media Foundation, a group of women journalists who want to build bridges with women journalists around the world. We raised money and put on a conference in DC to which we invited women delegates from fifty-seven countries. Our plan was to discuss the globalization of news and the new satellite technology. We held workshops to discuss the subject matter in detail. I moderated a workshop, which was held for women from underdeveloped nations. The participants were primarily from Africa.

We learned at the workshop that female journalists had a rough time. They make meager salaries, their profession is not respected, and they do not become famous unless they are jailed or harassed for criticizing a government official for corruption or some other wrongdoing. They want to be journalists because, even at their own risk, they want to help their people by exposing government corruption and other crimes committed by their leaders, police authorities, or the military.

African women are not "shy violets." They are very outspoken and took no time informing our panel that they couldn't care less about new technology and global media. They not only didn't have computers, they didn't have enough typewriters. I knew we would have to dump our topic and listen to these women's issues.

They described the patriarchal tribal system that still exists in most sub-Saharan countries. Women are considered inferior to men, objects of sexual pleasure, intended for bearing children and taking care of the home. Most men feel they own their wives and force them to do their bidding. And of course there is the problem of female genital circumcision, which cuts out sexual pleasure and desire so the women will remain faithful to their husbands.

A woman from Tanzania got up to tell about conditions in her daily newspaper office. She wanted to cover politics, but to get her foot in the door, she agreed to cover birth and death announcements, and social activities.

The Tanzanian said that one day she was trying to finish her assignment and was typing furiously on the keys of her beat-up Royal typewriter when her editor came beside her. She said he took one of her hands off the keys and placed it on his crotch where she could feel his erect penis. She said she was disgusted. She was on deadline. She said she couldn't look at him as he moved her hand in a circle over his pants. She said she didn't know what to do. She had seen him lead other women into his office and close the door. But she was married and the mother of a young boy. The thought of what her editor obviously wanted from her was unthinkable. She said she grabbed her purse and ran from the office. There was no one to tell about this embarrassing incident, especially not her husband. She went back to work and tried as gracefully as possible to refuse her editor's repeated sexual advances. She wasn't sure how long she could hold out before he fired her.

We Americans were shocked. We had laws against sexual harassment in the workplace. The African women have no recourse.

"What can you Americans do to help us in such a situation?" she beseeched us.

Another woman from Kenya related a story that was even more unbelievable. She worked for Kenya Broadcasting Company (KBC) and was the "Barbara Walters" of Kenya. She was the most visible woman in the country. She had her own show featuring interviews with significant figures. She also anchored the news. She told us that she was working in her office preparing for her broadcast when her husband arrived at the studios and came straight to her office.

"He started boxing me in the face till I fell to the floor. I didn't know why he was doing this. We didn't have an argument," she recounted, almost in tears. "He dragged me by my hair into the newsroom where all my co-workers could see, and he continued to hit and kick me."

We Americans were on the edge of our seats when she related the following:

"Not one of my co-workers did a thing. They watched. They didn't try to stop him from beating me. They didn't call the police. Nothing," she said and sat down.

We learned later that she had been hospitalized with a broken jaw and it was months before her face had healed sufficiently for her to return to her work in front of the cameras.

"I am chattel," she added, "just like an animal. My husband can do whatever he wants to me and it is nobody's business."

We realized that we had many issues in common with journalists from Western Europe, some Asian countries and Australia. But African women needed special attention. We at least had to get them computers and professional training, but there was nothing we could do to get laws passed in their countries protecting them from sexual harassment or providing them equal rights.

There have been many organizations working in Africa to improve its nations' economies, to provide food and health care, and to promote democracy. But we were the only group focusing exclusively on women journalists, whose reporting and views we considered essential for fledgling democratic societies. As a woman of color, with ancestors from Africa, I had great concern for my African "sisters."

Three years later I chaired an IWMF conference in Harare, Zimbabwe, for women journalists from countries in the southern region of the continent. There were delegates from South Africa, Namibia, Zambia, Malawi, Mozambique, Botswana, Lesotho and Swaziland, Uganda, Kenya, Tanzania, and our host country, Zimbabwe. We wanted to call the conference "African Voices: Empowering Women in the Media." The disgraced leader of Zimbabwe, Robert (President for Life) Mugabe objected to the title. We would not be allowed to "empower women" in his country. To ensure that we could have the conference we changed the theme to, "African Voices: Women in the Media."

It was a heated conference as tribal and country loyalties conflicted with American efforts to get the delegates to move beyond factional disagreements and focus on common interests and goals. Fortunately we had built in social activities such as tours of Harare, souvenir shopping in the marketplace, cocktail parties, and games. We came away hopeful. The women were bright, intelligent, courageous, and dedicated. We could help them.

I learned, however, that the African women journalists did not see me as a "sister." They saw me as an American. They reminded me that I lived a completely different lifestyle from them. They thought I was wealthy.

"Do you have a nice house with lots of rooms," I was asked at a late night rap session. "Yes." I thought of my thirteen-room house in Chevy Chase, Maryland.

"Do you drive a nice car, one that isn't ten years old?" "Yes." I thought of my Mercedes and my husband's BMW. "Do your children go to fancy schools?"

"Well, yes." I thought of my daughter at National Cathedral School and my son at Georgetown Day School, both expensive private schools in Washington, DC.

"Do you buy clothes in nice shops and pay the cost on the price tag?" "I do, but I always try to get them on sale," I explained lamely. In America, I certainly don't think of myself as wealthy, but in Africa, I felt like a Rockefeller.

They dismissed me. I had nothing in common with them other than journalism. To them I was no different from the white IWMF women who traveled to Harare with me. Yet, I still felt an obligation to press their cause in my organization. Their problems were so severe.

In 1997, the IWMF established the African Women's Media Center in Dakar, Senegal. We had an executive director, a staff and suite of offices. During a conference there to launch our new Center, I announced that I would donate thousands of dollars to establish the Carole Simpson Leadership Institute (CSLI). Its goal was to provide journalism skills, as well as leadership training, to women so they could advance in their careers and someday become executives in the African news media.

By now we realized that we could no longer take the role of the rich Americans coming to their countries and telling them what to do. We would have to find African women to do the training, women who understood the cultures and the nuances in relationships that were difficult for us to discern.

Most Americans think of Africa as one big country, but it is a continent made of fifty-four countries. In addition to the thousands of ethnic dialects or tribal languages spoken within each country, there are nations with official languages including English, French, Portuguese, and Swahili. Uganda is as different from Rwanda as Germany is from Italy, Ethiopia as different from the Ivory Coast as the UK is from Greece. The peoples' skin tones range from white to all shades of brown and black, and they are different in cultural traditions, religion, food, marriage rites and dress. Their climates, terrain, and crops are different. And lions and elephants don't inhabit all of the countries. Foreign nations covet the wealth of natural resources, which in addition to gold, diamonds, and oil (black gold) include titanium, copper, uranium, and magnesium. These resources keep the continent in turmoil while developed nations fight over who gets what, for how much, and from where.

The Carole Simpson Leadership Institute trained more than one hundred African women journalists; and some of them have assumed executive positions at their media companies. With my money and commitment I am confident that I helped make a difference in their lives. This is one of my proudest achievements. Even though these women who looked like me didn't accept me as one of their own, I accepted them as my own.

After the conference in Dakar, a group of American and African women journalists journeyed off the mainland to Goree Island, a hub of the slave trade dating back to the Sixteenth Century. A guide showed us the rooms in the fortress where men were separated from women and where women were separated from their children. We saw the ankle chains to which were attached large twelve-inch iron balls. The strong males were shackled with these monstrosities to keep them from trying to swim to safety. If they jumped in the waters of the Atlantic, the ball and chain would drag them to the bottom and certain death.

We were led to what is known as "The Doorway to Nowhere." It's an opening at the end of a long corridor where the slaves trudged thinking they were boarding ships taking them to plantations where they would do farm work. Instead, it was an opening to the gangplanks of slave ships that would transport them across the treacherous Atlantic Ocean to the "New World," where they would be sold at auction into a life of servitude and oppression. Men and women were separated from their spouses and children, frightened, alone, unable to understand the language that was spoken by the white men who ordered them about or the fellow slaves that lay beside them.

As the guide told us the stories, each of the women on our tour had a turn standing in the infamous doorway. I think we all shed tears as we looked out into the emptiness of the vast ocean. I tried to imagine myself in the position of a captured slave woman. It was a sobering experience. But to be honest, I was to some degree pleased that my ancestors got sent to America. Otherwise, I would be fighting the problems Africans face every day. I was not the only African American woman who came away with that opinion.

I have visited a total of seventeen African countries: Morocco, Tunisia, Niger, Mali, Sudan, Egypt and Ethiopia in the North, and in the sub-Saharan region, Senegal, Cape Verde, Kenya, South Africa, Mozambique, Angola, Tanzania, Botswana, Zimbabwe and the Comoros Islands.

I have a deep feeling for the African people but I sure am glad I was born in America.

THE DOUBLE WHAMMY

When would I just be Carole Simpson, a broadcast journalist? Nothing more, nothing less. Like clockwork I was reminded every six to nine months that I was either just a woman or just a black person. It could come in the form of an insult to my face, a slight, a piece of hate mail, an email, or a phone call. I couldn't understand why I couldn't transcend race and just become me, another human being.

I was continuously plagued by "the double whammy": the "whammy" of being black and the other "whammy" of being female. There were those who didn't like me because I was a woman and those who didn't like me because I was black. My employers didn't mind my twin identities because when the Federal Communications Commission enforced affirmative action goals in the 1970's and 1980's, I was a two-fer, meaning I could be counted twice on the FCC affirmative action forms—once as a woman, again as a minority.

Social scientists in the Eighties came up with a hierarchy of power according to race and gender. To no one's amazement, white men were at the top; black men were next, then white women. At the bottom were black women. When I saw it, I had further proof that to survive I would have to work harder and be better.

The history of television news shows that white males have always dominated the field. White men want to be surrounded by others like them. They want to hire as close associates people with similar

179

socio-economic backgrounds who attended the same kinds of schools and have similar interests or the same religion. They want to be able to talk about sports, their golf handicap, and what they'd like to do to the young shapely intern they just hired. Men can discuss those topics with other men, but not with women. That's why black men seem to fare better than women of color.

At the three major commercial networks, the late Ed Bradley had been a White House correspondent and then landed on "60 Minutes," the most successful newsmagazine show ever. The late Max Robinson of ABC became the first African American evening news anchor. Bryant Gumbel was a successful sports anchor at NBC before becoming host of "Today," the top rated morning news program. ABC made Robin Roberts a host on "Good Morning America," but a generation later than Gumbel had ascended the throne at "Today."

When you look for black women on the major networks, I was the only one to anchor an evening newscast, albeit on the weekends. I thought I had broken the barrier and there would be others to follow. So far, no such luck. A white woman briefly replaced me and a white man followed her, the way it was before I got the job.

People often ask me whether I experienced more racial discrimination or sex discrimination. Without hesitation I answer, "Sex discrimination." Don't get me wrong, I suffered both forms, but I was denied opportunities more often because I was female than because I was African American.

During my radio days in Chicago I found out that the men I worked with were making sometimes twice as much as I made for doing the same job. I asked my bosses about the disparity and was told that the men needed the higher salaries because they had wives and families to support. They told me I had a husband who could support me. No equal pay for equal work for me. Later I wanted to try my hand at management but was told I would never be able to get the men to perform well because they wouldn't take orders from a woman. When I wanted to anchor at WBBM, the CBS all news station in Chicago, I was informed that I couldn't have that job because "women don't like to hear other women on the air." At the time there were scarcely any women on the air, so I inquired, "How do you know that? Was there a study I never heard about?"

My news director, who didn't cotton to being challenged, dismissed me with, "That's a fact, so just forget about it."

Another boss said that, "Women's voices are shrill and not authoritative enough. News coming out of a woman's mouth sounds like gossip."

I knew that my voice was authoritative. I had worked on pitching it to a lower register, projecting the sound from my diaphragm. I got in the habit of always articulating my words carefully. Using my "TV voice" I could command attention and, yes, even respect. If I were verbally attacked, I could use my voice to wither some would-be opponent.

After the Three Mile Island nuclear accident occurred in Pennsylvania, I wanted to cover the story because my husband had worked on nuclear reactors at Argonne National Laboratory. Unlike other correspondents in the NBC News Washington Bureau, I knew something about nuclear power. Many reporters feared the possibility of radioactive fallout. So I asked the bureau chief if I could go. He said I couldn't, adding, "I'm worried about the effect on your reproductive system."

I couldn't believe it. "Why don't you let me worry about my reproductive system, SIR?" I responded. He sent a white male to report the big story which I was ready, willing, and able to cover. It turns out the male reproductive system is more susceptible to radiation than women's, for fairly obvious reasons.

Of course, there was sexual harassment from my male co-workers:

"What's wrong? Are you on the rag today?"

"The way you're looking I could fuck you on the spot."

"You're too emotional."

"Hmmm. Your butt looks so round, so firm, so fully packed."

"Boy, if you weren't married. I could spin you around the world and you know on what."

As if. And then there were the "accidental" contacts men made with my breasts or rear end.

I talked to other women and they had similar experiences, but they didn't seem as crude as mine. The myth of the "easy" black female, I believe, prompted them to display their most stupid and juvenile behavior. How was I supposed to concentrate on my job when the man I'm working with is stealing glances at my butt and breasts, or saying he wants to have sex with me? Thanks to a Supreme Court ruling, women now have legal recourse, but women of my era had none. We had to grin and bear it. Male bosses didn't appreciate how demeaning it was to be subjected to unwanted sexual advances. We had to work in a hostile environment and didn't dare complain for fear of being called another pejorative: a "hysterical woman."

I also never knew how and why men could make sexual references to whatever we may be talking about. "Speaking of the stay of execution, I want to stay with you tonight. We'll knock some boots." Why in the world did they think they could have their way with me? They weren't worth my time of day and all of them were married.

Why? Why do men have to express every sexual thought that passes through their minds?

The racial discrimination, unlike the sex discrimination, was subtler and more destructive because it could have an effect on your job or your salary. It was occurring behind the closed doors of executive suites. Black employees didn't see it but felt it. What I hated most were the racial insults I thought I had left behind in Alabama twenty years before.

There was a going away party in the ABC Washington Bureau for one of our correspondents who was leaving for a three-year stint overseas. I didn't really want to go, but decided to run upstairs and wish him well. As I entered the already crowded conference room, the first person I encountered was one of the leaders of the Bureau. As soon as he saw me and with no hesitation, he asked, "Where's your cap and apron? Aren't you going to serve?"

This man could take one look at me and first see a maid before he saw one of his correspondents. With race so prominent in his mind, could he ever see me as the Senior White House Correspondent? I was outraged. In my most powerful "TV voice" I asked, "What did you say to me?" Heads turned in our direction.

"Nothing," he answered flippantly.

"You did say something," I continued in *voce forte*. "Again, repeat what you said to me?" Everybody was looking in our direction now and you could hear a pin drop. His face flushed red.

"I'm sorry," he said softly. "I was just kidding."

I turned on my heel and walked away from him. This was the first time I didn't let comments like that slide, and they would never slide again. Colleagues gathered around me asking, "What did he say?" I didn't tell them. I described the confrontation as a little misunderstanding. Now, who was embarrassed? He never forgot it and our relations remained chilly until the day he left the company.

Minority employees were invited to New York to have lunch with Roone Arledge to discuss some of the same issues the ABC newswomen had raised with him earlier: career advancement, more minority employees and more of them in decision- making positions. Three of us Washington correspondents took the shuttle to New York and arrived early. We decided to stop by the assignment desk to say hello to the folks we most often dealt with over the phone. The woman running the national assignment desk looked at us and said, "You're here for lunch with Roone." We nodded. Then she asked, "What are you all having to eat? Chittlin's and watermelon?"

We were aghast. Did she really say that? How could she have said that to us? We each mumbled something. I said loudly, "I don't eat chittlin's and don't particularly like watermelon." Conveniently, her phone rang and she answered and began talking. Our signal, I suppose, that the conversation was over. I suspect one of her underlings on the desk saw her getting into hot water and called to help her escape our wrath. Later we talked among ourselves about this woman, who had power over who covers the big and important assignments. She could make or break a correspondent or producer. To her, we couldn't possibly be "star" material, just three chittlin' and watermelon-eatin' Negroes. During lunch with Roone, we named her and told him what she said to us: a demonstration of why we believed racism was alive and well at ABC. I believe she got a talking to, but not a formal reprimand, or suspension. Somebody up there liked her more than they cared about our bruised feelings.

This was another woman who got promoted after the ABC newswomen's group demanded more females in top positions. Her example disabused me of my belief that because she was a woman, she would be an agent of positive change. She could be as petty, hurtful, and discriminating as any man.

Many of my fellow correspondents were not happy that I got the Weekend News anchor job. One night on my way to the studio to deliver the news, I was accosted in the hallway by a white male correspondent who told me what he would have to do to become an anchor: "I'd have to put on a skirt, a kerchief on my head, and paint my skin black."

It sounded like a description, not of me, but of the early Aunt Jemima image on the box of pancake mix. He said something like that to me just before I was about to go on the air. He was trying to rattle me. I stood in my new burgundy suit looking at him for a long time and then I had to say it: "You're an asshole."

While working through lunch when I was covering the White House, I respectfully asked one of our technicians on his own way to lunch if he could bring me back a sandwich. Too quickly he asked, "What do you want, a collard greens sandwich?"

I was getting so tired of this. I wanted to know from him what kind of sandwich that was. I told him I had never heard of it. He heh-heh'ed and said "You people ("you people") like collard greens, don't you?"

I started softly but my voice rose in a crescendo, "I love collard greens but you don't put them in a sandwich, Mr. Charlie. Why are you asking me about a collard greens sandwich? Bring me, please, a tuna fish!" I finished sarcastically.

The red-faced technician grabbed the five-dollar bill out of my hand. An hour later I got my tuna sandwich without comment.

We often had working lunches in the Washington Bureau and they were usually pleasant affairs with a menu of sliced beef and turkey, Caesar and pasta salads, and iced tea or Perrier. The correspondents and producers were invited to one of these lunches and for the first time I saw a table with a platter of cold cuts, white and wheat bread, bowls of mayonnaise and mustard, cans of soda, and a plate of cookies. I remarked in the line, "We must be having budget problems. This is all we get?"

In a split second, a top producer snapped back at me. "What do you want, fried chicken and ribs?"

He wasn't talking to Carole Simpson. He was talking to someone black. I used my TV voice again and for all to hear I said, "What makes you think I want fried chicken and ribs? I don't even eat them. Do you ask because of my color?"

He knew he had stepped in it. "Carole, can't you take a joke?"

"No I can't. Not from someone who takes one look at me and sees a stereotypical black woman." He would suggest later that I was in the wrong for having no sense of humor.

The men would always say that about me. When I tangled with those in authority, they would downplay my complaints and label me a troublemaker, someone who was not a team player. If that would be my reputation for speaking out against racial insults, then so be it. Other black employees were experiencing worse acts of racism, but they were in no position to complain. I felt that I was established well enough and had the job security to speak on behalf of those who could not speak for themselves. One of my favorite gospel performances by Mahalia Jackson says in a song what I believe: "If I can help somebody as I pass along, then my living shall not be in vain."

Washington power player and former civil rights activist Vernon Jordan delivered a speech to black executives of major corporations from all over the nation. He told them that because they were successful and had "made it," they not only had to pay their income taxes but also had an obligation to pay what he called their "black taxes."

Jordan talked about our ancestors who risked and lost their lives in the cause of equal justice for black people. He said those executives stood on the shoulders of black heroes like Harriet Tubman, Frederick Douglas, W.E.B. DuBois, Fannie Lou Hamer, and of course, Dr. Martin Luther King. He pointed out to the wealthy black corporate executives they wouldn't be where they were today if it weren't for the sacrifices of those who went before them.

"Paying your black taxes," he explained, "is helping other black people succeed." He said it could be picking up a phone and putting in a good word for someone, or helping a person get a job, writing a recommendation, or providing scholarships for black students.

I never forgot that speech and began paying my "black taxes." I decided to set up scholarships for women and minorities. At the height of my money making, I had five different scholarships. I also decided to never miss an opportunity to mentor young people, to help them seek employment, and to help them with their broadcasting skills.

After I decided to fight for equality in the field of broadcasting, I was continually butting heads with top management. I had no choice. I would do what I could through my stories to help the helpless in our society, and I would do what I could in my field to get diverse perspectives, faces, and voices heard.

For thirty years I worked to bring to the table of news decision-making women and blacks, Latinos, Asians, and Native Americans.

Representatives of all those groups have been recipients of my scholarships.

The double whammy, double "No's," only made me more sensitive to the problems that still exist for women and minorities and more vocal in my efforts to help eradicate the barriers. There's a quote on a T-shirt I own that speaks to my activism: "No woman made history who was polite and quiet."

THE 1992 PRESIDENTIAL DEBATE

The fall of 1992. The presidential campaign was in full swing, with President George Herbert Walker Bush in a tough battle to win re-election against Reform Party Candidate Ross Perot, the quirky Texas billionaire, and Democrat Bill Clinton, the bad-boy governor of Arkansas.

George Bush had been resting on a ninety-percent approval rating after his victory over Saddam Hussein in the 1991 Iraq War, known as Operation Desert Storm. But on the way to the election he had not been paying attention to a big problem for the American people: the economy, since the war in a steady decline. By September of 1992, jobs and wages had gone south and the federal deficit had gone out of control.

I love political campaigns. How can you help but become a political junkie when you live in Washington, D.C? But after years of covering Congress, the White House, and campaigns, I wasn't covering politics anymore for ABC News. Not my choice. However, I was working on what I considered equally important stories about the nation's social problems, an issue the network news programs often overlooked.

Then one day my fortunes changed dramatically. Everything is so vivid to me. Friday, October 9th, was a beautiful afternoon. The fall foliage was beautiful, a typical warm autumn day in the nation's capital. I had walked to a downtown interview with Ralph Neas, head of the Leadership Conference on Civil Rights. Midway through the taping session, my pager started vibrating. I ignored it. Again it went off. Vvrrrmmm. Again, I ignored it. When it continued to tickle my kidney, I got concerned. Maybe something had happened to my son in school or my husband at work. I interrupted the interview and asked Ralph if I could use his telephone. Something is up.

I called our Washington Bureau television news desk and I was told to get in touch with our veteran political director, Hal Bruno, immediately. I wondered why he needed to talk to me so urgently.

"Carole," he said almost breathlessly, "they want you to moderate one of the presidential debates."

Who, what, where, when, why? My old reporter's "Five W's" flooded my head.

Hal didn't know much about it but he said "my" debate was going to be historic, the very first town hall debate, with real people asking questions. He said to call Janet Brown right now. Janet Brown? She was the executive director of the Bi-Partisan Commission on Presidential Debates. Though dazed I scribbled down the number.

Poor Ralph Neas, whose interview I interrupted, had watched all this with puzzlement. "What's going on?" he asked. I sputtered, blubbered that I was going to moderate the second presidential debate in the next few days and I was so excited. "Congratulations," he smiled. "That's a mighty big job and a credit to you."

I hadn't finished the interview with him. My mind was gone. I asked a couple of more questions but didn't know what I was asking.

I hurried out of his office and walked back to the bureau to make this all-important call to Janet Brown. I felt as if I were Dorothy, leaving the sepia tones of Kansas and entering the Technicolor world of Oz. This time I marveled at my surroundings. The wonderful crunch of the leaves with every step, the bright red maples, the remarkable golds and browns of the towering oaks, green leaves still clinging to branches which were not ready to part with them yet.

Why was I so happy? Because I felt that I had finally "made it."

What political reporter wouldn't want to moderate a debate that would be seen by ninety million people on all the networks in the U.S., as well as countless millions around the globe? The whole world would see my work.

The little black girl from a South Side ghetto of Chicago, who was told repeatedly she would never make it as a journalist, would be taking control of the world stage with three men, one of whom would become leader of the Free World, the most powerful man on earth. I could tell each of them when and when not to talk. And I could interrupt them when I felt they were not doing what they had been told to do: answer the people's questions. It was heady stuff.

Brown told me that I had been chosen by the Democratic and Republican campaigns and members of the Bi-Partisan Commission on Presidential Debates to moderate the second presidential debate occurring October 15th in Richmond, Virginia.

She said the Commission wanted someone with extensive live television experience, someone who had covered politics, and someone they thought could handle a live audience of ordinary people who would be posing their own questions to the candidates. A people person.

And they chose me? Janet said both major campaigns were enthusiastic over my choice. I had covered President Bush for eight years, and I had met and interviewed Governor Clinton on several occasions on education issues. Perot, I guess, had no say.

The debate would be at the University of Richmond and Janet said it was an experiment. It had never been tried before in presidential debate history. Oh, great. I had nothing to go back and review to see how it was done. Most often there was a moderator and a panel of reporters who would ask their questions of the candidates. But she said the Commission wanted to have real undecided voters in an audience and I would move among them with a microphone, "Oprah-style."

Janet faxed me a thirty-page set of rules governing the debate that primarily dealt with the selection of the audience, logistics, and the like. One page was devoted to my duties. She said my job basically was to make sure that this was a true example of democracy in action. I would have wide latitude in making sure the citizens got their questions answered. It was the people's debate and I could follow up if I felt the candidates had not answered fully. I was to make sure no candidate gave a speech and try to insure that each had roughly equal time to respond.

The first presidential debate was being held in two days at Washington University in St. Louis on October 11. The vice presidential debate, which Hal Bruno would moderate, was on the thirteenth in Atlanta. I had five days to prepare for this awesome job and Hal, our political expert, was busy preparing for his debate. I didn't want to call on him to help me.

It wasn't just a matter of standing up there and calling on undecided voters in the audience. I had to know everything: the candidates' positions on every issue, campaign activities, and who the Richmond audience was. I started to panic.

As soon as Roone Arledge gave his blessing, it was a done deal. A press release was issued immediately by the Bi-Partisan Commission, announcing the location, format, and my name as moderator of the Second Presidential Debate.

It had not gone without notice that I would be the first female and first minority to moderate a presidential debate. There had been criticism that in the past, minorities and women had not participated in the debates in the numbers they should have.

My phone started ringing. Television writers, media critics, political pundits, civil rights groups, women's groups all offered advice. The latter two reminded me that I was representing women and African Americans, and while they wished me luck, I better do a good job of representing my gender and color. The pride of women and African Americans was at stake. Now I really panicked. How could they put that additional burden on my shoulders?

I began to doubt myself. That was something I fought against and overcame my entire career. At the age of fifty-one I wasn't going to let it get me now. Panic was replaced by determination. Not only can I do this, I can do this well. I sounded like Al Franken's Stuart Smalley character on "Saturday Night Live": "I'm good enough, I'm smart enough, and doggone it, people like me."

I decided that until the debate I would not talk to anyone who wasn't helping me with research. I would steer clear of anyone associated with the three campaigns. No phone calls, e-mails, faxes. It seemed everyone in America had suggestions for me on what to ask, how to dress, how to act: be friendly, be serious. Be lady-like but strong; strong, but still a lady. Aaiiigghh! No matter what anyone said, I would be myself. That's all I knew.

While the candidates were furiously preparing for the debate, so was I. This format was new for them too. They weren't certain how it would work out or why they needed to have a format change. I later found out it was Bill Clinton's people who were pushing this format because it was where he could get close to people, turn on the compassion and his honey-drippin' southern accent, and win them over, regardless of what his answer was.

With Doug Adams, an associate producer assigned by ABC to assist with the research, I worked day and night familiarizing myself with the candidates' biographies, recent events on the campaign trail, positions on all the hot button issues, the lukewarm, and the cold ones. I read all the campaign literature from each camp. I read editorials and political columns. I got up to speed on the economy, the trade deficit, foreign relations, the environment, education, tax reform, crime, and every thing I thought might come up in the debate. I then wanted to find out about the 200 undecided voters who would make up the audience. I researched the demographics of the capital of Virginia and local issues of importance to voters. My fear was that during the debate the citizens might freeze when called upon. They weren't used to live TV and they had been specially chosen. It could be a bit daunting for them to go face to face with Bush, Clinton, and Perot.

So I made up a whole batch of my own questions with their interests and those of the American people in mind. Just in case. This was going to be a ninety-minute debate with no commercial breaks, no breaks period. The train was going to leave the station and there was no stopping it. And I wanted that train securely on the tracks for a smooth ride.

The day of the debate ABC hired a limousine to drive me and my little entourage to Richmond: my researcher Doug, my make-up artist Larry Drumm, and ABC senior producer Mike Clemente. I also took my eleven-year-old son, Adam, whose first reaction was, "Awww, Ma. Do I have to?" I wanted him to experience this thrilling event with me. What did he know from "momentous?" He brought Twizzlers, his notebook of creative writing, his Game Boy and enough games to last during his "ordeal."

I was a nervous wreck on the ride down, trying to recount facts and statistics, and then just told everybody to be quiet so I could think. I said a little prayer. I was so wrapped up in what I needed to do and how I had to perform with the whole world watching. I finally was able to get free when I reminded myself it was not about me. I heard inwardly, "Not my will, Father, but Your will be done." As my mother used to tell me when times got tough, "Let go. Let God."

Right away I felt better and enjoyed with my friends the rest of the two-hour ride to Richmond. When we arrived at the University at around 3 p.m., it looked like every reporter and camera crew in the country was there. Satellite trucks, mobile control rooms, crowds of reporters, security personnel, bomb-sniffing dogs, and campaign staffers form each campaign passing out banners, signs, and buttons.

We went to the press entrance and I heard a shout, "There she is." A horde of cameramen and women came running up. Like paparazzi snapping pictures and reporters (just as I had done in days past) yelling questions as to who I thought would win the debate. I got a little taste of Hollywood. I didn't like it.

The people staffing the door weren't going to let me in. I didn't have the proper credential. I didn't have any credentials. My handlers shouted, "She's the moderator."

I cooled my heels while they checked with "higher authorities." It seems they were expecting everybody but the moderator. We finally got in and were taken to my holding room in the gymnasium where I could stay till the debate began at 9 p.m. They would take me to the floor at 8:30 p.m. The audience would be seated at eight.

Unbeknownst to me, ABC News in New York had sent yet another producer to "help" me. Rick Kaplan was one of the highest-ranking producers at the network, having run "Good Morning America," "Nightline," "World News Tonight with Peter Jennings," and "Prime Time Live." What could he do for me six hours before the live broadcast? He did have the stage manager find a music stand and place it in the center aisle so that I would have a "home base" to which I could come back and forth to check my note cards. Thanks a lot Rick, but I probably would have made a similar request on my own. I didn't know what particular value he could provide because once the debate began at 9 p.m., it would run without breaks for ninety minutes. Once the train left the station I was the conductor.

Rick was in Richmond with me, because, it turns out, as my own sources within the company told me, my executive bosses were nervous about whether I would be able to pull this off. How infuriating. I was one of their award-winning anchors. But I believe they apparently thought I, a black woman, could never be as good a moderator as a white man or white woman. I believe with all my heart that had it been left to ABC News to pick a moderator, it would never have been me. The news chiefs would have certainly picked Peter Jennings, Ted Koppel, Sam Donaldson, or Diane Sawyer. I think I've reached the pinnacle of my career because of my ability, and they apparently thought I'd blow it. Ggrrrrr. I hated them for their lack of confidence in me. Another "No," another vitamin pill. I'll show you, I decided. After the debate *The New York Times*, in an editorial, praised my skills as moderator, and so did *The Boston Globe* and TV pundits.

The producer of the broadcast, Ed Fouhy, a former boss of mine at both ABC and NBC, took me on a walk-through of the set that had been constructed on the basketball court of the University's gymnasium. I had never seen such a big television production before. There were ten studio cameras, a state of the art control room, and microphones were placed throughout the audience. The 200 undecided Virginia voters would sit in a semi-circle facing the presidential candidates, who would be seated on fancy high-wooden stools. I had free run of the floor. Poor Ross Perot was so short, compared to Bush and Clinton, that when he sat on his stool, his feet didn't touch the floor. He looked like a bald-headed little boy. Behind the set, there were seats for VIP's and others with political connections to the campaign and university.

The voters had been asked to arrive at the University at 4:30 p.m. for the 9 p.m. broadcast. They had little to do, just sitting around and chatting, or milling about their holding area in the gym. At about 6 p.m., they would be fed pizza and sodas. Since I had been told I had a lot of control as moderator, I decided I wanted to talk to them as a group. I felt that we must all be feeling the same tension and I wanted to break it. If we could talk informally, I knew that I could help relax them and me.

So after downing their cheese and pepperoni and Cokes, the audience members all sat in folding chairs and I came out to greet them with no introduction. To my shock, they saw me and erupted in applause. I blushed and giggled like a schoolgirl. I applauded them back. I began, "I guess you all know that I'm Carole Simpson of ABC News, and your moderator tonight." They applauded again. It was a good feeling.

I had not worn the clothes I would wear on the air that night. I was in comfy slacks and sneakers. One of the men shouted out, "Are you gonna wear those shoes on the air?" Everybody howled. I assured them I would change into a proper suit and dressy pumps.

I was confident now that we were bonding.

I told them a little about my career and how we wound up together in this moment of destiny. Then I wanted to know who they were. What did they do for a living? Systems analyst, housewife, schoolteacher, tax consultant, house painter, retired construction executive, cafeteria worker, truck driver, nurse, ordinary folks from many walks of life with one thing in common: they were all undecided voters. I explained that this debate was historic and would be seen by millions here and around the world. They gasped. (Nobody had told them that.) My task, I told them, was to hold the candidates' feet to the fire if necessary to get their questions answered to their satisfaction.

To help accomplish that I told them I wanted to get an idea of the issues that concerned them most. They all went reaching for pieces of paper and note cards. They had all written up their questions. I said, "No, no. I don't want to hear your actual questions, just the issues you care about."

I also reminded them that it was very dull television if they were to read to the candidates. I said they would come off looking much better if they memorized what they wanted to ask so that it looked like they were speaking from the heart and not a note card. They all nodded in agreement. Nobody wants to look bad on television.

I decided to try them out on some of the issues that had dominated press coverage of the candidates. I asked if they were interested in the Iran-contra affair. President Bush turned out to have misled the public on how much he knew about the secret White House basement operation under President Reagan, which was selling arms to Iran and using the proceeds to support the guerillas trying to topple their government in Nicaragua.

"Are you interested in that?" The voters shouted, "No."

"How about the two Jennifers, one with a 'G' and one with a 'J?'" The reference was to the alleged sex scandals between George

Bush and Jennifer Fitzgerald, and the one between Bill Clinton and Gennifer Flowers.

The chorus of "no's" grew louder. I was playing the room.

"Then how about Ross Perot and his charge of a plot against his daughter by the Black Panthers?"

"No, no, no." They laughed almost in unison.

With fake exasperation, I asked, "Well, then what do you care about?"

"Health care." "The economy and jobs." "Social security." "Education." "Crime." "The budget deficit." "The trade deficit." "Moral values." The words and phrases coming from all directions peppered my ears.

"Okay, okay. I've got it."

Someone else spoke up saying he didn't like the candidates fighting among themselves and not offering the solutions to the problems that were making life difficult for too many Americans. At that particular time, President Bush and private Republican-financed groups had been running commercials casting aspersions on Clinton's character and trustworthiness.

I thanked them for their candor and promised them that they would be fine representatives of America, reminding them that we would be history makers. I told them I was going to go get dressed and added, "I'll see you guys later." They applauded loudly for the last time.

I knew we would all be fine and that the debate would be truly historic.

Time for the all-important "getting ready for air." Larry, my stylist, would always say, "Time to make the donuts." I had chosen a red double-breasted suit. Ed Fouhy thought it was a good choice because the camera operators could more easily spot me on the floor, when they needed a shot. To complement, a white silk blouse, large pearl and gold earrings, dark hose, and plain black pumps. So patriotic was I feeling about that night that I had chosen some blue underclothing.

Larry had a challenge with the makeup because I was not just being seen head-on, as if I was anchoring. I'd be seen from every angle because I would be moving about. There was thirty minutes allotted for getting miked, for final sound checks, and I asked for a few moments for my own mental preparation. Then we'd move directly into the ninety-minute live program. My make-up would have to last two hours. There would be no opportunities to touch up a shiny nose or lipstick smear. I begged Larry to work some magic because I didn't want to worry about how I looked on camera. Television viewers are so critical. He did a great job. I had on a face that would crack if I smiled too broadly.

A final fingering of my hair and I was ushered to my place. The lights were ablaze. The audiences were in place. The voters waved to me and the man who had wondered about my shoes said, "You look really nice." "Thank you, sir." Everyone smiled. I had this audience with me.

In order to not give preference to any candidate, they all were to take the stage at the same time coming from three different directions, but only after I had opened the program to give some introductory remarks about the historic nature of this town hall debate and our citizen questioners.

A sound engineer hid my mike gear. I was connected by an IFB (the ear piece you wear) connected to the studio through which Ed, the producer, could talk to me throughout the program. He would give me time cues and remind me to cut off a candidate or a voter who was hogging time. He had told me at the outset that he would be choosing the voters for me to call on so that the cameras would have a chance to get in place. That makes for a smooth, professional production. It would also insure that people throughout the audience would get their chance to speak. That was fine with me. I had no agenda.

The stage manager announced to everyone that there were five minutes to air. My precious minutes. I went over what I would say, because I didn't want to be seen reading any of my notes either. I had memorized my introduction. I thought of this as my shining moment. I knew I could handle this debate. I wouldn't blow it. I thought of all those obstacles I had to overcome in my career. I chuckled to myself and said to all those naysayers throughout my life, "Just watch me now."

Cue Carole: "Good evening, I'm Carole Simpson. Welcome to the University of Richmond for the Second Presidential Debate...."

DEATH THREATS

After the debate, I finally got a chance to talk to the candidates. I walked first to Ross Perot and apologized for having to interrupt him so many times. I told him the director told me to cut him off because he kept exceeding his time limits. He said in his heavy Texas twang, "Thas awriiight. Happens to me awl the tiiime."

President Bush gave me a big hug. The President said he was so happy to see me for the first time in four years. (Those four years of his presidency that I hoped to cover as ABC's Senior White House correspondent.) He told me that I had done a "great job." I was sorry I couldn't say the same for him.

To find Governor Clinton, I had to wander backstage to his holding area. He and Hillary were standing outside the room talking to each other when they saw me approaching. They both came forward with big smiles. The Clintons knew Bill had nailed it. They each gave me a hug and congratulated me for moderating the debate so well. They added that they liked the town hall format with voters posing the questions instead of journalists. I told them I liked it, too.

In my goodbyes to the candidates, I wished each of them good luck. The election was less than a month away.

Back in my holding room my colleagues clapped and shouted, saying things like "great job" and "you were terrific." I was concentrating so much on the candidates and maintaining control of the debate format, I really had not given a thought to what I was doing, nor how well. I was just glad, so glad it was finally over. It was shortly after 11 p.m. and I had to sit down and get out of my high-heels. I wanted to drink some water. "Where's Adam," I asked.

My 11-year-old was curled up on the floor in his little suit and tie sound asleep. My colleagues said he had fallen asleep just minutes before the debate began and hadn't moved. He had no idea that his Mom was making history that night. She had become the first woman and first African American to moderate a presidential debate.

I woke him up and we all made our way to the Richmond hotel where we had reservations for the night. I entered my room and there were bouquets everywhere. Friends and ABC co-workers, including Diane Sawyer, had sent them before the debate occurred. I was most appreciative. At that point, I didn't know how the media and political reporters would view my role as moderator.

During the drive back to Washington the next morning, my ABC supporters got on their phones.

"A *New York Times* editorial today gave you rave reviews, Carole," one of them shouted out.

"*The New York Times?*" I nearly squealed.

Others chimed in that newspaper and TV pundits were calling it one of the best debates ever. They all concluded that Bill Clinton won the debate hands down and may have clinched the presidency with his warm and folksy answers to the voters' questions. George Bush, they said, seemed distracted and out of touch. They wondered why he kept glancing at his watch during the debate. Where did he have to go? they joked. The political analysts also agreed I had done a good job as moderator.

We also heard that the debate had drawn 92 million viewers on every major channel in the United States and there were millions more watching around the world. That was terrifying. Eight million watched me every weekend. No problem. But 100 million in the U.S. and overseas freaked me out. I was glad I hadn't been thinking about <u>my</u> performance for once, concentrating instead on the voters' questions and the three presidential candidates' answers.

Once back in the Washington Bureau everyone greeted me with smiles and compliments. I was feeling pretty good when I got to my office and started receiving and returning telephone calls. My pride, however, was to be short lived.

Later that day I found out about hurtful things that happened. In the post-debate spin room Republican political operatives were apparently telling reporters that I had thrown the debate to Clinton, that I called on audience members I knew would ask Bush tough questions. The President's poor performance was totally my fault. They told the media that I was obviously a liberal Democrat and was partial to Clinton. The Republican strategy was to take attention off Bush and focus it on me. Talk about spin. They should have known that I had covered Bush for eight years, and although I personally didn't care for his policies, I cared for him very much.

In fact, I have among my prized possessions a handwritten note from President Bush on an embossed White House note card that I received a week after the debate. His greeting was, "Hi Carol." He said it was great to see me and that I had done a good job as moderator and added that he thought I was fair. It was signed, "Fondly, George." I displayed the note on television when ABC's "20/20" did a story about the national criticism of my objectivity.

On his afternoon radio talk show, Rush Limbaugh agreed with Republican spinmeisters, but in harsher language, calling me a "femi-Nazi liberal" who should never have been given the moderator's role. I was incompetent. Implied, but not verbalized, was racism. "Who is <u>she</u> to be questioning presidential contenders?" I was a political reporter for twelve years, that's one reason.

Worst of all, however, was hearing the rumors swirling in New York that before the debate several of the executives had serious doubts about my ability to do the job. They actually thought I might "mess up" and embarrass ABC News. In the end they thought I had done "okay." That sent me through the roof. I had been reporting and anchoring for the company for ten years, after many earlier years working at NBC News and for Chicago news stations. It made me so angry. I wanted to know exactly at what point I would finally gain the respect of some of my own executives. I guess I knew secretly, never.

There actually was something worse than that. I thought my life was in danger. After Limbaugh's radio tirade against me to his 20 million "ditto heads," about two hundred of them called and faxed me death threats. Some said, "You should be killed." "You do not deserve to be on this earth." "Watch your back. I'm going to kill you." "You're a nobody."

I know there is plenty of hyperbole by Limbaugh, but I also know there are crazy people in this country. I am afraid of crazy people. I'm not talking about those who suffer mental illness. I'm talking about the wackos, who delude themselves into thinking their distorted truth is the real truth.

I informed our head of security at ABC. He said he would have the mailroom and telephone operators screen my mail and calls so I wouldn't have to hear or read the hate speech and threats on my life. He said a security guard would escort me to the parking lot to get my car at night. He assured me I would be safe on ABC premises. Then I remembered I was scheduled to give a speech in a couple of days at California State University, Fresno.

Our security chief called my hosts at the University and explained the problem. He said his team would make certain I was safely on the plane from Washington and inquired if they wanted to help out at the other end. If they weren't, I wasn't going. I was afraid.

The University said they would be happy to hire some bodyguards to pick me up at the airport, transport me to campus, and remain with me through my visit. At baggage claim, two men about 5 feet 5 and 5 feet 6, respectively, greeted me and said they would protect me from harm for the next thirty-six hours. I hate to admit but I almost laughed out loud. In my heels, I towered over them. But I was gracious and thanked them for being there.

On the way to their car, they showed me their guns. Guns? Okay. I hadn't expected them to be carrying firearms. This is serious, I thought. On campus we were quite a threesome. They checked out every room before I entered. They scanned crowds looking for suspicious characters. They went into my hotel room and pronounced it "clear." It was truly a strange experience. I felt I had overreacted. As I bade farewell at the Fresno airport I looked at my slightly built, height-challenged protectors and couldn't help comparing myself to Whitney Houston in that movie about her "bodyguard."

The death threats continued after Clinton's election victory. But by mid-December they stopped. I had conquered my fear and the "crazies," I guess, just gave up.

There were academic post-mortems on the election at several major universities, which invited me to be a guest speaker. Among political analysts, the debate was considered pivotal to Clinton's win. I told them that I couldn't really tell who prevailed while I was in the midst of the debate. What I saw from my vantage point in the center aisle was a wide angle of the question-asking voters and the three candidates on stage. I could see Ross Perot's feet dangling from the stool that was too high for him but just right for his rivals. I saw Bush basically sit or stand at or near his stool. Clinton mostly stood. It wasn't until I saw the playback on television, that I saw what the viewers saw.

I finally saw President Bush looking at his watch. I saw him knocked off his game plan when one of the audience members asked the candidates to stop the mud slinging and just stick to the issues. It was as if the President were a life-size balloon that slowly deflated from an invisible pinprick. I saw him struggle with the question asked by the young black woman, Tamron Hall. She wanted to know how the national debt personally affected him. Her wording was not precise as it could have been, but Mr. Bush stumbled through a rambling answer.

Then I saw Clinton walk straight up to Hall and hit that question straight out of the University of Richmond gymnasium. He felt her pain, he said, and he showed it on television.

I could really appreciate Clinton's speaking and people skills and his mastery of facts and figures when I watched the replay. Many political scientists said the exchange between Clinton and Hall was "the moment" during the entire general election campaign that sealed Clinton's victory, despite another debate that followed with Jim Lehrer of PBS posing all the questions.

It wasn't my fault Clinton won the debate or the presidency. It was the exchange between a voter and a candidate that resonated so strongly with the electorate.

Even though ABC didn't have confidence in me, even though untruths were being spread about me, and even though Rush Limbaugh may have incited people to threaten my life, I have no regrets. Moderating the 1992 Town Hall Debate was the crowning achievement of my career.

I wish Mama and Daddy could have seen it.

LETTERS. I GOT LETTERS

After so my many years on television, I received thousands of letters, phone calls, and later e-mails from the viewing public. The vast majority of the communications were complimentary and positive. They boosted my spirits. When people see you on television, in their homes, they think they know you and can say whatever they want to you. Their messages included everything from death threats to marriage proposals, from fan letters to hate letters, from opinions on news stories to opinions on my clothes, hair, and makeup. Some of the letters were pornographic and deeply disturbing. I also received many interesting presents from viewers, including artwork (much of it from the incarcerated), crocheted items, tea cozies, hand-carved statues, silk scarves, several pairs of earrings, and even a diamond necklace. I had to return the necklace because there was a seventy-five-dollar limit on the value of gifts we could receive as ABC News employees.

I also received bizarre requests. Some guy in Buffalo, New York, offered to pay me $250,000 to bear the anti-Christ child. He said he would pay my airfare to Buffalo and put me up at the Hilton Hotel where he would impregnate me. He promised to then take care of me until the demon was born. The outside of the envelope was covered with pentagrams and three sixes he had drawn in red, blue, and green ink. The letter was written in the hand of an eight-year-old and went on for eight single-spaced pages explaining why he had chosen me for the unholy task. That letter I turned over to security. In fact, I gave all the really scary mail, including the death threats after the presidential debate, to our security office. Should I come to some harm, they might have some leads for law enforcement. Pleasant thought.

There were several requests for nude photos of me, full frontal and in color. The marriage proposals were very sweet and accompanied with photos of my would-be suitors. No Brad Pitts or Denzel Washingtons in the bunch.

Strange items were mailed to me. I received a small jar in a box. According to the sender I was to cut off some of my pubic hair, place it in the jar, and return it to him. He said he had a collection of all colors and textures. There was also the envelope with no return address but a postmark from Michigan. It contained one walnut. No message. A plain walnut. I tried to open it to see if something special were inside. But it really was a just a nut. I guess that's what that person thought of me. A nut.

Perhaps the most bizarre item I received in the mail was contained in an 8 x 12 gold envelope with Barbara Walters' return address, of all things. The only thing in it was a sanitary napkin that had been discolored with lime green ink. It definitely was not from Barbara. Who was trying to say what with that thing?

I have collected excerpts of some of the letters I received, with the spelling and grammar used by the writers, to give you a sense of what was on the minds of viewers when they watched me on television. They represent the good, the bad and the ugly.

> From New York, New York to the President of ABC
> *You will admit that we are a white nation. Why in hell must we have a damned nigger, such as Simpson, pitching us the weekend evening news. Is she an ABC token nigger that someone felt compelled to hire? Who needs the hideous creatures? Signed, WASP*

From Washington, DC to ABC News

I write in order to praise the performance of Carole Simpson on the Second Presidential Debate...She did the best job I've ever seen of live moderating and I hope that ABC will give her more opportunities to perform such an important service to the community. If there were more journalists with her tactful non-nonsense approach, politicians might have to act more responsibly when interviewed. Since there's only one Carole Simpson, though, you'd better make sure we get to see more of her.

From Phoenix, Arizona

WAKE UP! GROW UP! You ARE only a token. Maybe if you would STOP bitching and constantly referring to your color you WOULD be respected for your experience! Of course, your advanced age (and jowls and fat) is against anyone in any industry.

From El Paso, Texas

Carol Simpson. Black Nazi Cunt. ABC Leftist Whore. The Alamo is NOT a legend.

From Sharpsburg, Georgia

...I wrote a letter to tell you you are charming and a delight on tv. I hope, honey, you stay where you are. Your intelligence, your decorum, outright delightful smile and warmth is so contagious it almost melts the screen. You are truly beautiful and I love you.

From Oak Ridge, Tennessee

...Until the minority Afro-American population in America turns away from this belief that white America "owes" them and rids themselves of "I am being picked on by whitey", they are going to find themselves in a position where they surely will be equal and the white race will

*consider all minorities "free loaders" whether true or not.
Respectfully yours.*

From Tucson, Arizona

*Enjoy your Sunday news. No background music. Clear
diction without ups and downs. The older generation
enjoys same because we make our decisions when the news
is given clearly, such as you render.*

From Juneau, Alaska

*...I do not find myself needing a label other than American.
After all we are just people. Why do you not leave it at
that.*

From Newtown, Pennsylvania

*This is just a brief note to tell you how magnificently
you looked this Sunday...Everything was just perfect: the
dark-grey suit, your jewelry, the way you had your hair
-- everything was just fine. In the past there was always
something you should have done with your outfits, jewelry,
makeup and hairstyle...So when I saw you this Sunday
and everything was so perfect, I just thought I'd drop you
a note.*

From Ogdensburg, New York

*...About the discrimination that you say you still
experience. I can only say that your position in this life
must negate any sour notes you hear from those ignorants
who don't know any better. Human nature being what
it is, if all skin turned purple tomorrow we would still
have bigots. Be happy at your accomplishments. Your
tormentors will meet their due one day and it belittles you
to show your distress.*

From Lyman, South Carolina

You are my favorite anchorperson. I always enjoy your

newscast. *I haven't seen another newscaster that good since Walter Cronkite. You are much better than Dan Rather, Paula Zahn, Diane Sawyer and the rest of them...*

From Monroe, Georgia

First time I ever heard you on radio news. Right away I liked your distinct voice, no twang, no southern dialect. You also did not use N.Y. lingo, i.e. Thoity Thoid St. Must be a boid cause it choips like a boid. My wife and I enjoy your voice and your very attractive face, i.e. TV news. And we are white folks.

From St. Croix, U.S. Virgin Islands

Please don't think that I am a nut case. The purpose of my letter is in the hopes that one day I will get to meet you and get to know more about you. You can probably see that I am very nervous in writing this letter, because you are very special to me. As far as I am concerned you are the most beautiful black woman in the world...Next time I will send you a picture so at least you will know that I am not King Kong. (Smile)

From Menard, Illinois

I Send You My Very, Very Warmest Wishes for Inner Joy, Peace of Mind, Happiness and Good Health even in the Midst of a bitter and Troubled World! I Hope You Would "Always" have the Very Best That God has To Give.

From Los Angeles, California

It is evident that the President and his men are applying pressure on the men here to get me to stay. I don't wish, desire to stay here. I again must say I need the time away. Their using time against us in this, and would you please find out what they're doing... And yes, I'm upset. Make the <u>stalling stop</u>. <u>I</u> want <u>to leave</u>.

211

From Phoenix, Arizona

I am sitting in the Madison Street Jail on Armed Robbery and Kidnapping. I am going to give me story to you. Free! Please write me back to let me know when you can make an appointment. Please help!

From Birmingham, Alabama

This letter will probably not go over well, but I'm writing out of concern. Your wig is too wiggy-looking. It does not make sense for a woman with money, who lives in New York to wear a wig that screams "wig." Here's how to buy one. Go very, very short. Katie Couric short...Also stop wearing bold colors on the air. Let your blouses give you the color you need around your face. Do dark suits. They slenderize...Also you have always over-enunciated. Try to be more natural.

From Coal Township, Pennsylvania

I am writing to you today. I need your help if you can please...I was arrest for possion with the intent to deliever with 11.21 grams...I had just pulled my hot dog cart in. I walked to the corner to a telegram pole surrounded by weeds and grass. As I was walked there I look down and spotted something that appeared to be spotted. As I looked closer I realized it was a female hand bag. As I bent down to examine the bag a police office Jeep approached and the Office stopped and ask me what up I say Hi and he say what with the bag. I say I don't know...The Office then picked up the bag and look in it. After doing so he then instructed me to stand against his Jeep. So I did very unaware of why...Please help me to prove my insecure. I am begging to you. I am against drugs. I don't use drugs and against it.

From Columbia, Kentucky
As I do every other morning, I watched Good Morning America. When the network started the 8 AM ET news segment you had a beautiful silver (?) necklace/chocker which was so plain and simple that it attracted my attention. Please make sure that someone can let me know where I can purchase one. Granted you and your staff have much more important things to do, but I have searched (central KY is not the fashion capitol) and searched to no avail.

From New York, New York to Roone Arledge, President, ABC News
This is a short note of praise of Carole Simpson...As a follower of ABC News, I've always enjoyed her reporting. However, I feel you should use her talents more wisely by putting her more in the public eye than you do. I like Peter Jennings, but I would like very much to see more of Carole Simpson. Her style and abilities are too good to be hidden!

From Washington, DC
This is a belated note to say "Bravo" for your moderating triumph during the debate. I want you to know that my daughter, the 13-year-old, thought you were terrific. So thank you, thank you for giving our girls such a superb example of what women can do.

From Miami, Florida
Carol Simpson did a terrible job with the Presidential debates. Why would you have such a person on your Saturday news time. She turns everybody off your station. As soon as she comes on we tune off. What a sickening whore. Her voice. Her face--get rid of her.

From New York, New York

It is regrettable, not to mention downright criminal, that when in the presence of Europeans, some of our people (you) feel a need to disassociate themselves from the masses of black people…But I'm here to tell you sister, you can never cut the ties of your own community from which you were borne and bred. No matter how you think you've "arrived" or feel that you have successfully assimilated into "mainstream America", you are still one of us, although after your report many of us I'm sure would be reluctant to claim you.

From Phoenix, Arizona

WAKE UP! WISE UP! GROW UP!
Don't open your trap when you don't know what the hell you're talking about! ALSO: WHOM DO YOU THINK YOU'RE KIDDING?

From Glen Echo, Maryland

To a journalist and professional of your stature and experience, I need not have to tell you about the power of language…You described a young girl as "wheelchair-bound." Please pardon my sarcasm, but did you mean she was heading <u>toward</u> a wheelchair? Did you mean she was <u>chained and padlocked</u> to a wheelchair?…People use wheelchairs, they are not bound to them.

From Henderson, Nevada

Think of my idea for you. A little show. That gives a ALIEN VIEWPOINT. It could be a top show. And do what TV is ment to do. TEACH, what is wrong TV teaches wrong things. YOU TEACH NEW RIGHT IDEAS—NEW TO THE THINKING OF YOUR WORLD.

From New York, New York to ABC News

What a disgrace! Why would you place a real-world inexperienced, elocution graduate, plastered smile, giggling, minority driven "two-fer", news reader phony as the sole moderator in last night's debate to embarrass your network and our country to the nation and the world. She not only was simply not up to the task, she also was a <u>major</u> *distraction to the proceedings.* <u>Shame</u> *on you. Where was the* <u>distinguished</u> *moderator to bring respect to this inane format? You should be in the tank, sirs.*

From Lowell, Massachusetts

...When Bush attacks the draft dodger/womanizer/ liar from Arkansas, how come Clinton cries like a baby and you media call it a "negative attack?" Listen to that arrogant smiling jerk attack Bush and the dirty insults of Al Gore. Media says shit. Why? Because they wallow in dung anyway.

Speaking of "dung:"

From Baton Rouge, Louisiana

Your all pushy, jealous control freaks, copycats, wearing white style wigs, lightening skin, ingrates, ugly like the liar devil...P.S. God never said niggers are equal to whites! He told whites to exterminate you, all of you! They didn't get the job done but he will SOON at Armageddon. Your all miserable discontents. You might as well be dead anyway. Even skunks and rats will keep on living. Niggers are the lowest life on earth and manure-fertilizer is all a niggers worth! <u>Signed:</u> *Lilly White*

From Omaha, Nebraska

Dear Carole: *EMERGENCY NUMBERS*
When in sorrow   *Call John 14.*

When men fail you	*Call Psalm 27.*
When you want to be fruitful	*Call John 15.*
When you have sinned	*Call Psalm 51.*
When you worry	*Call Matthew 6: 19-34.*
Etc.	

From La Mirada, California

I think you were the worst M.C. in life. I could see you didn't like Ross Perot. Next time refuse and let some qualified like Oprah. You were embossing to say the least…
You were rude, rude, rude.

From Wichita, Kansas

I want to condemn you for the blatant lies you media clones perpetuate on the gun issue…Our nation's borders are like a siv. Those boats, planes that's bring in tons of drugs, bring in guns, thousands of them. Who gets them Carole? The savages, yes the savages. The basic scum who kill daily. I am so damn tired of the media, particularly whites who cannot get that word savages out of their damn mouths. Your people complain that more blacks are in the can serving time. Who the hell is doing the killing?…If I sound racist to you, that's crap.

From Cincinnati, Ohio

Women's issues…It appears all men are guilty unless proven innocent, by females. What consernes me is women can topple governments, capture Greek fleets, but nowhere in all of recorded history, has a fighting force of females ever held, captured, conquered, liberated land to live on. They have led as leaders. But never held.

From Washington, DC
Lose the bangs. You'd look much more intelligent if you got the hair out of your eyes.

From Steinauer, Maine
The number one issue is life. Do you support the unborn right to life or Do you support the unborn right to be killed? The USA was the wealthy nation on earth. When the USA was the wealthy nation, where did this wealth come from? The name of the game is control. Handle with Prayer.

From Boise, Idaho
I heard the Saturday newscast. It was biased. Just because someone has white skin and lives in South Africa doesn't mean they're racist. The news media should be neutral. Why does ABC News have activist newswriters?

From New York, New York
Shame on you ABC and Carole Simpson for the obscene report on Sunday night showing the carcass of a (Palestinian) 2-year-old infant with a bloody bullet hole in its chest, choreographically presented up to the TV camera in closeup, followed by its burial in closeup under a stone slab…No one will convince me that an Israeli took aim at a poor little baby and put a bullet through its breast. What possible agenda is served by this excessive image except to revulse America and further inflame against the "despicable Jew", incarnate as Israel?

From New York, New York
Your final broadcast as Sunday evening news anchor was a poignant moment for all of us who value the crispness-laced-with-humanity of your reporting…With high respect for your professionalism, I wonder if your change

217

in position was not motivated by this crazy age issue for women broadcasters—when the likes of David Brinkley can go on for years looking like an Egyptian mummy… Alas this country pays the price for the superficiality of this visual medium. Wishing you all the best in all your goals, thank you again for your both solid and humane professionalism as Sunday anchor. You are missed.

The viewers who took the time to write made me proud, sad, angry and amused. Letters like these reminded me that I was not just talking to a lens on the floor camera with a red light on top. I was reaching real live people who were intelligent, thoughtful, and helpful, but also ones who were bigoted, trivial, and, even some… What should I call them? Real crazies!

HAVING IT ALL

One of my most frequently asked questions is: "How did you manage to have a husband, a family and a demanding career?" Simple answer: "I don't know. I just did it."

I look back on the early 1970's when my daughter, Mallika, was a toddler; my husband was working at Argonne National Laboratory and pursuing his MBA at the University of Chicago evening Business School; I was reporting at WMAQ-TV, teaching a journalism course at Northwestern University and helping my father care for my mother, who was dying of lung cancer. Some days were unbearable. I was physically, mentally and emotionally exhausted. But you do what you have to do. Some women would never be comfortable with making the personal sacrifices I made. If I were able to do things over, the situation wouldn't have changed. What would I have given up? My husband, my mother, my daughter, my exciting job in television? Not one of them.

Seriously, there are two things that made it possible to "have it all": I married the right man and I had a job and income that allowed me to afford live-in childcare. I was extremely fortunate.

I married my best friend, Jim Marshall. My mother told me that Jim was the man I should marry and she was right. She had seen the procession of other boyfriends and concluded that he was the only man for me. He was not the kind of guy who made my heart go aflutter. What was more important to me was that we enjoyed doing the same things; we were competitive in a nice way; we were able to talk endlessly about everything under the sun, and he made me laugh. I also wanted a partner who was smarter than I. A good mind was more sexually attractive to me than biceps. Jim, at twenty-five, was invited to join Mensa.

There was only one solution for my childcare problem. I begged Mama to take care of Mallika during the day and I promised her that Jim and I would come by after work to feed her, play with her, and put her to bed. We would take her home on Friday nights and bring her back on Monday mornings. Although Mama didn't want any pay to care for her granddaughter, we said that was unthinkable. We were going to pay her a good wage.

I was reluctant to hire a stranger to care for my infant, so my mother said she would do it. What better surrogate could I have? She and my father were wonderful caregivers. However, when Mallika was close to a year old, I noticed that my mother tired easily and she had developed a nasty cough she couldn't get rid of. These were early signs of the lung cancer that would take her life a little more than two years later. Mallika, who began walking at nine and a half months, had become a real handful.

The situation had to change. We decided to move out of our small apartment and buy a house where there would be room for a live-in babysitter. When Mallika was almost a year old, we owned a four-bedroom townhouse in Hyde Park, the University of Chicago community and the city's only stable integrated community. We found a 50-year-old black woman from Memphis to take care of our daughter. We all moved in together and life became much easier. She stayed with us until Mallika was nine years old. There is nothing like trusting your caregiver and being able to provide stable care for your child.

Jim's job required little travel so he was always there when I had to be out of town. He was as adept as I at feeding, bathing, changing diapers and playing with a little girl. I played dolls and dress up with her. He played ball and video games with her. The only thing he couldn't do was braid her long curly hair.

Mallika was ten years old when we adopted our son, Adam. The age difference gave us the opportunity to raise our daughter and son as if each was an only child. At critical ages they both had the undivided attention of at least one of their parents, and I was never more than a phone call away.

My going on a trip was no occasion for disappointment for Mallika or Adam. They were happy. Dad was in charge. They could have cake or pizza for breakfast. He would take them to the park, to video parlors, to movies. Except on school nights, they got to stay up late; they got to sleep late. They each developed close bonds with their father, because he was not a man who believed raising kids was the woman's job. He appreciated the value of children having both parents present in their lives. He never missed a school open house, teacher conference, or musical program. While I provided the homework help in writing, spelling, and speaking, the kids went to Jim for their math and science homework, and he oversaw the science projects. Next to my Daddy, Jim was the best father I knew. But when I was home the kids were Mommy's girl and Mommy's boy. Oh, joy.

People were so critical of working mothers. It's true I didn't get to spend a great quantity of time with my daughter and son, but we had plenty of quality time. There was lots of love, lots of snuggling up with books in their beds, lots of trips to museums, zoos, and art fairs. I made certain they went to the best schools, took piano and Spanish lessons. They played sports and learned to swim. Adam began drawing and writing stories in notebooks he carried everywhere from the time he was six years old. It was a portent of his life as an adult, managing screenwriters in Hollywood.

We took vacations around the United States and overseas. My children travelled to the Caribbean, England, Scotland, France, Italy, the Netherlands, Morocco, Egypt, and went on safari in Kenya. My income, together with Jim's, made it possible to expose our children to experiences many families can only dream about.

They had a Christian upbringing. Both were christened and later confirmed in Grace Episcopal Church in Silver Spring, Maryland, where each served as an acolyte until each went away to college. I was a member of the congregation, but after being named the anchor of the news on Saturdays and Sundays, I was unable to attend services but continued my financial support. I missed going to Church.

One of the best things about having children is coming home after an awful day at work and having my toddlers run to the door, grab me around the legs, and shout, "Mommy's home. Mommy! Mommy!"

Mallika would grab my hand and drag me to the kitchen to show off a picture she had painted at pre-school. Later, it was Adam proudly showing off some disgusting bug or caterpillar he had caught in the backyard and saved in a jar. All the angst and stress of the workday slipped away, erased by the smiling faces of my energetic and spirited children. They gave my life balance. At work someone may have criticized one of my stories and I would go into a funk until I got home and saw what were the most important things to me.

Since I was able to bear a biological child, many of my relatives and friends couldn't understand why I would adopt a baby. It was a direct result of doing numerous stories on the number of black children available for adoption. At the time, for every one white baby awaiting adoption there were ten black babies. The statistic was startling. Un-adopted black babies were destined to spend their lives in foster care until they reached eighteen years of age and had to go out on their own.

The stories had such an impression on me that I convinced Jim we should adopt, and probably a baby boy because they were harder to place and we already had a daughter. We investigated some private agencies but then settled on the District of Columbia Social Services Department. It took two years, but on December 10, 1980, I got a call that they had a healthy baby boy available who was seven weeks old. I was ecstatic. "What do I do now?" I asked the social worker.

"Come to the office and see him, and if you like him, you can take him home," she replied.

"Just like that?" I couldn't believe what she said.

"Just like that," she repeated.

Jim and I were both at work and made plans to meet downtown at the Department. We were both nervous. We sat in a small room and the social worker brought in a tiny yellow bundle of baby and handed it to me. I pulled back the blanket to see what I was sure would be my new son. He wriggled and cooed and it was love at first sight. I handed him to Jim and he said, "He's smiling at me."

What was there not to like? This was a baby for whom we could provide a good home and a more than comfortable life. He would have all the rights of our daughter. We could make a difference in the life of one human being who had not been dealt the best hand.

My husband and I both thought he was perfect. We told the social worker we wanted him. She said, "Then take him."

"Now? I don't have a bed, or food, or clothes. No diapers!" I blathered. Jim had to rush back to work so it was all on me this time.

I said I would have to go home and get my housekeeper and buy some things at a store and we would be back to pick him up. When we drove back to the agency my heart was pounding. "My son. I have a son." I liked getting used to those words. We picked up my new baby. I drove the car with our housekeeper cuddling my baby son in her arms. She was as excited as we were. The baby didn't cry once. He just made happy baby sounds all the way home. He knew how to win our hearts.

Mallika couldn't have been more thrilled. No longer an only child, she had a baby brother. That evening we played with him, passing him back and forth between us and trying out names. He started to whimper and fell into a deep sleep. I had no crib, so he spent his first night in one of his big sister's large dresser drawers that we made up with bedding. By the following morning we had settled on a name. Our son would be Adam Earl Simpson-Marshall. I am the last of the Simpsons so I wanted the name to carry on in his hyphenated surname. We gave him the middle name of Earl for Jim's wonderful grandfather, and Adam because it sounded strong.

People used to say, "Yeah, he's nice, but he's not like your own child." Oh, yes he was. I walked the floor with him many a night during his colicky period. I taught him how to walk and talk and tie his shoes. I did for him everything I did for my daughter. And our love for Adam grew every day. Mallika and Adam—despite the age difference--became close as brother and sister. I had a biological child and an adopted child. I can honestly say I don't love one more than the other. They are both my beloved children.

Still, through their growing up years I was guilt-ridden. I used to wonder how much smarter my children might have been if I had stayed at home, at least for the first few years.

In my mind I was validated as a good mother when I watched Mallika graduate from Harvard University with honors. When she was handed her degree I was overcome with tears. I remembered all the men who said I was a bad mother by turning over the care of my year-old daughter to a "stranger." I remembered the men who said women belonged at home, that all the problems in society began when women went to work leaving their children behind and taking jobs away from men.

I experienced the same emotional release when Mallika graduated in the top ten percent of her class from the University of California, San Francisco, School of Medicine. She was chosen to be one of the two student speakers at Commencement. Her fellow graduate spoke humorously about medical school. But my daughter, who was introduced as Dr. Mallika Marshall, in her speech challenged the repeal of affirmative action in student admissions by the University of California Board of Regents. It was a brave and controversial speech to deliver with several Regents sitting on the stage. I thought she had delivered it well, until 15-year-old Adam leaned over and whispered in my ear, "She's better than you are, Mom."

Adam was extremely intelligent and creative but did not receive the grades his sister did. School was a struggle. We got him tested and at age twelve he was diagnosed with dyslexia. In a family of overachievers, it caused him some problems as an adolescent. He had to work so much harder than his classmates just to get a "C." We hired tutors who helped him overcome his problems with organization and reading. The special tutoring, Adam's winning personality and his superior oral expression were enough to keep him competitive in his academics.

My tears flowed freely again when Adam graduated with a degree in Visual and Performing Arts from Syracuse University. A week after he came home, he set out alone in his old Land Rover to drive to Hollywood to seek his fame and fortune. He had no job, just a dream. He took several temp jobs at production houses until he reached his goal of becoming a literary manager, now representing a stable of screenwriters.

Not bad for a working mother, Carole. But it was bad for Carole.

I didn't know how to say no. I was invited to speak here and there, to emcee a dinner, to serve on a panel, to chair a media organization, to join a professional group, to cook a cake for the school bake sale, to attend my children's plays and piano recitals, to work with the women and minorities at ABC, to attend a dinner party at the home of my husband's boss, and to provide the big meals during the holidays.

Participating in my husband and children's activities were top priorities, but many of the things I took on I could have refused. If somebody appealed to me that my presence as a speaker would raise more money than anyone else for homeless children, I would do it. I was always juggling my time and trying to wear three and a half hats: mother, career woman, wife and homemaker. I spent my life fighting the word, "No," so I didn't know how to say no even to myself.

However, I was in for a huge awakening during the unforgettable and life-changing year of 1990 to 1991. In February of 1990, I was in South Africa for the release of Nelson Mandela. As I explained earlier, I was terrorized after being beaten by a white South African policeman during a clash with black and colored supporters of Mandela's impending freedom.

In May, I received an honorary degree from Marymount College in New York and had to fly back to Washington to anchor the newscast that evening. I was traveling with my friend, Susan King, a Marymount alumna. We left the city in bright, warm, and sunny weather. Twenty minutes out of LaGuardia we hit a storm and the worst turbulence I've ever experienced. It was as if we were riding a huge metal bucking bronco. People were visibly frightened, and I looked down at my knuckles on the armrests and they were actually white.

All of a sudden the left wing dipped so low the passengers were briefly riding sideways. The plane shook violently. It had been struck by lightning. The passengers uttered sounds of fright when we all saw blue and orange electrical sparks crackle across the top of the cabin, exit the window across the other wing and end up somewhere in the pea soup sky. That was terrifying to see. I could tell the pilot was trying to go around, above, and under the weather system, but no matter which way he adjusted the plane's altitude, it was equally turbulent. We heard no word from the cockpit. We continued rocking and rolling in the sky, when about fifteen minutes later, lightening struck the plane again and played its light show across the cabin roof. Oh, my God. I always thought lightning doesn't strike the same place twice. I forgot we had been moving. Passengers were screaming. I believed I would die that day on that plane. I started praying.

The usual thirty-minute shuttle trip took two hours. We landed in Baltimore instead of Washington, where the wind shears were too dangerous. I grabbed a limousine and got to the studio ten minutes before I had to go on the air. A bathroom trip, a little powder and lipstick, a hair pat down, and I was in the anchor chair reading stories I had never seen and I didn't make one stumble. How? I don't know. Probably fear. I had thought I would be dead. I went home and couldn't sleep reliving the horror of the worst airplane trip I had ever taken.

In January of 1991, the first Gulf War was underway, and I had been up for forty-eight hours relieving Peter Jennings' anchor coverage, with short recaps on the war action at twenty-five minutes after the hour and five minutes to the hour. Local stations could broadcast their own war coverage or use my reports.

When I was finally released from duty, I went home where I hoped to sleep for twenty-four hours, but I had not been home for two days and there was virtually no food in the house. I asked my housekeeper to drive with me to the small local supermarket only a block and a half from my house. It was 11 o'clock in the morning, and the strip mall in which the grocery store was located was unusually quiet. The market was almost empty. We scurried around and picked up the food we needed. By the time we got to the checkout counter we had two full shopping carts.

I bagged the groceries while the clerk was ringing up the items. I was anxious to get back home and go to sleep. We left the store and I asked my housekeeper to watch the carts while I went to get the car and drive to the pick-up area.

I had a beautiful dark red Mercedes I bought five months ago. I backed it up and drove to the front of the store. I was turning off the ignition when I heard a tap on my window. Outside there was a well-dressed black man. I rolled down the glass and he asked, "You want some help with your groceries?" I told him, "Sure." My hand was on the door handle when I heard him say, "I don't care about no groceries. I want this car."

I thought it was a compliment and said, "Yes. It's a really nice car."

"Get out of the fucking car, you goddamn bitch. I'm taking this car," he said in a threatening voice.

I didn't get it. "What do you mean?"

"You fucking bitch. Get out of the car or I will blow your fucking head off."

I was still not thinking clearly and when I hesitated, he reached for his belt and pulled out what I later learned was a 9mm semi-automatic gun. When I saw the cold steel of the weapon pointed at head, I got it. I really got it. This is what I always feared: being the victim of a crime.

"Oh, okay," I said stupidly.

I was frightened for my life but I was still scatterbrained. I started fumbling with the keys, thinking to myself that he needs the car keys but I need my house and office keys, and I tried to separate them from the ignition.

He went crazy. "Get out. I will kill you, you dumb fucking bitch." I had never been talked to like this. And for God's sake, it was 11 o'clock in the morning.

"Okay, okay." I left the keys in the ignition, grabbed my big purse, got out and went to the back of the car and opened the trunk to get some movie videos I needed to return, and for some idiotic reason I started putting grocery bags in the trunk. Heaven forbid the armed robber not have food to eat. I just completely lost track of my senses.

"What the fuck are you doing?" I honestly wasn't sure. "I'm going to kill you bitch. Now get away from the car and drop that bag."

Was he talking about the grocery bag in my hand or my bag, I wondered? I held out my huge work purse and timidly asked, "This?"

"Yes, you fucking cunt. Are you stupid?" I was, under the circumstances. Then I thought, take the car but not my purse. I could live out of it for a couple of days. All of my identification and credit cards in the wallet, my make up, my medicine, my electronic diary, tooth paste and tooth brush, even disposable panties. I hesitated again. Why am I letting this man order me around? The gun, Carole. It's the gun.

"Now!!" he demanded and pointed to the ground. I dropped my bag. He came towards me and threw it in the trunk, slammed the door and got in the car. Another man in a hooded sweatshirt got into the passenger side, and they both sped off in my lovely car. I watched them turn the corner and drive out of sight.

Feeling like an idiot, I stood there with nothing but two carts of groceries and my housekeeper. Neither of us realized what was happening to each other. While I was looking at a gun, the robber's partner was distracting her. He had been making moves on my pretty young housekeeper, asking for her name and phone number. We grabbed each other, grateful that all we lost was the car and my purse. Then I realized he had my address and the garage door opener, my ABC identification with the address of my office building. What do I do now?

My mind suddenly cleared. I ran into the grocery store yelling that I had been carjacked. I asked somebody to call the police. The manager did. Then I phoned my husband at work. He was shocked to hear what happened but said he would come straight home to cancel the credit cards, get the keys changed, and disable the garage door.

Within a few minutes a Montgomery County Police car pulled up to the store. I explained what had happened. He asked for a description of the robber and my housekeeper provided one of his companion. It seemed so ridiculous. I was giving a description of the majority of black men in the DC area: black, short cropped hair, average height, average build, no facial hair, dressed in a leather jacket, between twenty-five and thirty years of age.

The officer radioed back that police should be on the lookout for the make and model of my car and the descriptions we gave of the suspects. He added that they are "armed and dangerous." I felt like I was in a television police drama. I told the officer I felt so stupid that I just let this guy take my car and purse and did nothing to stop him. He said I had done the right thing. He said if someone with a gun wants your possessions, let them take them, otherwise, "We might be drawing a chalk outline of your body on the street."

He loaded his squad car with my groceries and drove me home. He was sitting at the kitchen table when he got a radio call saying two men driving a car like mine had just robbed a bank with a hand grenade and two handguns. It appeared they had gotten away with about $250,000. A bank robbery meant that my carjacking case was of little consequence to the county police because bank robbery came under the jurisdiction of the feds. It turns out the suspected criminals had robbed three or four banks in the Washington area over the past two years. The officer said I should be glad they were professional criminals. They didn't care about me or my car. They only cared about money. He said if the carjackers had been young and inexperienced I really might have been killed.

The men were still on the loose, and may still be as far as I know, so I lived in fear for several months that they would find me. I still am leery of people approaching me. I watch my back all the time.

So, in the eleven months between February 1990 and January 1991, I had three traumatic experiences: being beaten up in South Africa, fearing I would die in a plane crash, and being carjacked at gunpoint. I started noticing when I woke up that I just didn't feel good. There was nothing specific, no pain, just a vague sense that something was wrong with the woman who had it all, and too much more.

WHAT'S WRONG WITH ME?

The U. S. Department of Education asked me to narrate a documentary it was producing for the nation's public schools about the problems of smoking and drug use among teenagers. I narrated most of the program but the producers wanted me on camera in several places. They came up with some locations in a disadvantaged area in DC. In one day I was to shoot five one to two minute stand ups, which I memorized.

It was a beautiful sunny day in April of 1992, after a three-week stretch of working without a day off. Of course, I was feeling tired. I drove to the first location feeling not only tired but also a little strange. I got through the first shoot okay. We moved to the next location, and then to the third. When I took my position to speak to the camera this time, I was woozy. I started to speak and blacked out for an instant and fell to the curb. Everyone encircled me to find out if I was okay and asking what happened.

"I don't know. Everything just went black. Did I fall?" I inquired.

They told me I just slumped to the ground in a sitting position. I couldn't explain what was wrong, but I was fearful. Nothing like this had ever happened to me. I felt light-headed and nauseous. This could be serious, I thought. We were outside a high school. I wanted to splash some water on my face, rest a bit, and get my bearings. I went inside to the faculty restroom where I felt the urge to throw up, then the urge to use the toilet. I discovered that my menstrual cycle had started and I attributed my "episode" to the monthly event and felt a little better about what happened.

The crew had gotten me cold water and ice and I sat in the car with the air conditioning running while I rested. I took two Tylenol and after about fifteen minutes I felt I could resume the camera shots. I re-tried the words that had put me on the ground and got through them this time. I was still light-headed and a little wobbly in the knees, but we finished the shoot. I probably shouldn't have been driving but I got home and lay down. The only way I can describe the way my head felt is "fuzzy." I went to sleep, but awakened with another symptom, dizziness. When I tried to walk, I was reeling. I decided I needed to call my doctor.

The next morning I called in sick and reached my internist, who agreed to work me in as soon as I got to his office. He said he didn't like my blacking out. He did a complete physical exam and prescribed a medication that was supposed to help vertigo. It didn't.

A few days later the doctor called me back to his medical suite and said the results of my physical were normal. His voice was very soft when he reluctantly told me there could be a brain tumor and I should see a neurologist. A brain tumor? My heart nearly stopped. I never considered anything as serious as that. I was hoping it was just my period.

The recommended neurosurgeon put me through a battery of tests, which included walking a straight line. I couldn't. She requested an MRI. All I could think was, "brain tumor, brain tumor...I won't see my children grow up."

With great gratitude I accepted her report that there was no evidence of a brain tumor. Perhaps I had an inner ear problem. She recommended an otologist. I went to the specialist who examined my ears and tested my hearing. In a dark room I was spun around and upside down in a space age chair where technicians blasted air in my ears at the same time asking me to answer questions, like how many states begin with the letter "M."

The otologist concluded there was no physical reason for me to be dizzy and "feel strange in the head." This couldn't be. Why was I feeling so bad? The doctors couldn't explain. Each of them said it would probably go away in time.

But it didn't go away. Some days would be better than others. I continued to work but often it was difficult to get through the day. The funny thing about the un-defined malady is that when I had to be "on" I could be "on." I would feel terrible getting ready for a newscast, but when the red light on the camera came on, I started reading and experienced no symptoms. The red light went off, and I felt weird again.

A month after all the tests proved negative I was scheduled to give the Commencement Address to the College of Literature, Arts and Science at my alma mater, the University of Michigan. The venue was the huge football stadium where the crowd of graduates, parents, and relatives in the stands numbered 35-thousand. The view of all those people from my vantage point on the stage was daunting.

New symptoms became manifest. A fast-beating heart and "butterflies" in my stomach joined the dizziness and unsteadiness. I was absolutely certain I wouldn't be able to go through with my carefully crafted speech. But when it was my time, all the symptoms disappeared and I gave a hum-dinger of a commencement speech about the Los Angeles riots that followed the Rodney King police beating trial and the nation's unfinished business with racism. Some of the people who attended are still telling me about how much they enjoyed my spirited talk. It was a real phenomenon that I could return to my normal self-control when I had to.

I continued my work feeling terrible and waiting for the symptoms to go away like the doctors said they would. In October, after six months of depression about my condition, I was tapped to moderate the 1992 Second Presidential Debate in Richmond, Virginia. I got through the worldwide-televised event symptom-free.

The next year I was working at home with a CNN interview show on in the background. I heard a psychoanalyst talking about people who had dizziness, fast pulse rates, stomach upset, and heads that felt like they were "full of cotton." She said these sufferers also had a sense of impending doom. I perked up immediately. The woman was being interviewed about stress-related illnesses. She said millions of Americans had symptoms like mine because they were suffering anxiety or panic disorder.

"Eureka!" That's it, I thought. The doctors couldn't find a medical reason for what was happening to me because it was psychological. She went on to say that if people with the disorders can become so upset with how they feel that they frequently become clinically depressed. I listened closely to the name of the guest and wrote it down. I had a new lead. I was stressed out.

The next day I called the psychoanalyst, thanking her for providing some answers for a condition that plagued me for almost a year, then I asked her for places I could get help. She recommended The Center for Anxiety Disorders in Washington.

I called and asked for the earliest appointment I could get. A week later I met with the director of the program, a psychotherapist. This was new territory for me. Did I have a mental problem? Thank goodness she didn't have me lie on her couch. I sat, instead, and described what I had been going through. She listened thoughtfully and then asked if anything frightening had happened before I developed what I had taken to calling "my crazy head." Of course, that horrible year of 1990-1991.

I recounted the beating in South Africa, the near airplane disaster, and the carjacking at gunpoint. She responded with, "That's an awful lot for your mind to process over such a short period of time."

She recommended that she teach me behavior modification, as well as see a psychiatrist to prescribe medication to help ease the physical symptoms. I was relieved that finally there might be a solution at hand.

The psychiatrist explained to me that I already led a very stressful life as a television journalist, a mother, and public speaker. On top of that, to have three traumatic events in less than a year had, as he put it, "burned out some of your brain circuits." That didn't sound good. He further pointed out that what I was experiencing was similar to suffering post-traumatic stress disorder. But in my case anxiety and panic disorder were the result of my brain's being unable to handle so much trauma and so much daily stress. He prescribed anti-anxiety medication and sleeping pills. I hadn't had a good night's sleep in almost two years.

Over a six month-period, my psychotherapist taught me breathing techniques and methods to manage my stress. Among the first things she prescribed was, "Time for yourself. You've been serving everybody and everything else, but neglecting Carole."

I had to admit that was true. I seemed to never have time to do what I wanted to do.

She suggested I hand over even more parental responsibilities to my poor husband, who had been worrying about me for a long time. She said I should set aside time when I could get massages, manicures and pedicures. She said I should put away my newspapers and journals for a while and read a novel. She wanted to know what I enjoyed doing as a child and I told her, coloring.

"Fine. Go buy a coloring book and get some crayons and when you feel anxious just think about making a pretty picture and start coloring," she said.

"Think about your favorite place in the whole world and close your eyes."

I told her it was a garden at a resort we frequented in Jamaica. She asked me to describe it. I told her it had lush tropical foliage and brilliant flowers. I could feel the trade winds and hear the soft "whoosh" of the Caribbean Sea. By the time I finished my description I was totally relaxed.

"When you feel your heart pounding in your chest go to your favorite place," she said. "You see how easy it is." And she gave me a lecture not about others saying "No" to me, but my saying "No" to other people.

It was all great advice and I practiced it right away. I was determined to feel like my old self again. With the medication and the behavior modification I slowly felt the symptoms dissipate. They return every now and then, but now I know what to do.

I tell younger women not to fall into the trap I did. They must make time for themselves and take care of their health. Men get their relaxation. They play golf, poker or video/computer games. They go fishing, get catnaps, and never have qualms about watching sports. But women are caught up in making the trains run on time in their households and staying ahead of the game at their jobs, as well as taking the kids to buy new shoes and school supplies, making cupcakes for the Cub Scout troop. How many men have all that to take on? Not very many.

Now I feel no guilt at all when I kick off my shoes and watch some damsel in distress movie on the Lifetime channel. I have facials and massages and get my nails done. I read a Stephen King or Patricia Cornwell mystery. If I want to take a nap, I tell everybody to leave me alone and turn the ringer off on the phone. If I don't want to cook, I don't. Everybody is on his/her own or we order a food delivery. I no longer think of it as time that should be spent on more important tasks. I've learned that nothing is more important than taking care of my mental health, which adversely affects my physical health. They say stress kills. I won't let it be my demise. After knowing how to take care of everyone else, I finally learned how to take care of me.

MY FALL FROM GRACE

The 1990's were my best decade. I was a respected anchor and correspondent with both national and international reputations. My weekend show was top rated among the major networks. I was recognized everywhere. People asked for my autograph in restaurants. They wanted to pose with me for pictures in the airport. Taxi drivers, store clerks, and ordinary people on the street hugged me. They said I was the best, and some wondered when I would replace, in my opinion, the best anchorman, Peter Jennings. I thought I would continue to grow at ABC News with more opportunities coming my way. But a funny thing happened on my way to enjoying my success and dreams of the future. I believed there were moves afoot, not only to bring me down to size, but to force me out.

In 1996, Disney purchased the ABC Television Network from Capital Cities, Incorporated. There was the inevitable change of executives who brought in their people, who hired their people. They had their favorites among ABC personalities. I am not blaming Disney for what happened to me. It was the monumental change. An entertainment company bought a television network with a proud News Division and a tradition of quality news programming. But for a company known for its theme parks and resorts, its movies and merchandise, the News Division wasn't of particular importance to Disney. It bought the ABC Television Network to get the popular

237

and profitable ESPN, which came with the deal. News was not special anymore. News programs accounted for only ten percent of the network's daily programming. The News Division became just another budgetary unit and was being held responsible for its bottom line. The days of Roone Arledge's "do it at whatever cost" were so over.

How does a News Division keep to a budget when so many unexpected events occur: the wars in Iraq and Afghanistan, Hurricane Katrina, the earthquake in Haiti, the BP oil spill in the Gulf of Mexico? It costs money to bring the stories, pictures and sounds of war and disaster to the American television audience. The stories I covered on social problems were not considered important enough to spend the money necessary to do a quality job. Besides, hadn't all the focus groups said they didn't want to be upset by seeing the problems of the poor and homeless? So the stories that were my specialty dried up. There was no appetite for them or me on any news broadcast.

During the week I could get money from the weekend news budget to do some of those stories for my own shows. But cutbacks continued and before the end of the 20th century, unions, salaried employees and those of us with personal contracts were seeing our salaries cut or frozen. We were hemorrhaging audience and advertisers, and cable news channels were growing at our expense. Why wait for the evening news when you could see news anytime you wanted? And with the addition of on line news sites, doomsday appeared on the horizon for network newscasts.

All of this sets the stage for the shocking events that would rattle me to my core. As I have recounted, I spent much of my career trying to get more women and minorities into executive positions. It was my belief that our news products would improve by including different perspectives on the news. We should produce programs that were more representative of our audience. How would I know that the two people, who perhaps did more damage to my career than any white man at ABC, would be a white woman and a black man? Both probably owed their jobs to me. I put my own career on the line to advocate for women and minorities to be promoted to the jobs they had.

The white woman became my boss at Weekend News in the mid 1990's. I was so happy that for the first time in my life I would be working for a woman. She wouldn't have been my choice because she came from a major daily newspaper and had no previous television experience, but all the news executives said she was "so smart." They wanted her to gain experience on the weekends because they were grooming her to take over "World News Tonight with Peter Jennings." During the week, she worked on the daily show in New York and then traveled to Washington to produce the weekend newscasts.

I was so thrilled with her hiring that I decided to have a party introducing her to people she should know in the Washington Bureau. It was an elegant catered buffet dinner in my home for eight-five guests. I hired a well-known local jazz pianist and his bass player to entertain. Everyone had a good time and called it one of the nicest parties they had attended. The guest of honor seemed genuinely happy and told me no one had ever thrown such a lovely affair for her.

The following Sunday was her first weekend in charge. She had a reputation of not being "warm and fuzzy." I was prepared for that, but I was used to being asked my opinion of the show rundown, the stories that were included and in what order they should air. She didn't ask; she told me. If I had a strong opinion on something I would have spoken up. But I was anxious to see how she "stacked" a show. Everybody said she was "so smart" and all. Once I was on the air she was tentative in how she gave me direction from the control room on what was coming up next, or changes we would have to make in the rundown while the show was underway. That Sunday we got on and off the air without any hitches. She was okay.

A few weeks later, my director, responsible for all the technical aspects of getting the broadcast on the air, came by to tell me that this woman ordered her to prevent the studio crew from talking to me during the broadcast, unless it had to do with a technical problem.

"What are you talking about? You must be kidding?" Kibitzing with the studio crew during commercial breaks was one of my tools to keep me continually aware that I was talking to ordinary people out there in TV land.

The director emphasized her point: "Seriously, Carole, she doesn't want any talking on the floor during the broadcast and I told her you're the one who initiates conversation with the floor crew."

I asked, "What's the reason for this new edict?"

"She said she wants to have your full attention during the show," the director answered.

I was so angry. "Let me talk to this bitch." I don't use that word against women, but I felt it was fitting for her intrusion into my work style.

For seven years I had successfully anchored the program and no executive producer complained that I wasn't paying attention. Why would I not pay attention? I'm the one that would look stupid if the wrong story came up, or if there were black holes in the broadcast, or if the copy I was reading didn't match the pictures being shown.

I caught the woman in a hallway and I angrily said:

"What is this mess about my not talking with the studio crew?"

She responded, "Peter Jennings doesn't do it." Funny she would say that. He didn't talk much to any people on the set.

"That's Peter's way," I said. "My way is to talk to people in the studio because it helps me remain conscious of the fact that I am not delivering the news to an impersonal camera, but to real live people out there. It helps me maintain an affinity with the audience."

She came back with, "I don't know about that, but I need to have your undivided attention when we are on the air."

I enlisted my TV voice and said, "I have been anchoring for seven years and you've been producing for seven minutes. How in the world do you think I'm not listening to you? I have an earpiece in my ear and the sound goes directly to my brain. There is no way I can miss anything you say." I added, "What in hell's name do you think I'm talking about with the crew? We're not talking about the latest movies. We're talking about the stories that just aired. Or I'm telling them about problems with the teleprompter, or my microphone."

She said, "Well, we'll see."

I asserted, "There is nothing to see. I will continue to talk to the crew." Just by how she was standing there while I was talking, I could tell that I really set her teeth on edge. Of course, I would always wonder if it were because, like her, I was another strong woman, or an uppity black, or both.

I'm sure she went back to our executives who wanted her to succeed and reported our conversation. I believe she spoke to them with contempt for me.

After commuting between New York and Washington for several months, she tired of it and persuaded the network brass to move the Weekend News to New York. According to my New York sources, she made an argument that it would be cheaper, but she really thought the Washington staff was not as good as the New York staff. She claimed she could produce a better show there, especially with a different anchor, a man in New York. Thanks to Roone Arledge, my removal was non-negotiable.

She got her way on the move. Now I would have to do the traveling from Washington to New York every weekend. Because I was covering stories out of town during the week, this was going to be more than I wanted of the hassle with planes, trains and taxis. But I wanted to anchor and I had to do what I had to do.

One Sunday, after I had been doing the show from New York for a few weeks, I was sitting around the rim with the writers and producers, all of us waiting for lunch, when she came out of her office and said for everyone to hear:

"Carole, you can have a makeup artist but you can't have a hair dresser, anymore."

"You're joking, right," I said with a smile.

"I'm not joking," she replied sternly. "With our budget, we can't afford it."

I said, "Hey, I do a national newscast. Surely you want me looking my best."

"I've made my decision." She walked back into her office.

As if I were the senior President Bush in 1990 talking about the Iraqi invasion of Kuwait, I shouted, "This will not stand."

Later that afternoon I went into her office and sat down. I explained to her calmly that every show had hairdressers, even if the anchor was a man with little or no hair. I told her I really needed one.

She mentioned a white female correspondent who sometimes filled in for Peter Jennings during the week.

"All she has to do is wash her hair and blow dry it. Why can't you do that?" she asked. I thought about the girls I envied in high school.

"Surely you know black hair is different from white hair. My hair needs working with and more attention for it to look stylish and professional."

I was reluctant to recount that I was almost begging. Here I was, the only African American woman doing a newscast at ABC, and I was about to be the only anchor without a hairdresser. Of course, I suspected she wanted me to look bad so she could argue that I didn't look good enough to be anchoring.

There were established union wages for hair and makeup artists in New York. I think for both of them, ABC was charged a thousand dollars for them to work weekends. It wasn't my fault they got paid that much. But I couldn't believe I was arguing with another woman about my need for a hairdresser.

A producer tapped on the glass and said she was ready for me to track narration for a piece of video we were receiving from an overseas story. I excused myself but told the woman that this discussion was not over.

"Oh, yes it is," she taunted.

I think for the rest of the day tiny puffs of smoke were coming out of my ears. I was truly steamed. How dare she? How could she?

I decided that I would stay over in New York and spend the next day talking to two executives I considered my supporters.

When I asked for appointments to see them they didn't seem surprised. I think she had alerted them about our conversation. I hated that I had to go to them. I didn't want them thinking women couldn't work together, that we were in a catfight. But I had to stand up for myself, and I knew about the problems older women faced in television when they no longer make men orgasmic or women wanting to look like them. I had fought for all women and minorities against sexism and racism, and if I had to fight ageism, so be it.

I told the executives about the conversation the day before. They stopped me from further describing the details by assuring me I would have a hairdresser. Not to worry, they were taking care of it. Whew!

Then they wanted to know my assessment of how good a producer she was. I said she was all right but didn't solicit input from me, just her two male senior producers. I questioned some of her decisions on news stories, like a six-minute segment we ran about a Louisiana leper colony that aired during dinnertime. The poor unfortunates profiled in the piece looked grotesque.

"Doesn't she know I am a veteran journalist with worldwide experience? I have ideas," I explained. "I know what makes a good newscast. I could produce the show myself if I had to."

But she's "so smart," I heard them say, again.

"And I'm smart and you're smart and a whole lot of people that work here are smart. They should be," I responded.

My two bosses said that obviously my producer and I had a "personality clash" and only we could work it out. I got the message. Solve this yourselves. We are not getting involved. At least I got my hair stylist.

After I left the executive suite, I went directly to the woman's office and asked cheerily, "Can we have dinner later this week? I'll fly back to New York."

She made a quick scan of her calendar and said, "How about Thursday?"

I told her that would be fine and I would meet her after the "World News" broadcast. I flew back to Washington, wondering what I could do or say that would help us get along. I decided I would be conciliatory, even though I thought she was a "control freak."

On Thursday I met her at the news rim and she said she would get her things so we could leave. "Do you like Indian food?" she asked.

"I love it," I responded. She said we would go to her favorite restaurant on the East Side.

We grabbed a taxi on West 66th Street and chatted congenially about the news in that evening's broadcast, critiquing what was good and what wasn't. We arrived at the restaurant and because she could not go without a cigarette every fifteen minutes to a half hour, we had to be seated in the smoking section near the bar at the front of the curry house.

The waiter came by to pass out the menus and take our drink orders. I asked for my usual, a glass of Chardonnay. She had lit up a cigarette by now and was puffing away when she requested a double Martini, straight up. I blinked my eyes. I had never heard a woman order such a strong drink. We sipped our drinks as we studied the menus and then placed our food orders. These simple actions were prelude to a knockdown, drag out confrontation.

Since I had invited her to dinner I decided I should open the discussion. I told her that it seemed as if we had gotten off on a bad foot and I was anxious to resolve our differences for the sake of the broadcast and for the success of our individual careers. "I think I can help you and you…"

Something came over her and she interrupted me with her eyes bulging and nose flaring to say, with what seemed uncontrollable anger, "You can have fifteen fucking hairdressers and we won't cover the news."

I was trying to be calm but she was acting like she was possessed. After her nasty comment, I fired back, "I only want one fucking hairdresser and we can cover the news!"

The issue was expense. Given the big scheme of news budgets, 500 dollars a week for a hair stylist would not break the budget of Weekend News.

She reprimanded, "How dare you go over my head and report me. What are you trying to do, destroy me?"

"Whoa. Settle down. I think you're the one trying to destroy me by trying to kick me out of the anchor chair and trying to make me look bad."

Things continued to deteriorate and our raised voices attracted the attention of the bar flies and restaurant patrons. We must have been quite a sight: a white woman and a black woman, obviously professionals, both "dressed to the nines," in a heated and animated argument.

"This all began because of my hair," I reminded her. "If you hadn't denied me a stylist I wouldn't have gone over your head. You were unreasonable. Nobody's going to look out for me, but me."

She responded, "Yes, you and your hair."

We were getting nowhere. We were two tough "broads" who had both had to struggle to succeed in our careers. We did have that in common, and I pointed that out. I was older than she and more experienced at ABC News so I had to "pull up my big girl panties" and be the grownup.

We mostly ignored our meals and talked for more than an hour. I told her it would hurt women for years to come if we couldn't work together to put out the best news show on the network. That would help both of us. I asked for her respect, and to consider my suggestions for the show. I indicated I would provide the same respect for her. She reluctantly agreed. We reached a ceasefire. I knew it would not hold, but at least we could tell our bosses that we were adults and agreed to work together. Neither of us wanted them to hear anymore, "Meow,

Meows." She was afraid what happened between us would hurt her. I was afraid it would hurt women.

After reaching an uneasy truce, we only worked together a few months more and she got her dream job with "World News Tonight with Peter Jennings."

After assuming her new position it was not long before she did herself in, according to my sources in New York. She was so disliked by the staff and so difficult to get along with that she didn't keep her coveted position long. She was taken off "World News," put on a project, and before long it was common knowledge she was out the door. I blame her for being the first to poison the well against me among top management. Well, I'll be damned. It was a woman. A woman "so smart."

PAYING THE PRICE

When my nemesis left the job on weekends, a woman who could not have been more different than she was succeeded her. My new female producer actually liked me, respected my work, and was always looking for ways to promote the broadcast and me. The fact that she was a "television person," who had worked her way through the ranks of ABC News, gave her a more accommodating perspective of an anchor. In television you learn that it is an interdependent enterprise. We all have to work together, and with her, we did. Sundays were fun again. We did our work but there was camaraderie on the news rim from which could be heard easy banter and laughter. Under her producing skills, Weekend News won a national Emmy, a rare event for a weekend show. While she was succeeding on weekends, her predecessor was having some difficulties with the staff during the week. Ah, justice.

After three years my favorite producer was promoted to one of ABC's more prestigious shows. She deserved it. While her stock in the company was rising, I felt mine continue to decline. I had been anchoring the Weekend News for twelve years. I began getting signals that the company had "plans" for the broadcast, which it saw as a training ground for future anchors. As one executive put it, "We have a lot of talent getting a little long in the tooth."

After every broadcast I watched the tape to critique my performance and the broadcast. I was always trying to improve my delivery and presentation. I started noticing that my eyes were drooping and my double chin was starting to show. I didn't have a problem with wrinkles. "Black don't crack," they say. I had struggled against racism and sexism throughout my career and I wasn't going to let age derail me now. I knew that "everybody" in television was getting plastic surgery. In 1998, I decided it was my time.

I did research and found one of the best plastic surgeons in the Washington metropolitan area. He had done work on members of the Saudi Royal Family. I thought if he were good enough for them, he was certainly good enough for me, because the Saudis could afford to go anywhere in the world for plastic surgery.

I scheduled a consultation and developed a nice rapport with the surgeon right away. I told him I didn't want to look different or more attractive, just less droopy. The doctor sketched my face and showed me how he would lift my eyes and reduce my double chin through liposuction. He would do a half-facelift. From his assistant I learned that the procedure would cost 13-thousand dollars, not covered by insurance. I got over my fear of the pain and potential medical mistakes and scheduled the surgery.

As far as anybody at ABC was concerned I was on a three-week vacation. The surgery was done in the massive operating suite in the doctor's offices. It took a couple of hours and I woke up from anesthesia with deep throbbing pain and my head swaddled in layers and layers of cotton and gauze. I could scarcely open my mouth to take the painkillers. For a week I looked like the "Bride of Frankenstein" with a Technicolor face of reds, yellows, blues and purples. I began to think I had made a terrible error. I looked in the mirror and was certain I would never look right again. The doctor removed the bandages and the staples that held my skin together and he said I was healing just fine.

In two weeks, I couldn't believe the difference. No more colors. The swelling had gone down and was looking like myself again, no, better than myself. My eyes were open and bright and the unsightly double chin was gone.

I decided I wasn't going to try to hide my surgery like most people in television. I didn't want people whispering, "I bet she had plastic surgery." So when I went back to work three weeks after the surgery, looking pretty good I must admit, I told everyone about my mini-facelift. The word spread rapidly throughout the building and people started showing up at my office wanting to see the "new" me. They all thought I looked "great."

ABC's "Good Morning America" was intrigued and wanted me to tell my story on the show. I appeared live and showed the photos I had my husband take of my appearance each day after the surgery. They demonstrated how quickly I healed. I told the viewers I wanted to look—not younger—but better.

Another reason I had the surgery was to test the prevailing opinion that men could stay on TV until they looked almost mummified, but women, once they showed their age, were no longer welcome on the small screen. With few exceptions, Barbara Walters is one, I now believe it's true. My plastic surgery probably bought me another four years as anchor of Weekend News.

But as the Millennium approached my stature at the network continued its downhill slide with top management.

I was in my office during the fall of 1999 when one of my producers told me that there was a commercial running on the in-house channel promoting ABC's 24-hour coverage of the turn of the century, with anchors and correspondents reporting from the far-flung corners of the planet. The producer said she didn't see any mention of me among the reporters who would be in Fiji, China, Australia, Paris, London and places in between. Others were tracking Y2K to see if all the computers in the world crashed at midnight. I couldn't believe that all the anchors were participating except me.

It took a couple of phone calls to find out who was producing the extravaganza. I got him on the phone—another so-called friend of mine. I told him I had heard about the commercial. I asked in a friendly tone, "Did you forget to include the only African American anchor?"

He stumbled around and finally said, "No, I didn't." I'm not sure today if it were a deliberate move to make me crazy or his unit really did forget. It was clear to me that I was no longer on the radar and that was a bad thing. The News Division was about to produce the biggest television event in its history, and I was an afterthought.

I told him, "You must have forgotten about me, because you have already shot the commercial."

I could almost hear the wheels turning in his head as he responded, "I was going to call you next week. We have already selected people for the foreign assignments and now we're working on the United States. And, uh, since you're from Chicago, we want you to cover Chicago's celebration."

After New York's big to-do, how many people are going to stay awake to see me welcome the 21st Century in the all-important central time zone? The audience would drop off significantly and my role in the coverage would be diminished. But I wanted to be part of the TV spectacle, and if I were going to be in my hometown, I was grateful for small favors.

During this period, I got my fifth boss at Weekend News. This time it was a black man, one I had been promoting for years as an excellent producer who should be an executive at the network. He was also a friend. We worked together with Roone Arledge on minority complaints of racism in the News Division. I was very excited that we would be a team on the weekends. I was also delighted that barriers kept falling at ABC News, even though it was Weekend News. I was sure this black man would do everything he could to support my remaining in the anchor chair.

In the beginning everything seemed to be going fine. He did choose two men to be his senior producers, and as time went on, Sundays in New York was like the boys' club. The men were all competent, but now on the rim there was lots of talk of sports and cars and golf. Often the conversations made me feel like an outsider because I couldn't participate fully. But I had gotten used to that from my early days in the business. I was content with letting the boys be boys.

How this friend of mine, this black male producer, felt about my talent ultimately became apparent after the 9/11 terror attacks on the World Trade Center. ABC was all over the story, trying to keep the public informed, but of course also trying to beat the competition on the biggest stories to occur on American soil.

September 11th was on a Tuesday. I helped cover the story of the plane that crashed into the Pentagon. It was a soul-searing horror. The rest of the week I watched all the TV coverage and read all the major newspapers in order to keep myself completely up to date on all the details in preparation for Sunday's broadcast. Friday I got a call from my producer saying he would not need me to anchor that weekend.

"Why not?" I asked. I had been looking forward to anchoring a broadcast full of news about the disaster.

He told me that he had asked Charles Gibson, co-host of "Good Morning America," to anchor.

"But it's my show," I argued.

He said, "It's not your show, it's ABC's show and we want Charlie to anchor. After all he does two hours of live television every day. He's more experienced than you are. You only anchor once a week."

I love Charlie Gibson, who is a fine newsman, but as the host of "Good Morning America," he did some news but primarily conducted interviews with chefs, movie stars, fashion consultants, and the occasional oddball newsmaker.

Didn't my producer remember that I was on the air with Peter Jennings for forty-eight straight hours during the first war with Iraq in 1991; that I anchored fourteen straight hours of testimony in the Clarence Thomas Senate confirmation hearings for a seat on the Supreme Court; that I anchored live, with Ted Koppel, the release of Nelson Mandela in South Africa; and that I was part of the coverage of the last four presidential elections? There were no Teleprompters for live, breaking news events. I had to adlib from my own knowledge, putting issues in historical perspective and then current context for the viewers. It's a tough job, but I had done it successfully for many years at ABC. Why in 2001 was I no longer good enough?

I don't know for sure if it were the producer or ABC executives who made the decision. I suspect the producer, my good friend, read the tea leaves on my status in the News Division and was trying to curry favor with the brass. If he intimated to top management that "Carole can't hack it," he would be demonstrating his lack of support for my capabilities. If it weren't his idea, why wouldn't he level with me and say he had nothing to do with the decision? And if it weren't him, why wouldn't he fight for my right to anchor? I had fought for him. That really hurt.

From my bedroom in Washington I watched Charlie anchor the broadcast I had delivered for thirteen years. I was so disheartened.

The next week my producer told me my services would not be needed the next weekend. "Charlie did such a good job." How could anybody have known how well I would have done if I hadn't been given the opportunity? He acted as if one day I suddenly lost my broadcast skills which had been honed for so many years. I felt I was better than ever.

After one of my broadcasts I had dinner with a male news vice president who said he wanted to have a talk with me. I asked him why I was having trouble with my producer. The executive knew I had pushed for this well-qualified black man to get the job. He explained that my producer thought my delivery was too slow and that I could not ad lib well. All of a sudden? With criticisms like that, it seemed to me my producer was setting me up to be removed from the anchor chair. I wondered why he couldn't tell me himself. He made it sound to management that I was somebody showing her age, somebody no longer sharp enough. If he wanted a faster delivery all he had to do was tell me, and as for ad libbing, I was no Peter Jennings, but I had always done it well.

It struck me that a white woman and a black man were the two people who first began to cast doubts on my talent. I felt both of them owed their jobs to me. I put my own career on the line to get more women and minorities into positions of authority, the kind of authority they exercised against me. Fortunately, I have been around long enough to see many of the people who tried to hurt me experience their own declines and falls. Both of them suffered that fate.

Three weekends after the height of the 9/11 developments, I was able to return to the show. I was frosty with my black producer. In the past I would have taken him aside and asked what was going on. But this time I felt the writing was on the wall. "It's time to get rid of Carole." I believe he, the man I promoted for so many years, was a party to the plan.

THE ANTHRAX DEBACLE

After the 9/11 attacks on New York City's World Trade Center in 2001, there was an anthrax scare a week later. Letters containing white powder spores of the deadly infectious agent were sent to two U.S. Senators and several news organizations. Five people were killed by anthrax, and twenty-two others fell ill. At the time I was co-chair of the International Women's Media Foundation and our major fundraiser every year is the Courage in Journalism Awards held every October. Each year we conduct a worldwide search for women journalists who endured terrorist acts, prison sentences, and death threats for reporting the wrongdoing in their countries, committed by people ranging from heads of state to crime bosses to guerilla fighters.

The luncheon was held at the Waldorf Astoria Hotel on October 16th, where the awards were presented to three courageous foreign journalists and a lifetime achievement winner from the United States. It is always one of the media events of the year, drawing about 700 media owners, print and TV luminaries, corporate sponsors and rank and file journalists, most of them women.

I flew to New York the night before the awards ceremony for a small dinner with the awardees who that year came from Sudan, Colombia, and Spain, together with members of my organization. While we were enjoying dinner, I got a call from my close friend Judy

Woodruff, who was working for CNN. She was coming to New York the next day, but that night she wanted to alert me to the news she just heard that the infant son of an ABC producer was in the hospital with a case of suspected anthrax poisoning.

"What producer?" I worriedly asked Judy. She said she hadn't heard any names because ABC was keeping that confidential.

"Carole, I thought you would want to know," Judy said sadly.

Of course, I wanted to know. A baby? The child of a producer? It was too horrible to imagine. I immediately called the New York news assignment desk and requested the editor in charge. I told him what I had heard from Judy Woodruff and asked if it were true and which producer's baby was sick. He told me without hesitation. She was one of my favorite producers. We had worked together on several stories.

I hung up the phone and my fellow dinner guests saw me get emotional. They wanted to know what was wrong, and I recounted the startling news to them. I excused myself from the dinner. I wanted to get back to my hotel and try and call the producer to express my concern and to pray for her and her baby.

I couldn't reach her. From what the New York editor reported to me, the incident had happened a few days earlier when she was working in the New York offices. Her husband was out with their son, and they stopped by ABC so her baby could say hello. Her son and baby were there for just a few minutes. Her baby's arm became discolored and swelled up to twice its size. They called the pediatrician, who told them to rush to the emergency room. Doctors ran tests and began treating the baby right away for a cutaneous anthrax infection. The doctors said the baby apparently had been exposed to anthrax. Later, when I got a chance to talk to the producer, the baby was doing much better and the swelling was going down. She described the whole incident as the most horrible time of her life. She feared her baby would die.

The morning of the luncheon I checked in with the Washington Bureau to find out what was going on there. It was something I did every time I was out of town. I talked to one of our assignment editors and she said, "Oh, my god, Carole. You should be here and see what's happening."

"What? What's happening?"

She told me there were police cars and fire engines blocking DeSales Street, where the Washington Bureau is located in downtown DC. She said there were TV crews, local and national, along the sidewalk outside, and that there were "guys" in HAZMAT suits doing a floor-by-floor search of the building.

I asked her why and she answered it was because a couple of correspondents had received suspicious mail. She said everyone was panicking because the letters had a New Jersey postmark, just like the letters confirmed to contain anthrax that were sent to Tom Brokaw at NBC News, Senate Majority Leader Tom Daschle, and Vermont Senator Patrick Leahy.

As I got dressed for the luncheon I was extremely anxious. I was getting a small taste of what our Courage in Journalism awardees go through day after day. I knew that I would have to change my opening remarks at the program to reflect the fear that American journalists were now experiencing in the face of anthrax threats. During my discussions with the desk editors and the producer, there had been no admonition that this was privileged information and not to be made public.

All my life I had been a reporter whose job it was to inform the public. Since Judy Woodruff had picked up the anthrax story at CNN and I had confirmed it with desk editors in New York and Washington, it never occurred to me not to discuss it with all the journalists at our luncheon. It was a story I believed was already "out."

My IWMF co-chair and I were introduced to the hundreds of media movers and shakers from both New York and Washington at about 12:15 p.m. When it was my turn to make remarks, I said I now understand the fear our honorees face daily and I have even more respect and admiration for them than I ever had before.

Without revealing any names I told the crowd about my conversation with Judy and our desk editors. (The story about the ABC producer's baby had been reported in that day's *New York Times*.) I told the luncheon guests about the hubbub outside the Washington Bureau that morning and the suspicious letters. The crowd reacted with visible shock. Murmurs could be heard from the dozens of tables on the floor. I noticed people leaving the ballroom. What I didn't know at the time was that they were leaving to phone their news organizations.

I introduced the next speaker, who would profile our first awardee. Forty-five minutes later I started getting messages from an IWMF staff member saying I was to call one of the ABC executives as soon as possible. I put it off, figuring she knew where I was and what I was doing. What could be so important? But the calls kept coming. I had to leave the ballroom to find a phone. I called the female executive and she said sternly, "You need to get back here right now."

"I can't leave in the middle of the program. What's so important?" I asked. "Can't it wait an hour, until 2 o'clock? I have to finish the program," I implored. I wondered what had happened and couldn't come up with any reason I would need to see her so urgently. She agreed to wait until the program was over, but told me to hustle back. It was extremely important. I began to worry. "Is something wrong with my husband or my children?"

"This has nothing to do with your family. It's about you," she said impatiently.

"Okay. I'll see you as soon after 2 o'clock as I can make it."

About me. About me. What have I done? I wondered. I still couldn't come up with anything.

The luncheon ended, and the IWMF had put on another inspiring program honoring the courage of women journalists. I was planning earlier to go straight to the airport, but now I had to lug my suitcase to our New York headquarters to meet with the female executive.

Decked out in the elegant suit and stylish boots I chose to wear to the luncheon, I went to the executive floor and told the secretary that her boss had summoned me. Well, of course, I had to wait. It was so urgent, but I had to cool my heels outside her office. It's a trick I found employers often play to get the upper hand. You can wait. You're not all that important.

The secretary told me I could go in. There was not only the female executive awaiting me, but also an ABC lawyer. The executive I had always considered a friend of mine. Today I was greeted with stern looks and stiff postures.

I asked why an ABC corporate attorney was there and whether I needed my own attorney present. I was told that was not necessary. The executive who sent me all the messages at the luncheon said that I was called in because I had discussed an anthrax scare at ABC at a public forum. She began lambasting me for providing false information and details that could lead to the identity of the mother of the baby infected with anthrax. I said that was ridiculous because I just said, "a producer I used to work with" and added that I had worked with dozens of producers over the years. I was told that management was furious that I released information about the letters in Washington. She said what I stated at the luncheon was false and this was "a very serious situation." Management had to spend valuable time knocking down my false information, time that could have been much better spent.

The executive accused me of committing "transgressions," of "wrongdoing," of "poor judgment," and she said that I was "irresponsible" by having violated some ABC News policy that I not talk about what goes on at ABC, especially as regards anthrax.

"ABC policy? What ABC policy? I've never heard of it," I explained.

"You had no business discussing the internal affairs at ABC News. You told the people at the luncheon that a producer's baby got anthrax here and that there had been an anthrax scare at the Washington Bureau. That's not true. You had no business talking about what happens at ABC."

"Wait a minute," I said. "I've been working here for twenty years and I have never seen, read or heard of such a policy. I talk about ABC all the time when I give speeches. No one has ever said I can't talk about what goes on in my workplace or what I do here and how I do it."

I continued almost breathlessly, "And I did not tell anything false. I talked to the Washington desk about the HAZMAT teams at the Bureau and the letters that were intercepted." I had information from what I considered reliable sources and it was my considered judgment that it was appropriate to discuss what was happening at ABC during a luncheon where we celebrate courage in journalism. "Don't you understand?" I pleaded. "What better sources could I have than our own assignment editors who had first hand knowledge or were eyewitnesses?"

I was talking to two brick walls. This was the executive fror whom two years ago I had made up in cash the difference in her coach fare and a first class fare, just so we could travel from the Philippines together. What a fool I was. Just like the 6000-dollar party I threw for the producer who didn't want me to have a hairdresser. Stupid me.

Nothing I said got through to her. The lawyer mostly sat and listened, jotting down the occasional note and chiming in from time to time on the serious nature of my behavior. I suspect she was there to be witness to my dressing down and my reaction.

The female executive said the anthrax story was being "carefully controlled" by top management and "official pronouncements could only be made by David Westin or other executives." Westin replaced Roone Arledge as president of the News Division, and I had clearly stepped on his toes.

I got angry when they told me that the ABC PR person had been telling reporters all morning that there were no suspicious letters delivered in Washington. Then I realized why the huge "magilla." When I spoke about what I had learned, journalists at the luncheon called their news desks to report my remarks. The ABC spokesman had to field questions from the news media all over again based on what "Carole Simpson said." The reporters wanted to know who was right? I had been an anchor for thirteen years and had achieved a high level of credibility. That's why the reporters wanted clarification. The spokesman now had reporters questioning his assurances that nothing was wrong in Washington. The decision was obviously made to cast me as the one who was "wrong." To show the world that what ABC News management says is trustworthy, I had to be the sacrificial lamb. I stated falsehoods. I didn't know what I was talking about, they would say.

I apologized profusely, saying I would never knowingly violate ABC policy nor would I ever do anything to hurt the mother of the baby. I left the office in tears, but thought after I took the verbal whipping and after my apology, that was the end of the matter. I took the train back to Washington, feeling chastened and embarrassed.

Two days later, October 18th, I got a late afternoon call from the female executive's assistant saying that I had to be in New York the next day at 1 p.m. for a meeting. Now what was this about? The executive could not talk to me, so I called the lawyer. I was worried about the nature of another meeting and having to fly to New York for it. She urged me to come because it would "be in your interest" and "the company's interest" to have the session. She said it would only take about twenty minutes and I would be free to return to Washington. Twenty minutes? That was even more mystifying.

On the plane I decided it would be another meeting to yell at Carole and make her formally apologize to Westin. Little did I know that I was coming to hear the results of an official inquiry into my remarks at the luncheon. I had not been made aware that my statements and actions were being scrutinized, that people were being interviewed and that decisions about my future were being made. Had I known, I could have better prepared myself.

When I got to ABC News, I was ushered into another female executive's office, another friend of mine, I thought, and awaiting me were the first executive and the lawyer. Three white women all in a row. The first executive said management had completed its review and decided to punish my "wrongdoing." They asserted that I had reported false information, violated company policy, and for those transgressions I was being suspended for two weeks with pay.

This was beyond the pale. "Suspended? You've got to be kidding."

"We're not kidding. It's the company's decision." "Company decision" must have meant Westin either ordered or concurred with this punishment.

"But it's wrong. It's unjustified," I argued. I felt like a little kid suspended from school for talking back to a teacher.

I had a spotless record for thirty-five years as a broadcast journalist. Oh yes, I often challenged management on issues regarding equal opportunity and news judgment, but when it came to my work, I was the one who never got a fact wrong in a story, who never broadcast something in error requiring the News Division to issue a retraction, who never padded an expense account, who never missed an assignment, and who always volunteered for extra work. I was "Miss Goody Two-Shoes."

The executive said employees had been fired for actions as egregious as I committed (funny, but I never heard of such a case in my twenty years there), but she added the company had taken into consideration my long service and that's why my punishment was not more severe.

I was told that a full investigation had been conducted. "An investigation?"

My eyes now began to well with tears. "How could you conduct an investigation without hearing my side of the story? You interviewed other people, why didn't you interview me?"

"We know your side of the story," the executive told me. "We got the tape of your remarks, and you were completely out of line." They must have requested the IWMF videotape of the event that was shot for our archives.

Sputtering through my tear-filled eyes I said, "I would never knowingly violate ABC policy. I only spoke of the incidents to illustrate how precarious the job of a journalist was becoming after the 9/11 attacks. There is no way I could have known this was secret information."

"Yes, there was a way," she emphasized. "You should have called me and told me about your plans to reveal this information."

I had no plans to "reveal" any information; I was just speaking about what I believed to be the facts. I thought the story was already in the hands of the news media. "And besides, I have never called you with questions about what I can and cannot say in public, and I give speeches all the time on many subjects," I reminded them. "Why would I have done it this time?"

"In the future, it may be necessary in your case. You will just be away for two weeks and nobody has to know why. You don't tell, we don't tell. It's a personnel matter which is privileged information."

They said no one had to know. Hah. My suspension would demonstrate that the company was punishing me and making me pay for my "mistake." I would take the fall for telling the truth as I knew it and violating, a heretofore unknown to me policy. That's what they would tell the media, and my name would be splashed in newspapers everywhere. I just knew it.

I told the women that this was totally unfair and I asked for the opportunity to state my case in writing to be part of the "file" on me.

"Sure. You can write whatever you want. But the suspension stands and takes effect immediately," she said. I then left immediately.

I was devastated. My emotions were a complex mix of hurt, bitterness, embarrassment, righteous indignation, and profound melancholy. I was beaten. My mascara was running down my face when I left the office, and I found the back ways to exit the building so I wouldn't have to see anyone. I was sneaking out of the building like a thief, a criminal. Then I ran into one of the Weekend News producers. He could tell I was distraught. I begged him to come with me and take me some place where I could get myself together, because at that moment I was a complete mess.

"How about lunch nearby," he suggested.

"That would be good," I replied, "but not a restaurant that ABC people frequent."

I told him what had happened, that I was suspended, and that I had broken out in hives. He offered words of solace. After I was able to talk about my distress and the ruination of my career, I thanked him for being there for me. He is among the many wonderful white men I have worked with. We parted and I called my husband. I always needed to talk with him for support when bad things happened. He told me: "Just come home, honey, and we'll talk about it. Don't work yourself into a dither. I love you and everything will be alright."

Jim always knew what to say, always trying to make me feel better, but in my heart I knew everything would not be all right and that my career was irreparably damaged. I boarded the Delta shuttle to Washington and somehow managed to get home. I don't remember how. I threw myself into Jim's arms and boo-hoo'ed. He helped me get undressed and into my nightclothes. I climbed into bed. But I was not going to let ABC have the last word. Still crying (I think I cried a total of nine hours), I couldn't turn my mind off and I knew it was just a matter of time when I would be news. An anchor suspended. I would lose the public trust and that is what I worked for over my entire career.

Sure enough, the morning papers around the nation had stories about my false information on anthrax and my suspension. Gee, I wonder who released that information to the press. Not I.

Only weeks later did I see some of the press articles. The Associated Press published the following headline: "ABC Suspends Carole Simpson for Anthrax Remarks."

The New York Post had more details: "...ABC News execs were annoyed that Simpson made her comments without checking with them first, particularly since the infected baby and the way ABC screens its mail were internal matters. Simpson's comments turned an already 'edgy' situation even worse, sources say."

I bet knew who the source was.

The ABC News PR man called me later that morning after the stories ran about my suspension. He said I needed to issue a statement to the press. For my consideration he read a statement he had prepared. It would have me say that I had misspoke, that the information I talked about at the luncheon was false and that I apologize.

I couldn't believe it. A journalist who heretofore had sterling credentials for speaking the truth was now being asked to say that I lied. I wouldn't do it. The PR guy told me it would be much better for me in the long run to admit I made an error.

"I didn't make an error and I'm not telling the American people that I did. I will lose all the credibility that I have carefully built," I explained.

According to press accounts the man received forty calls from reporters on the Simpson luncheon remarks. "They want to hear from you why you said those things," he urged. "Did you say the letters that supposedly went to ABC in Washington were postmarked from Trenton, New Jersey?"

"I remember saying they came from New Jersey, because that's what an ABC editor told me," I replied.

He said the media reported that I said "Trenton," from which the early anthrax letters to Capitol Hill had been mailed. I told him I don't remember saying Trenton and I wanted to "go to the videotape." He said there wasn't time because the TV writers were on deadline. I was so depressed that I said I would only admit to not getting the exact postmark. I told him I stood by everything else I said. If he wanted me to issue a statement confined to that one detail, it would be okay. I hung up and put my head under my bed covers and that's the way I stayed for four days.

The Associated Press later reported on the statement I issued: "Simpson in a statement issued Thursday said she regretted the mistake about the Trenton postmark. 'My goal as a journalist is to always try to get it right,' she said. 'When any of us in this profession makes a mistake, it's important to say so.'"

Funny. I don't remember agreeing to that last sentence or agreeing to make that part of my statement. He put his own words in my mouth.

After my first four days of being in a funk, I mustered enough energy and anger on October 22nd to write a six-page single-spaced memo to ABC Management, setting forth my version of the events leading to my suspension. I started by calling my treatment "unfair and unwarranted." I said I was sorry about what happened and requested a further review taking into consideration my point of view. I ended by asking for a reversal of the suspension. I heard nothing, so I went back under the covers.

Meanwhile, during the second week of my depression over the suspension, my husband persuaded me to take a trip to Rehoboth Beach, Delaware, for a few days. I have always enjoyed the ocean resort in the off-season. But we spent one night there and I was ready to go home and get back in bed. I was still in a deep funk.

On Maryland Highway 50, we stopped at a small souvenir shop where I found a three-foot high doll. She had on a straw hat and had long brown pigtails, a blue and white pinafore, thick white stockings, and chunky black patent leather shoes. She looked like me when I was a three-year-old. The doll had no facial features. The hands were covering it and she was designed to stand with her face to the wall or in a corner. She looked from the back as if she were crying and had been punished.

"Bad Carole," I told my husband. I had to have her. I plunked down the fifty dollars she cost, lifted her gently, and placed her on the back seat of the car. I decided that from that point on, she would do all the crying for me. I was finished. I was no longer "Bad Carole." She made me laugh at myself. I kept her in my office for several years to remind me of one of the worst experiences of my career.

What hurt most during the two-week suspension is that none of my friends at ABC called to see how I was doing or to offer moral support. They later told me that they were afraid they might upset me further. I believed, however, that in their eyes I had become a pariah. My colleagues thought it wise to keep their distance from me.

On November 1st, the day before I was to return to work, I received an e-mail from Westin. He said he reviewed the basis for my suspension and concluded:

"You disclosed to the public internal, confidential information that had not been vetted through any editorial process. Your actions exhibited extremely poor judgment and violated a fundamental tenet of ABC News policy – to report the news accurately and after editorial review. Accordingly, I concur with the decision to suspend you."

Well, I tried. This was a "No" I couldn't use for energy. I was depleted. When I returned to work, I was treated like a wounded bird. People whispered when I came into a room. I think some of them were happy I got my comeuppance, while others felt I may have been wronged but still would just as soon not be seen talking to me.

Isn't it ironic that ABC News got itself into some anthrax difficulty in late October, the month of my discontent? Brian Ross, the highly respected ABC News investigative correspondent, reported on the Peter Jennings show that the anthrax letters that were mailed a week after 9/11 contained a substance called bentonite, which his anonymous sources linked to Saddam Hussein and Iraq. Other media outlets could not confirm the story and the White House and research scientists denied the presence of bentonite. Did Brian report "false information?" The main suspect, Dr. Bruce Ivins, a scientist at Fort Detrick, Maryland, committed suicide and the FBI closed the case in February of 2010. But ABC News, dogged by questions about Ross' story for years, never issued a retraction.

THE NEWSLADY IS BANISHED

I t was no surprise that ABC wanted to get rid of me. I was a thorn in their side. I knew it. However, I believe top management decided it would be impolitic not to renew the contract of the first black female anchor of a major network newscast, who was also the outspoken advocate for women and minorities at the network. Not renewing a contract is tantamount to firing. The executives chose a strategy of trying to make me leave on my own. They tried to make me so unhappy that I would quit. No, I would not make it that easy for them.

My agent would soon be negotiating a new contract scheduled to commence in 2002. I expected the worst and that's about what I got. I was asked to meet with David Westin and one of the female vice presidents I had tangled with before. I've always been a student of body language. It was very handy in television news to be able to assess the best way to approach strangers I needed to interview for a story. This day the message I read was, "You're not going to be happy." This was not going to go well for me.

Westin began by saying ABC wanted to sign me to a two, not my usual three-year, contract, but I would have to give up my anchor slot. He pointed out that I had held the chair for fourteen years, which was a very long run in television. That was true. He carefully avoided any reference to age or the desire to use my broadcast to train new anchor talent. That already had been intimated to me for years in the most legally appropriate terms.

I then expected to hear about a new position I would have with the network, but I thought I would remain on television, maybe reporting for Weekend News or another show. Instead, I was told that they wanted me to work with young people. Everyone in the company knew that I love working with children and youth. I mentored many of our entry-level employees and was always ready to talk to students visiting the Washington Bureau. I guess they thought they were doing me a big favor. But I was flabbergasted. I would not be on the air anymore?

The woman vice president said they wanted me to be an ambassador to the public schools and travel around the country talking to high school students.

"Talk to the students about what?" I wondered. She said I could decide that. Or instead, she said, I could work for Radio Disney. Radio Disney? The radio network aimed at 8 to 12-year-olds?

"And just what would I be doing for Radio Disney?" I asked.

"Well, you could have discussions with kids about the issues of the day. It would give them a chance to get involved in current affairs," she answered happily.

I have never been more insulted.

"How much of this offer is negotiable?" I asked Westin.

"I'm afraid not much," one of them answered.

I knew that this "non-offer" was intended to be so upsetting that I would refuse this ridiculous contract and leave ABC. My thighs started itching fiercely as we wound up our conversation. I was holding back the tears of embarrassment I felt, refusing to let them have the satisfaction of seeing me in a weak position.

I didn't characterize the offer. I just said I would have to talk with my agent, Stu Witt, who would get back to him. I left the executive floor and rushed to the Ladies Room to look at my thighs. Hives, I guess. Big red, raised splotches itching like crazy. I tore at my upper legs with furious scratching, which made it worse. There it was, the turmoil in my mind having an adverse effect on my body. How could ABC News have so much power over me? Then I realized I had spent twenty-one years of my adult life working there. It was like home. It seemed like my parents saying they didn't love me anymore and banishing me to the backyard.

After I got over the initial shock, I decided that since ABC had raised my discomfort level, I would raise its discomfort to a higher level. I called super lawyer Johnnie Cochran. Before he passed away, just his name struck fear in the hearts of anyone on the opposing side. I knew what his involvement would mean to the company. I didn't know Johnnie Cochran, but he knew me from television and was a big fan.

I was never interested in suing ABC News, but Cochran--after he heard my stories-- thought I had grounds. Top executives were playing hardball with me and I was going to play hardball back. Johnnie said he would send a letter to ABC News suggesting they not "mess" with me.

In a letter he sent to Westin on December 17th of 2001, two months after my anthrax suspension, Cochran wrote the following about the contract offer made to me:

"This development is shocking, given her long and distinguished tenure with ABC News, and her reputation as a national television personality. I do not have to tell you that she is highly regarded as a journalist and a news anchor in many communities across the nation and the world. She is well known for her integrity, honesty and compassion as a journalist and a person. Miss Simpson has been hurt by these developments both professionally and personally."

Cochran then requested to have a meeting with Westin. It was never held.

The letter apparently sent parent company Disney and ABC News into a panic. I heard that Disney wanted no legal problems with Cochran and me and told the News Division to "fix this."

My agent went into negotiations with ABC over the provisions of the contract. They made a better offer and we reached agreement. I decided to sign it and make the most of the silly little assignment I was given as ABC's Ambassador to Schools.

My last day of anchoring World News Sunday, October 19, 2003, was a tough day. Except for the executive producer, I loved the staff and my studio crew and makeup team. I wanted to end the newscast with a goodbye to my audience. ABC management, fearing what I may say on my last broadcast, had to clear my final words to my fans. It was poignant and heartfelt, and once again I was fighting tears and the quiver in my voice. Instead of my usual sign off, I said at the end, not "Good Night" but "Goodbye." After the lights were off, I dissolved on the anchor desk in tears. But within a few seconds the whole staff surrounded me on the set with a big cake, flowers and champagne. I hugged each and every one on the staff. Then I packed up my rolling suitcase, put my coat on, and walked out into the night weepy and alone. The car to take me to my hotel for the last time was waiting.

The following week, Westin decided to have a get-together for me in New York on the floor of the executive offices, in recognition of my fifteen years as a weekend anchor. I didn't want to go, but my Washington bureau chief thought I should not refuse the President of the division if he were trying to do something nice for me. Traveling to New York was always a pain and going there for an hour and a half afternoon reception was even less appealing. On the shuttle to New York, I decided to continue my pattern of catching the executives by surprise.

It was a nice little event and many of ABC's top executives and "stars" showed up to wish me well. It didn't feel like a "You've done well" party, but a "Goodbye, it's been good to know you" party.

After the toasts and well wishes I broke into the song I memorized on the plane: Gloria Gaynor's anthem from the Seventies, "I Will Survive."

I'm not a singer but I can carry a tune so I began:

"At first I was afraid, I was petrified, thinking I couldn't live without ABC on my side…"

Some people smiled, others looked disgusted.

"I spent so many night thinking how you did me wrong, and I grew strong, I learned how to carry on."

By the time I got to the chorus I was rockin':

"I've got all my life to live and I've got all my love to give and I'll survive. I will survive."

There was tepid applause when I finished, but I felt great.

Before Westin left the gathering he leaned over to me and said, "You'll do just about anything, won't you?"

"Just about," I smiled, "and thanks for the party."

Now that I was no longer reporting or anchoring, I worked for a couple of months coming up with a program that I hoped would be useful in the public schools. Our public high school students, I knew, were not watching TV news or reading newspapers or seeking news on line. I decided that I could go into the nation's high schools and teach classes on the importance of the First Amendment and a free press, and the importance of keeping up with the news.

I had one of our young interns go out with a camera crew and visit a school in suburban Maryland school and another in Washington, DC. He asked the students about whether they pay attention to news and the majority from each school said they didn't care about the news because it was all depressing and they didn't understand who and what reporters were talking about. Some couldn't name the countries where U.S. troops were fighting.

I produced an eight-minute tape with the choicest and funniest answers from the students we interviewed and I explained the information explosion. I would show that to every class to get the discussion going.

With the help of publicists at ABC affiliates in various cities we were able to identify schools that would benefit most from my classroom presentation. For the next two years, a producer and I travelled to thirty-one cities from Raleigh, North Carolina, to Oakland, California. I delivered my free press seminar in forty high schools and probably reached close to 5000 students.

I created this assignment for myself. I felt it was important. The students were especially turned on when I had them check the labels of their clothing, purses, shoes, and cell phones to find out where they were made. They were shocked when they read out countries like Honduras, Pakistan, Romania, Macao, Russia, Nicaragua, Mexico, and, of course, China. In almost every classroom, only one or two students had clothing items Made in the USA. This led to a discussion about work being lost in America because companies, seeking cheap labor, exported the jobs overseas. We discussed what it might mean for their futures.

In 2005, I got word that there was no longer any budget available for us to travel around the country anymore. My Ambassadorship was over. Now I had nothing to do. I tried offering stories to various broadcasts but I was clearly persona non grata. I would never appear on ABC News again.

I would go into the office maybe once a week and check my mail, visit friends, and get the latest gossip. I wanted to do something, so I started writing this book.

OLDER, WISER AND HAPPIER

My retirement from ABC News was demoralizing. After thirty years on national television, it was hard to imagine myself no longer having any visibility. I knew what happened to folks who left their lives on TV. People would ask, "What ever happened to…?" And few, if anyone, ever knows.

The Washington Bureau threw a going away party for me, and I was presented the gift most correspondents receive upon their leaving: a beautiful glass box on which is etched the U.S. Capitol, engraved inside my name and the date of my departure, January 29, 2006. That date was also close to the date I began at ABC twenty-four years earlier. At the get-together in the conference room, my Washington colleagues made kind remarks and then I had to speak. Despite the fact that I was ready to leave, I looked at the sea of faces that included correspondents, producers, writers, editors, business staff, researchers, technical crews, secretaries, and security guards, and I began to choke up. These were people I saw and worked with almost every day. I would probably never see them again. As that thought took hold, the tears spilled from my eyes. This book must make me sound like one of the biggest crybabies in journalism. I blame it on hormones. I cried when I was hurt or angry, but the men I saw at work, cursed, smashed fists through walls, or went out and got drunk. Men and women experience similar emotions but express them differently. I would rather "cry me a river."

I have never been short of words, but on this last day at ABC, I was. I could only stammer through the tears that I would miss everybody and that I appreciated all they had done to help me with my work through the years. When I could no longer speak, I found myself embraced by my longtime co-workers. Some of my closest friends were crying, too. It was one of the most heartrending days of my life.

I drove myself home with the last pieces of memorabilia from my office and began to feel the onset of an anxiety attack. What was I anxious about? Well, what the heck was I was going to do with the rest of my life? I wasn't ready to retire. I couldn't see myself living in a condo in Florida, or joining the ladies who lunch. What would I do at home? I remember asking the iconic David Brinkley about when he planned to retire. He said, "Never." I asked him why.

"If I ever retired I know I would sit around in my pajamas all day and watch TV." I agreed with Brinkley that it was an unpleasant prospect. I knew there was more I could do and more I wanted to do, even if it weren't on television.

My husband and I lived in the Washington, DC, area for thirty-two years. But my daughter, Dr. Mallika Marshall, was living in suburban Boston, and my son, Adam, had moved to Hollywood to become a talent manager. There was really nothing to keep us in Washington except old friends, but there was a strong draw to Boston, our first grandson. My husband and I talked about getting older and wanting to spend more time with our family. In June, five months after I left ABC, we had sold our condo in DC, bought another in Boston, packed up our belongings, including the dog and cat, and moved to Boston to be near my 18-month-old grandson, James, and of course, my daughter and son-in-law, Jason Hurd.

It took a while to get settled in a new city, especially one as different as Boston is from Washington. I was surprised to find so many

Bostonians cold and unfriendly. The weather also was horrendous: too many rainy, foggy, windy and gray days. But I had a little boy to love and spoil, and my daughter, who helped pay off her medical school bills by answering questions from her parents like, "What's this weird rash on my arm?" or "What should I do for my stomach ache."

It is great to be a part of her life again. She never neglects to invite her father and me to her social events and keeps trying to find people our age "to play with." She wanted us to be happy in Boston. As if she were still a teenager, we started arguing again, this time about how to discipline Baby James. She didn't like my meddling at all, but it was so hard for "MeMe" and "Pop Pop" to stay out of it. She later blessed us with two more grandchildren, Jackson and Savanna Rose. We love and enjoy our little "grands" so much. In fact, I told my daughter I love them more than I loved her. It's a joke but she doesn't appreciate it.

She and I also have something else in common, television. She never wanted to follow in my footsteps. She went into medicine because she wanted her own thing. Now she practices medicine and was the medical correspondent for WBZ in Boston for ten years. She still practices urgent care at a medical clinic for the underserved but also does nationally syndicated medical reports for local stations around the country and maintains a website, "Ask Dr. Mallika," to answer the public's medical questions. It makes me so proud that she is a medical broadcast journalist. I did have an impact on her career.

However, back to our early days in Boston, I was determined to find work and two months after we arrived I was in the process of setting up a media consulting company. Out of the blue I got a call from Linda Peek Schact, a friend from the International Women's Media Foundation. She told me she was teaching political communication at Emerson College, the only college in the nation specializing in Communication and the Arts. Linda said she was delighted to hear that I had moved to Boston, and she wanted to know if would I be interested in teaching journalism. I had not thought of teaching even though I was in the area with the highest concentration of colleges and universities in the nation. I recalled my days teaching at Tuskegee University and Northwestern University and remembered how much I enjoyed teaching college students.

I told her I would be interested. Who wouldn't be interested in working at a job which was only a two-block commute from home? Linda made it known to the administration that they had an amazing opportunity to bring Carole Simpson to the journalism program. She really sold me. By fall I had a formal offer from Emerson's vice president for Academic Affairs. I would be named Leader in Residence, teach two journalism courses, and host on campus conversations and panel discussions on current affairs. It sounded perfect. I would be working with the future journalists of tomorrow, and I wanted to expose them to the passion I felt when I was studying journalism in college. I signed a contract and began teaching at Emerson in January of 2007, almost one year to the day I left ABC. I had a new home where people admired me, respected me, and were grateful to have me.

Professor Simpson, my students call me. How's that ABC? One door was closed but thanks to God, another one opened on a brand new life of service. My students keep me young and sharp. Teaching college may be among the hardest work I have done. Writing syllabi, preparing lectures, grading papers, and critiquing students' broadcast assignments. Then there is the challenge of keeping students engaged in the classroom. They are social networking all the time. I struggle to get them as turned on about writing a newscast as receiving a silly text from their boy and girlfriends.

I love teaching. I love the students, who think they know everything but scarcely know anything because they were born as recently as 1993. To drop some knowledge on them and watch their growth over the length of a semester is as rewarding as any honor I received for my television work. What I do now isn't like last week's broadcast or the most recent story I reported, which goes on the air for fleeting moments then wafts away in the atmosphere. What I do now has a lasting impact on hundreds of young people's lives.

Surprising as anything is the fact that I have been back on television. During the 2008 presidential primary season, I appeared frequently on "Larry King Live" as a Hillary Clinton supporter. Sorry, President Obama. I have also done WGBH, the public television station in Boston, and CNN. It's great to get miked and feel those bright lights in my face again, and better still, to give my own opinions, which I had assiduously avoided as a practicing broadcast journalist.

For extracurricular activities, my interest in international affairs and children has earned me a seat on the Board of Trustees of the national and international relief agency, Save the Children. My dear friend Cokie Roberts recommended me to the Board because we both felt we wanted to help children in our older years. It has been most gratifying to see our organization leap into action when disaster strikes anywhere around the world, providing children and their families safe spaces, shelter, food, water, medicine, and even toys. Our organization has been there for the tsunami in Indonesia, the floods in Pakistan and China, the earthquake in Haiti, and hunger in Sudan, as well as disaster areas in the United States. My work with Save the Children—despite the scope of the tragedies we hope to ameliorate—is another area in which I can fulfill my continuing ambition to do good works.

My life has completely changed. I have a new career that is a joy every day. I'm getting used to my new city and most important of all, I have the love of my husband, my children, and grandchildren. What more could anyone ask?

I remain a news junkie, devouring news stories from TV, radio, newspapers, and the Internet. I am a different woman now in a different age, but one who will always try to make a difference, and, because it's in my blood, one who will always be a "NewsLady."

TAKE-AWAYS

When I was coming along, I had no mentors, no role models, and no godfathers. Everything I learned I had to learn by bumping my head into brick walls and deciding, well, that didn't work. I want to close my story with some practical tips I learned the hard way, which I believe may be useful for anyone working in corporate America, no matter your color or gender.

1. Know yourself. Develop a realistic view of your strengths. Acknowledge your weaknesses and try to overcome them. Don't overpromise, but don't sell yourself short. Either extreme can be hazardous to your career.

2. Don't let anyone steal your dream by telling you "no." Have confidence in yourself. If you believe it, you can achieve it.

3. Never compromise your principles. You won't be able to live with yourself. If it feels wrong, it is wrong for you.

4. Toot your own horn. If you don't nobody else will. Tell your employers and co-workers when you succeeded

where others failed, or when you have built a better mousetrap.

5. Determine who your adversaries are. Understand what motivates them and strategize to prevent them from doing damage to your reputation in the workplace.

6. Find out who your friends are. The truth might surprise you. The enemy of your enemy is not necessarily your friend. All your skinfolk aren't your kinfolk.

7. Pride goes before a fall. Don't rest on your laurels. Don't become complacent and satisfied. Continue to set goals for yourself, if you want to reach the top.

8. Know when to hold 'em and know when to fold 'em. You can't fight all the time. Pick your battles.

9. Don't forget the people who are not at your level. Your subordinates can be of tremendous assistance and support and besides, today's mailroom clerk could be tomorrow's CEO.

10. It's never too late to change course in a career. If things don't work out, then leave. Somewhere out there somebody is looking for you and exactly what you have to offer. Never, ever give up.

EPILOGUE

I have taken you on a forty-year journey through my career as a broadcast journalist. From the South Side of Chicago, a little black girl with a dream and determination made it almost to the top ranks of her profession. I have taken you through the high points and the low. Without a doubt there were many more highs.

Despite my many struggles, I would not have changed much. I consider my career one of the most exciting, challenging, and rewarding anyone could have. I travelled to sixty-five nations on five continents and to forty-eight of the fifty states. I have seen America and I have seen the world. Every story I reported was an education. I find myself able to talk about virtually any subject.

I interviewed Presidents and Kings, death row inmates and Nobel Prize winners. I covered stories that made viewers cry or laugh, get angry, or take action. My work influenced policy decisions in local, state, and federal governments.

Every day was an adventure. Nothing was more exciting to me than going into the field with a camera crew in tow and becoming the eyes and ears of the public. Then back at the studios it was downright thrilling to write the story and add the pictures and sound we gathered into a compelling, interesting, and engaging story.

I did not seek fame, but I became famous. I got the nice tables in restaurants and the prized theater seats. I signed autographs and posed for photos with people on the street. I was always uncomfortable in these situations. I am a journalist, I wanted to say, not a celebrity.

To the employers who gave me the opportunity to showcase my work on television, I am thankful. Having the opportunity to inform the public of the things they wanted to know and the things they should know was an important responsibility. I worked hard to earn the public trust and to live a private life in service to others.

I have recounted events in this book that show how many tried and how many succeeded in doing me harm. Please know that before, during, and after my television career, the NewsLady overcame and prospered. I was blessed.

CPSIA information can be obtained at www.ICGtesting.com
Printed in the USA
BVOW071743071211

277513BV00002B/28/P